TNP Even when that laughable Abner Doubleday creation myth of baseball's origin—foisted on the American public by Albert Spalding for crassly commercial reasons—is justly dismissed, still the reputed "American origins" of the national game are tough enough to shake. Most current sports histories merely substitute one "creation myth" for another. Thus Alex Cartwright gets full credit and—presto—the American birthright of the national pastime remains largely intact. But the Cartwright claim itself rests on shaky enough ground: the Elysian Fields contest of 1846 was no more an instance of "fully evolved baseball" than were numerous earlier matches held throughout the northeastern states and provinces of Canada. This native game of "base-ball" was never immaculately conceived but, instead, slowly and painfully evolved—"stool ball" to "rounders" to "town ball" to "Massachusetts game" to "New York game"—and the germinating seeds were always demonstrably European.

Events of the past decade have made the international elements of our adopted national game simply indisputable. A near tidal wave of Latin American imports has inarguably provided the biggest single story in major league baseball during the 1980s. Rival Japan boasts a long-standing professional league which, while never a serious match for our own, nonetheless solidifies the cross-cultural appeal of diamond play. In world amateur contests it is Castro's Cuba that has long been the ranking world power, while USA amateur teams are beaten out with disturbing frequency at world-level competitions by squads from Puerto Rico, Venezuela and Nicaragua as well. Throughout the Caribbean basin "beisbol" enjoys equal status as the ordained national game.

This Olympic year—in which baseball first (and at long last) debuts as a medal sport—seems, then, a most appropriate occasion to focus the attention of SABR scholars upon the world baseball movement. Even major league baseball—long a bastion of provincialism—now looks pragmatically in that very direction. Major League Baseball International Partners has recently been created by MLB, NBC and Pascoe Nally (a leading British sports marketing firm) to regulate broadcast and promotion of the international game. The International Baseball Association, based in Indianapolis, has been actively spreading the world baseball message for more than a decade with clinics and tournaments held around the globe.

As the world grows smaller and cultures find themselves drawn more tightly into a web of interdependence, it is again the miraculous game of baseball which marches at the forefront of this inevitable parade toward a world community. Baseball in 1992 ironically seems poised to fulfill its global mission at the very hour when runaway salaries and shopping mall stadia have disaffected so many American fans. Yet, as our Canadian SABR colleague Bill Humber has often reminded us, "Who ever said that baseball is an American game, anyway?"
—**Peter C. Bjarkman, Editor**

THE
National Pastime
A REVIEW OF BASEBALL HISTORY

Editor: Peter C. Bjarkman
Fact-checkers: Pete Cava, Frederick Ivor-Campbell

THE NATIONAL PASTIME (ISSN 0734-6905, ISBN 0-910137-48-X), Number 12. Published by The Society for American Baseball Research, Inc. P.O. Box 93183, Cleveland, OH, 44101. Postage paid at Birmingham, AL. Copyright 1992, The Society for American Baseball Research, Inc. All rights reserved. Reproduction in whole or in part without written permission is prohibited. Printed by EBSCO Media, Birmingham, AL.

Baseball in the Olympics

Pete Cava

This summer in Barcelona, baseball makes its official debut as an Olympic sport, four years short of a century since Baron Pierre de Coubertin revived the Games in Athens in 1896. Return with us now to those thrilling days of yesteryear: as the good Baron pondered the possibilities of an Olympics with no cable television revenue, across the waves the National League was preparing for its 21st season as America's top baseball circuit.

While some 311 athletes from 13 nations convened for the Games, Ned Hanlon and the Baltimore Orioles were embarking on a third straight drive to the pennant. That year, Greece's Spiridon Louis raced to the Olympic marathon title and Cleveland's Jess Burkett took the N.L. batting crown. Baseball and the Olympics were as far apart as Tippecanoe and Timbuktu.

For the next four score and seven seasons, that, for the most part, remained the status quo. Baseball was added as a demonstration sport at the Los Angeles Games in 1984 and again at Seoul four years later. This was a prelude to baseball's current status as a medal sport. Between Athens and L.A., however, baseball has provided some of the more fascinating and underexplored corridors of Olympic history.

Some historians include baseball as an exhibition or demonstration sport in the St. Louis Olympics of 1904. The Games were part of that year's Louisiana Purchase Exposition, and virtually every amateur sporting contest in St. Louis from May to November was packaged as part of the fair or the Olympics. *Spalding's Official Athletic Almanac* for 1905 includes a report from Olympic director James E. Sullivan that boasts: "this is the largest entry that has ever been received by any one organization or corporation that ever held an athletic meeting." Yet only twelve nations sent athletes, and in many events only Americans competed.

Sullivan's list of "Olympic" events includes the Interscholastic Meet for the State of Missouri on May 14; an amateur baseball tournament in June and the Athletic Games in Honor of Cardinal Satolli on July 1. Thrilling events, no doubt, but none can seriously be considered part of the Olympics.

Debut in Stockholm—In 1912, as America's major league clubs were gearing up for a new baseball season, the Swedish capital of Stockholm was preparing for the Games of the Fifth Olympiad. Two years earlier Sweden's first baseball club, Vasteras, had begun play. At about the same time the U.S. professional teams were heading north from spring training, Sweden's Olympic Committee contacted Vasteras officials about the possibility of a baseball exhibition during the Games with some of the American Olympians.

Vasteras players must have turned cartwheels at the thought of displaying their talents during the Olympics. Some of the club's best players, however, had recently moved away—a harbinger, perhaps, of the era of free agency?—and club officials fretted over whether or not they could field a competitive team. Determined to do their best, the enthusiastic Swedish baseballists soon began to prepare for their Olympic moment with thrice-weekly workouts.

Pete Cava *is press information director with the Athletics Congress of the United States, has appeared as St. Louis Browns manager Jimmy Burke in the film* "Eight Men Out", *and has authored a recent scholarly history of the New York Mets.*

Meanwhile, according to the organizing committee's report on the Stockholm Games, U.S. Olympic team members were making plans of their own for the exhibition. The American baseball squad, made up of volunteers from the track and field team, would bring their own baseball uniforms to Sweden along with special handouts. The flyers they'd had printed were intended to explain to Swedish spectators the intricacies of the bunt, the hit and run and, possibly, the wave and the Tomahawk Chop.

Original plans called for playing the game on the evening of July 10, during the track and field competition. The American Olympic Committee, however, forbade the U.S. players from taking part in any exhibitions until they'd finished competing in their primary events. The game date then shifted to Monday, July 15. The Ostermalm Athletic Grounds (site of the equestrian events) would be the site.

The game started at 10 in the morning. To even the sides, the visiting Americans provided a battery for the home team. The Swedes immediately inserted their new recruits—catcher Wesley Oler, a high jumper from Yale, and pitcher Ben Adams, who'd won a bronze medal a week earlier in the standing long jump—at the top of their batting order. The game was to be a six-inning affair.

The Americans got to Adams early, scoring four runs in the first. One of the big guns was Abel Kiviat, who played short and batted third in the order. Kiviat stole a base and had a pair of hits in four at bats, including a triple. Kiviat, Jim Thorpe's shipboard roommate en route to the Games, was a great athlete in his own right. Born in Manhattan's Lower East Side to an immigrant peddler, the five-foot, three-inch Kiviat had been the silver medalist in the 1500 meter event. In 1909 the bowlegged "Kivvy" was an all-city baseball player for Staten Island's Curtis High School. Kiviat, who for many years served as a press steward for track meets at Madison Square Garden, lived a long and merry life. At the time of his death in August, 1991, at the age of 99, Kiviat was America's oldest Olympic track and field medalist. The last surviving member of America's 1912 Olympic team, he was inducted into the National Track and Field Hall of Fame in 1985.

All told, eight Olympic medalists took part in the game. First baseman George Bonhag, who went oh-for-two in the game, had won a gold medal running the anchor leg in the since-discontinued 3,000 meter team race. Fred Kelly, the centerfielder, had led a U.S. sweep in the 110 meter hurdles. Kelly had a single in three trips and made one of two U.S. errors afield.

Silver medalists included Kiviat and starting pitcher Richard Byrd (discus), who notched three strikeouts and started the first double play in Olympic history. Ira Davenport, who caught the entire game and went two-for-three, was the 800 meter bronze medalist. High jump third-placer George Horine played half a game in

OLYMPIC GAMES AT STOCKHOLM, SWEDEN, 1912.

The Olympic base ball team (members of American team from the East) which defeated the Finland base ball team (members of American team from the West) in the match game in Stockholm; score 6—3; left to right, back row, Howard P. Drew, James J. Thorpe, Ben Adams, Wesley M. Oler; center row, John Paul Jones, Platt Adams, Abel R. Kiviat, Charles Brickley, George V. Bonhag; front row, Harold W. Holden, Kenneth McAleenan, mascot; E. L. R. Mercer.

left while Lawrence Whitney, the shot put bronze winner, took over in right halfway through the game.

One of the batting stars was a non-medalist. Sprinter Ira Courtney failed to make the finals in the 100 and 200 meter events and was part of a sprint relay team that was disqualified in the qualifying heats. Courtney vented his frustration on the baseball field, going two-for-three. His double and Kiviat's three-bagger were the only U.S. extra-base hits.

The Americans scored again in their half of the second to go up by 5-0. The Swedes got on the scoreboard with a pair of runs in the fourth. The Yanks put the game out of reach with an eight-run fifth inning. The Vasteras club managed a final tally in the sixth, aided by the fact they were allowed six outs in the frame. The U.S. won by a 13-3 score.

Swedish officials praised the local boys who, according to the final Games reports, "did not at all make such a bad figure in the field." The Swedes made five errors plus a few other mistakes, notes the report, "excusable on account of nervousness, etc."

Legend has it that Olympic great Jim Thorpe, a future major leaguer, played in the game. Thorpe's name does not appear in the boxscore, and with good reason. The USA-Sweden match took place on the last day of the decathlon competition. Competing in both events would have been an incredible feat, even for Thorpe.

The game received little coverage in the States. The July 17 edition of the *New York Times*, however, describes a game held the day after the USA-Sweden game. In this contest, two teams of American players squared off with the East squad topping the West, 6-3. "Platt Adams, New York Athletic Club, and C.E. Brickley, Harvard University, composed the battery for the East, notes the *Times*, "while Walter McClure, Olympic Athletic Association, San Francisco; R.L. Byrd, Adrian College, and Edward F. Lindberg, Chicago Athletic Association, were in the points for the West." Platt Adams was the brother of Ben, who'd been loaned to the Swedish team the day before, while Byrd and McClure had pitched for the U.S. team.

"The game was a novelty to the Swedes, and a large crowd was present," according to the *Times*. Ironically, the organizing committee report says the previous day's USA-Sweden match had "no great crowd of spectators, and those that were present were mostly Americans or Swedish Americans."

Thorpe managed to get into the second game, playing right field and ripping a double in two official trips to the plate.

All but forgotten in the USA–Sweden game was the umpire: George Wright. In the official report on the Stockholm Games, his name is listed unobtrusively at the bottom of the boxscore. Wright had been baseball's first superstar with the Cincinnati Red Stockings. He'd become a wealthy sporting goods entrepreneur after his playing days. In 1912 he was a spry 65 years of age. Al-

BASE BALL AT STOCKHOLM, 1912

SWEDEN VS. UNITED STATES.

The Swedish team was augmented by a battery consisting of Ben Adams and Wesley Oler, Jr., furnished by the American players.

SWEDEN.	AB.	R.	H.	P.	A.	E.		UNITED STATES.	AB.	R.	H.	P.	A.	E.
Oler, c.	4	0	1	7	2	0		Drew, rf.	1	1	0	0	0	0
B. Adams, p.	3	0	1	2	2	1		Whitney, rf.	1	1	0	0	0	0
Nelson, p.	1	0	0	0	1	0		Courtney, 3b.	3	2	2	1	0	0
Holden, p.	0	0	0	0	0	0		Kiviat, ss.	4	2	2	2	0	0
Sapery, ss.	4	0	0	0	0	0		Jones, 2b.	3	1	1	1	2	0
Welin, 1b.	3	0	0	2	0	1		Kelly, cf.	3	1	1	0	0	1
Wikman, 3b.	3	0	1	0	0	0		Patterson, cf.	1	0	0	0	0	0
Landahl, 2b.	3	0	1	3	0	2		Davenport, c.	3	2	2	7	0	0
Larson, rf.	3	1	1	0	0	0		Irons, lf.	2	0	1	1	0	0
Torsleff, lf.	1	1	0	1	0	1		Horine, lf.	1	1	0	1	0	0
Johannson, lf.	1	1	1	0	0	0		Bonhag, 1b.	2	0	0	6	0	0
Axell, cf.	3	0	0	1	0	0		Blanchard, 1b.	1	1	1	2	0	1
								Byrd, p.	0	0	0	0	1	0
								Haff, p.	2	0	0	0	1	0
								McClure, p.	0	1	0	0	0	0
Totals	30	3	7	15	5	5		Totals	27	13	10	21*	4	2

* Sweden allowed 6 put-outs in last (sixth) inning.

United States	4	1	0	0	8	x—	13
Sweden	0	0	0	2	0	1—	3

Two-base hits—Courtney, Wikman. Three-base hit—Kiviat. Stolen bases—Kiviat, Jones 2, Davenport 2, Johannson. Bases on balls—Off B. Adams 1, off Nelson 3. Struck out—By B. Adams 3, by Byrd 3, by Haff 3, by McClure 1, by Nelson 3, by Holden 1. Double plays—Byrd to Bonhag. Wild pitches—B. Adams, Nelson. Hit by pitched ball—Drew, Kelly. Passed balls—Oler 2, Davenport 2. Umpire—Mr. George Wright.

UNITED STATES TEAMS—EAST VS. WEST.

The exhibition game of base ball, arranged by the athletes of the American Olympic team, was played between representatives of the Eastern and Western portions of the United States, who called themselves for the occasion "Finlands" (West) and "Olympics" (East).

FINLAND.	AB.	R.	H.	P.	A.	E.		OLYMPIC.	AB.	R.	H.	P.	A.	E.
Irons, 2b.	4	0	1	0	4	1		Drew, rf.	3	1	1	0	0	0
Courtney, ss.	3	0	0	1	1	0		Kiviat, ss.	3	1	2	1	2	2
Davenport, lf.	4	0	1	1	0	1		Brickley, c.	3	0	0	14	2	0
Lindberg, c.	4	0	0	12	2	1		Mercer, 3b.	4	1	0	1	0	0
Haff, 1b.	4	0	0	7	0	0		P. Adams, p.	4	1	0	1	2	0
Kelly, 3b.	3	2	2	2	1	3		Jones, 2b.	2	0	1	0	1	0
Horine, cf.	4	1	1	3	0	0		Bonhag, 1b.	4	0	0	8	0	1
McClure, rf., p.	4	0	2	0	1	0		Holden, lf.	4	1	0	2	0	1
Byrd, p, rf.	3	0	0	1	1	0		B. Adams, cf.	2	0	0	1	0	0
								Oler, cf.	2	1	1	0	0	0
								Thorpe, rf.	2	0	1	0	0	0
Totals	33	3	7	27	10	6		Totals	33	6	7	27	8	4

Two-base hits—Kelly; Thorpe, Kiviat. Stolen bases—Irons, Haff, McClure 3, Kelly 2; Drew, Kiviat, P. Adams, Jones 2, Oler 2. Bases on balls—Off McClure 1, off Adams 2. Struck out—By Byrd 6, by McClure 4; by Adams 11. Hit batsman—Byrd 2. Passed balls—Lindberg 3. Left on bases—Finland 6, Olympic 4. Umpires—Messrs. Bonine and Sweeney.

though no evidence had turned up that history's first Olympic ump was *the* George Wright, all indications are that it was. Frederick Ivor-Campbell of the Society of American Baseball Research (whose brief account of Wright's life appears in *The Biographical Dictionary of American Sport*) asks rhetorically: "Who else would it be? An Englishman? Hardly. Some other George Wright with enough interest in and knowledge of baseball that he would officiate at a ball game in Sweden? Maybe, but I'll bet not." [*Confirmation of* the *George Wright as the umpire in the first 1912 Olympic contest came shortly after this piece was completed. The confirmation came from two very disparate sources. Darryl Brock, author of* If I Never Get Back *and one of the foremost authorities on the Cincinnati Red Stockings, called to report a conversation with one of Wright's descendants, who confirmed that his ancestor was indeed the arbiter in Stockholm. Ironically, a day before Brock's call, the author discovered a poster that had appeared in Stockholm during the Olympics. The poster hawks a game between the "Amerikanst Baseboll-lag" and the "Vasteras' Basebollklubb," and mentions "Georg" Wright of the "Champion Baseball Team of the World."*] George

Wright would live another 25 years, long enough to witness baseball's next Olympic appearance.

Kaatsen **and curveballs**—Four years after the Olympic baseball contest in Stockholm, the Games were canceled due to the First World War. Baseball didn't appear at Antwerp in 1920 or at Paris in 1924, but the game sometimes gets a mention in reports of the 1928 Games in Amsterdam. No reputable sources concur. Bill Henry, sports editor of the *Los Angeles Times*, was an eyewitness to the Amsterdam Games. As sports technical director for the next Olympics, Henry was in town to give a report on L.A.'s progress. His definitive work, *An Approved History of the Olympic Games*, (first published in 1948) doesn't include baseball as a sport in Amsterdam. Neither does the American Olympic Committee report for the Seventh Olympiad, nor do any of the works of Erich Kamper, the noted Austrian Olympics expert. A possible explanation for the confusion: one of the demonstration sports on the docket in Amsterdam was *kaatsen*. Perhaps it was this sport—a Dutch version of cricket—that some mistook for baseball at the Games of 1928.

But baseball would make a brief, post-World War One Olympic comeback, and there is evidence that, but for the Second World War, baseball might have become an official medal sport in the Olympics much sooner than it actually did.

M.E. Travaglini's fascinating account ("Olympic Baseball 1936: Was es Das?" *The National Pastime*, Winter 1985) cites Leslie Mann's efforts in bringing baseball to Berlin in 1936. Mann had hoped to make baseball an exhibition sport in 1932 (Los Angeles organizers went instead with football and lacrosse). A 16-year big-league outfielder, Mann dreamed of baseball as an Olympic sport. He had a prominent role in his own dream. An ambitious soul who brought along a publicist to Berlin (*Miami Herald* sports editor Dinty Dennis), Mann, claims Travaglini, "liked being at the center of attention." Longtime U.S. Olympic Committee member Bob Paul described Mann to Travaglini as "a hot dog. With the mustard." In Mann's report to the Olympic Committee on the baseball team, the old flyhawk mentions himself (in the third person) no less than nine times.

Mann's breakthrough came in 1934 when Berlin organizers invited the Americans to engage in a challenge match with Japan. The "challenge"—engineered by Mann, Travaglini believes—never materialized. The game in Berlin would turn out to be an all-American affair.

"Trials" for the Olympic baseball team took place in Baltimore during early July. Years later, one player told Loel Schrader of the Long Beach *Independent Press-Telegram* that "they wouldn't send you (to Berlin) unless you could come up with $500 for expenses." Stanford University's Harry Wolter would coach the 21-member squad. Mann took the title of manager, with Dinty Dennis as assistant manager.

"Men blaspheme what they do not know," opined seventeenth century French philosopher and mathematician Blaise Pascal. Pascal obviously wasn't one of the more than 90,000 spectators at Berlin's Olympic Stadium on August 12. Mann (whom Pascal probably would have blasphemed) reported the attendance as 125,000. No matter. The German fans, seeing baseball for the first time, loved it—but for the wrong reasons. "Here's somebody running down to first base and the crowd's cheering—and it's a pop-up," one surviving player told Travaglini. "But belt one out beyond second base and go for extra bases and there's no reaction at all."

The game was played at night on a makeshift diamond with no mound and bad lighting ("I think they had one 20-watt bulb in centerfield," quipped Gordon Mallatrat, one of four Stanford players in Berlin). Through a loudspeaker system, an announcer kept the crowd informed of the game's nuances. The players had been divided into two teams, the "World Champions" and the "U.S. Olympics." An inside-the-park homer by former Bowdoin College player Bill Shaw gave the Olympics a 2-0 lead in the first. After the homer, said Dick Hanna, another Stanford alum, "there was a big pause. Then there was an announcement in German that...hitting a home run was a big deal. So, everybody cheered."

The novelty was beginning to wane by the seventh inning, which the announcer told the fans would be the final frame—to great applause. The U.S. Olympics managed a run in the top of the seventh to knot the score at 5-5. Les McNeese of Fort Lauderdale, Florida, settled matters in the last of the seventh with a homer to give the World Champions a 6-5 win. Relying on his curve, Carson Thompson of the Penn A.C. hurled four shutout innings in relief of starter Bill Sayles of the University of Oregon.

A four-letter man from Temple University, Thompson's most vivid memory from Berlin had come a few days earlier. He'd been selected to explain the game to one of the narrators of an Olympic documentary film. Thompson told Phil Elderkin of the *Christian Science Monitor* that the narrator turned out to be "a charming woman," with whom Thompson spent an entire afternoon. The narrator was Eva Braun, the mistress of Adolf Hitler.

The game received mixed reviews. Most reporters panned it ("There is reason to believe that Germany has been made immune to baseball," wrote Joe Williams of the *New York Times*). The 1912 contest in Stockholm had at least been an international affair.

Mann remained undaunted. His report mentions Japan's plans to include baseball as part of the 1940 Games, which were set for Tokyo. Mann's agenda included a series between the U.S. and Japan in 1937 and in 1939. The 1940 "World's Tournament" in Tokyo would involve seven other teams: China, the Philippines, Hawaii (a U.S. territory at the time), England, Germany, Mexico and Cuba.

World events over the next nine years would snuff out Mann's dreams, not to mention some 55 million lives. But Bill Shaw, interviewed by Travaglini, was certain that Mann had almost pulled it off. "Without the events that interfered with the 1940 Olympics," Shaw told Travaglini, "Baseball would now be as much a part of the regular Olympic program as soccer is."

Pesapallo **and the game Down Under**—In ancient times, wars were postponed so that the Olympics could take place. In this century, it's been the opposite. In 1948, after the world had pulled itself together again, the Olympic Games resumed. By now basketball, another American sport, was thriving in the Olympics. Baseball was still feeling its way. Left out entirely at the 1948 Games in London, baseball took a back seat in Helsinki in 1952.

That year the Finns unveiled their own brand of baseball, called *pesapallo*. Developed in the twenties by a Finnish professor named Lauri Pihkala, *pesapallo* resembles baseball about as much as baseball resembles cricket. The Finnish pastime has a pitcher stationed to the right of home plate; a catcher who stands a few feet in front of home plate and a first baseman located halfway between third and home. Second base in *pesapallo* is where first base would be in American baseball. There are a pair of positions called "left shortstop" and "right shortstop." The entire field is shaped like an overgrown home plate. The pitcher, standing not far away and to the right of the batter, tosses the ball in an upward spiral. As the ball descends, the batter takes his cut and the pitcher ducks out of the way. The result looks like a two-man fungo operation, with spaghetti-bowl baselines that go from home to first (which is halfway down the third base side) and from there diagonally across the field to second. To get to third, a runner cuts straight across the field and from there to home, crossing first base in the process.

Erich Kamper's *Encyclopedia of the Olympic Games* cites a *pesapallo* contest on July 31 in which the Workers' Athletic Federation topped the Finnish League, 8-4. The rosters include immortals like Eero Vuorlu and Osmo Juntto. Not included in Kamper's tome are a pair of good old-fashioned baseball games played by an American pickup team.

According to Phil Elderkin, the Helsinki organizing committee invited the Americans to play the champions of Finnish baseball. This time the U.S. soccer team would furnish the personnel. Walter Giesler, the soccer manager, was pressed into service to organize the baseball squad. The Yanks scrimmaged a team from Venezuela to prep for the game with the Finns. The American win streak remained intact as the U.S. players whipped the Venezuelans, 14-4.

The game with Finland was a rout. Played in the Helsinki Football Stadium before some 4,000 fans—well below expectations—the Americans scored seven runs in the first inning en route to a 19-1 triumph. U.S. Olympic Soccer Committee chairman W. T. Hobson, Jr., reported that the highlight of the game was Charlie Colombo's homer. Colombo, a soccer standout from St. Louis, knocked the ball "over the top of the grandstand," noted Hobson.

Summer comes late in the year to the Antipodes. When the Australian city of Melbourne hosted the Olympics in 1956, the events took place November 22 through December 8. By 1956 W.R. (Bill) Schroeder had been director of the Helms Athletic Foundation for almost a decade. Schroeder was a west coast sportsman who, in the forties, had been one of the founders of the California League. The Helms Athletic Foundation (the forerunner of today's Amateur Athletic Foundation in Los Angeles) was an altruistic organization funded by a wealthy Los Angeles bakery. Through the Foundation, Schroeder had strong ties with the Amateur Athletic Union and the U.S. Olympic Committee. When Aussie organizers asked for an American team to put on a few clinics and play in a demonstration game, officials contacted Schroeder.

Schroeder scarcely had a budget. But he came up with a brilliantly simple idea. The armed forces played an important role in America's Olympic movement. Schroeder would put together a team made up of servicemen from the U.S. Far East Command. Military transports would bring the players to Australia from around the Pacific. The all-service team played a series of exhibition games with local teams around the countr prior to the Games.

The big game was scheduled for the morning of December 1 in the main stadium. Track and Field events—always the Olympics' centerpiece—were scheduled for later that day. Most newspaper accounts of the day's activities make no mention of the baseball game. "Poorly advertised and poorly timed, only a few thousand fans saw the first few innings of U.S. vs. Australia," writes Phil Elderkin.

As the game progressed, track and field fans began arriving in droves. By late in the game there were an estimated 114,000 in the stands—believed to be the largest ever for any baseball game.

The Americans beat the Aussies, 11-5. The big blow was a bases-loaded home run by a sergeant named Vance Sutton. The U.S. Olympic baseball win skein, which spanned five decades, now stood at 4-0.

The great U.S. '64 squad—By 1964 Rod Dedeaux, the legendary University of Southern California coach, was well known in Japanese baseball circles. Dedeaux's 1955 USC squad had barnstormed through Asia. The affable Dedeaux's Trojans had taken on all comers, including U.S. military teams and native ballclubs in Okinawa, Korea and Japan.

The 1964 Games were the first in Asia. The Japanese take their baseball seriously, and Tokyo's Olympic organizers invited Dedeaux to bring an amateur team for an exhibition. The team would be the best to date to play baseball in the Olympics. After Tokyo, ironically, there would be no more Olympic baseball for two decades. By then the old era of Olympic baseball, when the sport was buffeted about like a red-headed stepchild, would be over.

Dedeaux's 1964 team boasted a better roster than several expansion teams of the sixties. His collection of collegiate all-stars included eight future major leaguers. Among the U.S. pitchers were left-hander Alan Closter of Iowa State (who later played for the Senators, Yankees and Braves); Dick Joyce of Holy Cross (Athletics) and Chuck Dobson (who won 74 games, mostly for the A's, between 1966 and '75).

The position players included Jim Hibbs, an All-American catcher from Stanford (Angels); rifle-armed Florida State receiver Ken Suarez (A's, Indians, Rangers); slugging University of California first baseman Mike Epstein (who pounded out 130 homers for five big-league teams over a 9-year career); outfielder Shaun Fitzmaurice of Notre Dame (Mets) and one of Dedeaux's USC stars, second sacker Gary Sutherland (a capable utilityman for seven major league clubs from 1966-78).

The baseball squad wasn't considered part of the official U.S. Olympic contingent. Instead of quarters in the Olympic village, the baseball players found themselves staying in an antiquated YMCA. Eventually the team moved to more suitable lodgings in a Tokyo hotel. They soon became the envy of the other American athletes. Unlike their brethren in the Olympic village, the baseball players weren't subject to curfew. One team member recalls attending a party with sprinter Bob Hayes and Walt Hazzard of the basketball team. When Hayes and Hazzard had to leave early to make curfew, the baseball player continued to boogie to his heart's content.

More than 50,000 fans turned out for the game with a Japanese amateur all-star team on October 11. Dedeaux positioned himself in the third base coaching box, wondering how his team would fare. "Shaun Fitzmaurice was the leadoff hitter," Dedeaux told Loel Schrader. "He hit the first pitch of the game for a home run over the left-centerfield fence." The U.S. was en route to yet another Olympic victory, this one a 6-2 triumph.

Again, hardly anyone noticed or cared. The Olympic exploits of Bob Hayes and Walt Hazzard are legendary. All that's remembered of Shaun Fitzmaurice, if anything, is a .154 lifetime major league batting average.

Try, try again—Why did it take so long for baseball to win full status as an Olympic sport? While baseball started, sputtered and stopped in the Games, basketball had flourished. One stumbling block was Avery Brundage, the venerable head of the International Olympic Committee. Brundage, Olympism's answer to Judge

K.M. Landis, ruled the Games for years with an iron fist. To Brundage, the Olympics were for individual athletes. To him team sports—and the Winter Olympics, for that matter—were anathema.

Another problem was baseball's near-total lack of popularity outside of North and South America. While Americans played baseball and measured in feet and inches, the rest of the world used the metric system and played soccer. Curiously, as soccer began to boom in the U.S., the rest of the world began to discover baseball.

The final stumbling block was the lack of a viable international organization. Each Olympic sport has its own world governing body. Going back to Les Mann in the thirties, several organizations had tried this role and failed. It wasn't until the mid-seventies, with the founding of the International Association of Amateur Baseball (eventually renamed the International Baseball Association) that the sport would enjoy worldwide organization and unity.

AINBA officials almost immediately began lobbying for baseball in the Olympics. Avery Brundage had stepped down as the IOC head after the 1972 Olympics. Slowly, the complexion of the Olympics began to change. In 1981 the IOC Executive Board approved baseball as a demonstration sport for the 1984 Games in Los Angeles. A six-team format was adopted at an IOC session in New Delhi in March, 1983. Five months later the six teams were selected. They would come from South Korea, Italy, Cuba, Nicaragua, Chinese Taipei and the U.S.

Cuba no! Japan si!—Some 385,000 fans would watch the baseball games of the Los Angeles Olympics. Only track and field and soccer would attract more. The contests were played at Dodger Stadium, quite an improvement over the makeshift diamonds of the past.

Rod Dedeaux, again the American team coach, knew Cuba would be tough to beat. "They've got pitching, power and defense," he said. Forbidden to sign with major league teams since the early days of the Castro regime, several Cuban players could have easily commanded megabucks on the free agent market.

Cuba, however, joined the Soviet-led boycott, and the Dominican Republic replaced them in the Olympics. The tournament had also been expanded to include two more teams, Japan and Canada. With the Cubans gone, Dedeaux figured the Asian teams—especially Korea—would be the toughest competition.

The American squad included future major leaguers like Will Clark, Mark McGwire, Cory Snyder, Barry Larkin, Shane Mack, Bobby Witt, Scott Bankhead and Billy Swift. After a close 2-1 win over Chinese Taipei, they beat Italy, 16-1, and the Dominican Republic, 12-0, in the preliminary round.

Japan had gone 2-1 in the prelim round, losing to Canada. The Japanese won their semifinal game with Chinese Taipei in a 10-inning, 2-1 contest. Oddibe

McDowell's homer sparked a 5-2 win over Korea in the other semi.

Dedeaux's ace, John Hoover of Fresno State, started the championship game while Japanese coach Reiichi Matsunaga's choice was Atsunori Ito. Matsunaga also inserted Katsumi Hirosawa at first base, where the incumbent was in a three-for-15 slump.

The Americans scored first, but Japan nicked Hoover for two in the fourth and another in the 5th. It stayed that way until the 8th when Hirosawa lit up Hoover for a three-run homer. In the 9th the U.S. scored twice, but it wasn't enough. Japan won, 6-3. Ito, with relief help, got the victory. A streak that dated back to the Stockholm Games of 1912 was over.

Popcorn and smoked squid—While most of the American players went on to the pro ranks, the Cubans kept on winning at the amateur level. Cuba took the Intercontinental Cup at Edmonton in 1985. At Amsterdam in '86 they claimed the World title. At the following year's Pan American Games in Indianapolis, the Cubans survived a 58-minute rain delay and wiped out a 3-run U.S. lead in the gold medal game. Two months later they captured another Intercontinental Cup title.

Cuba joined a North Korean boycott of the Seoul Olympics, however, much to the dismay of U.S. coach Mark Marquess and his players, including nine veterans of the '87 Pan Am Games. Stung by the 13-9 loss to Cuba in the Championship Pan Am game, the Americans wanted a rematch. Australia replaced Cuba, joining the U.S., Japan, Korea, Chinese Taipei, Canada, Puerto Rico and Holland in the Olympic tournament.

Marquess (a Stanford coach, like 1936 mentor Harry Wolter) had a starting rotation of Ben McDonald, Andy Benes and Jim Abbott, but was wary of Japan. "No matter who you pitch, they have good balance," said Marquess.

The concession stands at Chamshil offered smoked squid and seaweed rice balls as well as popcorn, candy and Coke. There was music and dancing in the stands during games ("It gets a little irritating," griped Ben McDonald). Somehow Olympic organizers—who had spent $3 billion preparing for the Games—forgot to purchase a tarp for the baseball diamond. An early game between Canada and Australia, following a rainstorm, was played on a soaked field. Aside from these aberrations, it was baseball as usual in the Land of the Morning Calm.

The Americans went 2-1 in preliminary play, good enough to advance to the semifinals. They beat a tough Korean squad, 5-3, and pasted the Aussies, 12-1, before losing, 8-7, to future big league hurler Rheal Cormier of Canada. In the semifinal Ben McDonald, the 6-7 Louisiana State pitcher, handcuffed Puerto Rico, 7-2. Japan's 3-1 win over Korea set up a rematch of the 1984 championship game.

Lefty Jim Abbott of the University of Michigan, born with only a partial right hand, was a favorite of the Asian press in Seoul. Abbott had ended Cuba's win skein at home one year earlier. Coach Marquess handed Abbott the ball for the title match.

Ex-University of Tampa first baseman Tino Martinez gave Abbott all the support he needed with a pair of homers and 4 RBI's, and the U.S. had a 5-3 win. Abbott pitched the whole way, allowing 7 hits. "I didn't come in here thinking home run," Martinez told *Baseball America's* Danny Knobler. "They just happened."

The absence of Cuba didn't dampen the American victory celebration. "They're not here," said U.S. third baseman Robin Ventura. "That's their own problem. They know we can beat them."

Barcelona: Maybe not a Cuban dynasty— Cuba will finally make it to the Olympics in 1992. The Cubans went undefeated in the '91 Pan Am Games in Havana ("Cuba," says '92 Olympic coach Ron Fraser of the University of Miami, "is better than the Cleveland Indians.") Ironically, Barcelona could be the Cubans' last chance for Olympic glory. Without Soviet aid, how long will Castro's regime last? Without Castro, will Cuban players be permitted once more to sign with big league teams (and, if they are, will the Washington Senators mount a comeback?) How badly would the drain of talent affect the Cuban team?

Even if Cuba maintains the status quo, the cracks are showing. A Cuban team at the 1991 World Junior Championships in Brandon, Manitoba, finished fifth. ESPN's Peter Gammons reports that scouts were "shocked at the low quality" of the Cuban squad.

The field is set for baseball's first true Olympic tournament. Japan, Chinese Taipei, Puerto Rico, Italy, Spain and the Dominican Republic are entered, along with Cuba and the U.S. Baseball's international popularity is at an all-time high and the game is played in more nations than ever before.

If Cuba wanes as an international power, will the U.S. fill the vacuum? Or Japan? What about Chinese Taipei, whose youth teams always dominate in Little League play? Or Australia, the team that handed the Japanese their only loss at this year's Asian tournament? Has anyone noticed that three Aussie natives—Craig Shipley of the Padres, David Nilsson of the Brewers and the Yankees' Mark Hutton—played in the majors or high minors in 1991?

Stay tuned!

Jorge Pasquel and the Evolution of the Mexican League

Gerald F. Vaughn

The author wishes to acknowledge SABR member Jorge Menendez of Merida, Mexico, for special assistance in researching and writing this article.

The Mexican League has thrived as a top minor league since coming into U.S. organized baseball in 1955. The name of Jorge Pasquel is often associated with evolution of the Mexican League. Yet mystery still surrounds this most central figure in the administrative history of Latin America's own national pastime. He is described in Mexico itself as a tempestuous man whom nobody could understand, a man who would always help the needy but ruthlessly walk over anyone who opposed him.

Who was Jorge Pasquel, this man who raided major league baseball for talent in the 1940s? What impelled him to take the lead in Mexican baseball? Was it a desire to advance the professionalism of Mexican baseball, a businessman's pursuit of profits, or a nationalistic passion to compete with the United States? What was his lasting contribution to Mexican League baseball? To provide answers, this article begins by tracing events leading to Pasquel's ascendancy to the presidency of the Mexican League and then examines the consequences of his colorful reign.

Beginnings—Mexican baseball historians say that the first game played in their country took place on July 4,

Gerald F. Vaughn *is an economist at the University of Delaware and a past contributor of SABR research articles on various aspects of Mexican League baseball history.*

1889, near Monterrey. Its organizer reportedly was Treadwell A. Robertson, a former U.S. Army colonel turned businessman.

Interest in baseball in Mexico accelerated after visits by the Chicago White Sox in 1906 and important Cuban teams around 1917 or perhaps 1918. Local amateur teams soon formed leagues. In 1925 the semi-pro Mexican League, forerunner of today's professional circuit, was founded through the efforts of Ernesto Carmona and Alejandro Aguilar Reyes. Connections with professional U.S. baseball were also increasing. In the 1920s Black Americans were paid to play baseball in Mexico, and Black teams from Texas often performed south of the Rio Grande border. By the early 1930s all-star teams of white major leaguers and minor leaguers also were coming to stage exhibition games in Spanish-speaking venues like Yucatan and Campeche. And in 1933 Melo Almada, a fine hitter and adequate outfielder, became the first Mexican-born native son to play in the stateside major leagues. All of this contributed to the continuing rapid rise of baseball's popularity within the proud if impoverished Mexican nation.

Enter Jorge Pasquel—Just as baseball first boomed, Jorge Pasquel had himself first become influential upon the Mexican scene. Pasquel's own influence is founded in his family's vast wealth and in his relationships with leading political figures, most especially his nearly lifelong friendship with Miguel Aleman, president of the Mexican nation from 1946 through 1952.

Jorge Pasquel was born into substantial wealth on April 23, 1907, in Veracruz, one of five brothers and three sisters. His father made his money first through owning the

Jorge Pasquel

when Aleman maintained office as president of the republic, ten pictures hung on Jorge's own office walls in Mexico City—five were of Aleman and still another was of the president's son. Jorge was even to be found on the ceremonial stage at Aleman's formal inauguration and reportedly could casually drop in at the head-of-state's private residence, a privilege which none of the other leading politicians in the land enjoyed.

What, then, was Jorge Pasquel's true interest in Mexican League baseball? Had Aleman already decided some years before 1946 to run for the presidency? Had he received Pasquel's aid in every way possible, including exploitation of the Mexican League (by then a professional circuit), a league which Pasquel essentially controlled beginning as early as 1940? Was the plan which Pasquel (and perhaps Aleman) soon launched to buy up American ballplayers in reality no more than a thinly veiled effort to buy up the baseball-crazy Mexican voters? Let us examine Jorge Pasquel's relationships with the game still more closely.

Jorge Pasquel played sandlot, school, and amateur baseball as a young boy; later he would work out on occasion with the Mexican League team that he owned and sometimes also managed. In manhood he on occasion expressed the desire to bring Mexican League baseball up to the competitive level of U.S. professional standards. His ultimate hope seemed to be a "world series" played between the U.S. major league winner and his own Mexican League champions. By 1940 he had acquired controlling interest in the Veracruz Blues team of the Mexican League and also majority ownership of Mexico City's Delta Park, the finest baseball stadium in the country, though admittedly inferior by American standards. All of the other club owners wanted access to Delta Park as well, so Pasquel's control of the stadium gave him in effect virtual control over the entire league. He was not officially president of the Mexican League, however, until the 1946-1948 seasons rolled into view.

The Mexican League showed a financial profit for the first time in 1942. Quincy Trouppe, an outstanding Black catcher and third baseman, recalled years later Pasquel's mounting influence at the outset of the forties. In 1943 Negro leaguers Trouppe and Theolic Smith (a fireballing pitcher and good-hitting outfielder) sought draft exemptions in the U.S. so they could play baseball for cash down in Mexico. They were turned down by their wartime draft boards, and Trouppe wrote to Pasquel personally before he unhappily returned to work in a stateside defense plant. Soon the talented Negro leaguer was contacted at his home by the Mexican consul, who personally informed him that the neighboring nation of Mexico was lending the U.S. (obviously at Pasquel's arrangement) an impressive total of 80,000 war laborers in return for the baseball services of Trouppe and Smith (Rogosin, 1985, p. 174).

most profitable cigar factory in Mexico, then with a customs brokerage begun in the late 1890s. His estate (estimated at around a million dollars) upon his death became the base of the family's expanding business empire. By the mid-1940s the Pasquel holdings were measured in the tens of millions of dollars, perhaps as high as $60 million, due primarily to the burgeoning business sense of Jorge himself.

On July 25, 1932, Jorge was married to Ernestina Calles, daughter of former Mexican president Plutarco Elias Calles; they would subsequently be divorced, but not before Pasquel benefitted substantially from this nuptial arrangement of convenience. Most importantly and immediately, Jorge's connections with the Calles family brought federal patronage to the Pasquel customs brokerage. The Pasquel firm eventually handled more government shipping than any competitor and benefitted greatly as well from trade with the U.S. The company reportedly was the largest liquor importer in Mexico. Dealing primarily in imports and exports, shipping, banking, tobacco growing, newspaper publishing, cattle ranching, contracting and real estate, Jorge and his brothers also ran the National Lottery in Veracruz for awhile and were even officially sanctioned agents for General Motors.

Some of Jorge's business ventures secretly were in partnership with Miguel Aleman. During the stretch

American baseball itself in turn became more aware of Pasquel that very same year. The powerful Latino entrepreneur began hiring into the Mexican League a number of unemployed umpires who had been left out in the cold when the U.S. minor league circuits had shut down for the duration of the world war. Some of these "Yanqui" umpires would stay on in the Mexican League long after global hostilities had come to a complete halt and the cry of "play ball!" was again being heard everywhere north of the Rio Grande.

Tensions meanwhile increased on the Latin baseball circuit because some major league owners—principally Clark Griffith of the Washington Senators—had assigned scouts to the Latin American countries and had begun signing many players from Cuba and several from Mexico and other countries of the region. Baseball clubs within Latin America simply couldn't hope to compete against such inroads from wealthy U.S. pro teams, so they collectively and vehemently complained to Commissioner Kenesaw Mountain Landis who in 1943 mildly rebuked Griffith's practices and temporarily maintained an uneasy truce for hemisphere baseball relations.

The Mexican League attracted still further attention in 1944. Cooperstown Hall of Famer Rogers Hornsby was hired to manage briefly at Veracruz, and Chicago Cubs catcher Chico Hernandez came into the Mexican League to play for an entire season. Respectability finally seemed to be camping on the doorstep. Faced with such encroachments from the North American game, Pasquel decided he simply had to learn more about North American baseball technique, so he came to the U.S. for a full eight months for the sole purpose of observing, first-hand, big-time "Yanqui" diamond action. Expenses for Jorge and his entourage amounted to $285,000, he himself would later estimate. It was on this trip that he first realized precisely what an influx of major league talent might indeed do to elevate the game of baseball in Mexico, and he knew it would take plenty of money—money which his family had, even if the Mexican League itself didn't. In 1945 Jorge Pasquel started luring Latin Americans playing in the U.S. majors to come to the Mexican League, two of the best being outfielder Roberto Ortiz (a native Cuban) of the Washington Senators and pitcher Tommie de la Cruz (another Cuban, and focus of a separate article on Black Cuban ballplayers by Peter C. Bjarkman found elsewhere in this volume) of the Cincinnati Reds. The 1945 season, now bolstered by such recruits, was financially very successful for Pasquel's second-class circuit, netting around $400,000 in pure dollar profit.

Pasquel, Aleman and Nationalism—Max Lanier, the modestly talented St. Louis Cardinals pitcher who was soon enticed to depart the major leagues in 1946 to play in Pasquel's infant circuit, is quoted by author Donald Honig as follows:

I stayed in Mexico about a year and a half. We found out later why the Pasquel brothers were after the big leaguers to come down there. At the time Aleman was running for president, and I think there was some family relationship between him and Jorge Pasquel. Now the people of Mexico loved baseball. It was worked out so Aleman got the credit for us coming down there. They figured he'd get some votes out of it. And he did get elected. So I think the whole thing was strictly a political deal. After the election Pasquel started cutting everybody. He cut me from $20,000 a year to $10,000. That's when we started jumping back to the States. (Honig, 1975, p. 219)

The story of Jorge Pasquel and Mexican baseball thus also seems to be the story of Miguel Aleman. It is at the very least a story of nationalistic feelings and actions against U.S. interests that should be viewed against a backdrop of experiences shared by Pasquel and his compatriot, Miguel Aleman.

Pasquel's experiences with the United States had been from the first a strange mixture of the good with the very bad. He had begun making yearly trips north by 1931 and was favorably impressed by much of what he saw and learned about America's singular path of progress. However, he had reason as well for some negative impressions built up over the span of his years in public life. Unfortunately the U.S., for decades prior to adopting a "Good Neighbor Policy" toward Latin America in the early thirties, frequently intervened in the affairs of South and Central American nations and was considered blatantly imperialistic to many who didn't share the paternalistic view emanating from government circles in Washington. In one 1914 experience that both Pasquel and Aleman knew all too personally from their own childhoods, the U.S. Navy had bombarded and then seized the Mexican port of Veracruz. As a small boy Jorge cowered in a cellar in Veracruz while U.S. warships fired upon his home city and killed hundreds of its residents. The subsequent Good Neighbor Policy of Franklin Delano Roosevelt was a concerted effort, beginning in 1933, to improve relations with all of Latin America. The U.S. government thereafter refrained from direct intervention for many years. Yet such changes only partially healed old wounds for Jorge Pasquel and Miguel Aleman.

U.S. business influence was also still strongly present in Latin America, and in Mexico it was oppressively felt, resulting in expropriation of U.S. oil company holdings in 1938 by President Lazaro Cardenas. It was Miguel Aleman, then Governor of the state of Veracruz, who took the initiative to call together the governors of all Mexican states, to meet in the nation's capital shortly after the oil expropriation and declare their solidarity with President Cardenas; Aleman even became chairman of a formal union of governors. The Roosevelt administration did not question the right of the Mexican government to expropriate foreign-owned property but simply asked instead that a fair compensation be paid. The compensation issue took a period of years to resolve itself, stretching into the presidency of Mexico's Avila Camacho. Camacho was elected in 1940 with Miguel Aleman first serving as his campaign manager and subsequently as his Minister of the Interior.

John Gunther, in his 1941 book *Inside Latin America* observed:

> The most powerful minister in President Avila Camacho's administration is probably Miguel Aleman...the boss of the government machine...Alert, smooth, friendly, he had more to do with engineering Camacho's election than any other man. (Gunther, 1941, p. 47)

Also born on the outskirts of the city of Veracruz, Aleman became friends with Jorge Pasquel in early childhood. Aleman's father was a distinguished general who fought in the 1911 revolution against dictator Porfirio Diaz. Aleman graduated from the National University of Mexico in 1928, holding a law degree and displaying particular interest in labor law. He rapidly gained the posts of federal attorney, Supreme Court justice, senator, and governor of the important state of Veracruz, all by the relatively raw age of thirty-five. His record as Governor was exceptional, Cardenas liked him, he was known as a friend of labor, and he enlisted the backing of two-thirds of the governors to support Camacho's successful candidacy for president in 1940.

As Minister of the Interior under Camacho, Aleman controlled the federal police and cooperated closely with Washington officials during World War II, aiding especially in smashing Nazi and Fascist elements active in propaganda, espionage, and sabotage along the Mexican-Texas border region. He resigned as Minister of the Interior in June 1945 to launch his own candidacy for the presidency. He was elected to serve as president on July 7, 1946.

Miguel Aleman and Jorge Pasquel were not in any true sense fervently anti-American; rather, it would be more fair and accurate to claim that they were fervently pro-Mexican. Mexican nationalism would be asserted wherever necessary because the U.S. historically had not treated Mexico as a true equal hemisphere partner. Negro league historian Donn Rogosin has written on the matter: "Pasquel, an important financial backer of Mexican President Aleman, hoped to fan the flames of nationalism by proving that the Mexican League was the equal of the major leagues, and by analogy, that Mexico and the United States were in the same league, too." (Rogosin, 1985, p. 170)

At War with the Majors—Jorge Pasquel was described as "one of Mexico's shrewdest businessmen and most skillful showmen" in the 1946 volume of *Current Biography*. Assisted by his older brother, Bernardo, and younger brothers—Alfonso, Gerardo, and Mario—Jorge ran the family's business enterprises from his regal office suite, located at the prominent address of Ramon Guzman 71 in Mexico City. One large room of that impressive complex was devoted to board meetings of the Mexican League, where Pasquel conferred with owners of the other seven teams: Mexico City, Monterrey, Tampico, Torreon, Puebla, San Luis Potosi, and Nuevo Laredo. Jorge and/or his brothers were understood to have financial interests, though not controlling ones, in some of those remaining league teams and in many of their playing fields to boot.

Jorge was also admittedly an admirer of French emperor Napoleon Bonaparte. In the reception hall of Pasquel's mansion at Hamburgo 32 in Mexico City stood a statuette of General Napoleon. Jorge claimed to have read 25 books about his hero and considered himself a ranking authority on the famous French power-broker.

In 1946 Jorge Pasquel became himself emperor of Mexican League baseball and promptly went to war with U.S. organized baseball. For two years he and his brothers wooed top U.S. players to come to Mexico, drawing the wrath of major league club owners. During 1946 and 1947 about one-fifth of the Mexican League's 150 or more players had served in the U.S. major leagues or high minors; major leaguers included stars such as the aforementioned Max Lanier, Sal Maglie, George Hausmann, and Lou Klein. The Pasquels attempted to

Pasquel with the Bambino

upgrade the league to the point where it could hope to compete with the majors. Clearly they did not succeed. (For further details see the article entitled "George Hausmann Recalls the Mexican League of 1946-47" by the present author in SABR's *Baseball Research Journal* 19, 1990). The effort, of course, was doomed from its inception. Puebla team owner Castor Montoto complained in April 1946 that the Mexican clubs simply couldn't afford so many major leaguers. Sports columnist Joe Williams in New York—also in 1946—wrote:

> The Mexican League can never seriously threaten the balance of our two big leagues. The population isn't there, nor the facilities, and no matter how much money the many Pasquel brothers have at their command, there must come a time when they will grow weary of throwing it away.

So why did Jorge do it? Milton Bracker writing in *The New York Times* in June 1946 offered this answer:

> The real significance of Jorge Pasquel to Mexican baseball is not so much the handful of good players he has brought down. It is the prestige he has gained for the sport and for the nation by his skillfully impudent handling of the squabble with the majors.

Two years later the Mexican League was in complete disarray. By the end of the 1947 season, Pasquel's authority was diminished, though he continued to vie successfully for power. The 1948 season was, in turn, a full disaster. The league was reduced to only four teams by July, and all games were played in Mexico City where there were still sufficient fans. Quality players had left in mounting numbers. The season was scheduled to run through October 24, but the league abruptly disbanded September 19 and Pasquel resigned as president of the fallen circuit on October 28.

The Mexican League's total losses for 1946, 1947 and 1948 were estimated at $362,000, most of which perhaps was absorbed by the Pasquels. If Jorge sought profits from baseball, he had to be deeply disappointed. But as an astute businessman, he must have known that profit potential was modest at best. Neither he nor the Mexican government invested the huge sums in building modern stadiums that were essential to make Mexican baseball more competitive, and that lack of investment indicates they didn't really expect an adequate return. What began for Pasquel as a sincere interest in developing professional baseball in Mexico, with modest if any expectations of profits, became much more a mere exercise in nationalism. When the nationalistic purpose had been served, economic realities brought an end to his futile dream of equality with the major leagues.

The Aftermath—The Mexican League was reorganized in 1949 under new leadership. Jorge Pasquel retained his interest in his Veracruz Blues and from time to time would cause a stir that made people think he was perhaps seeking league control yet again. But he was less active in the league after 1951 when he was hit by a stone thrown during a game in San Luis Potosi. His popularity and influence in Mexico waned further in consequence of a distasteful financial arrangement that had substantially benefitted him alone at the clear expense of his fellow Mexican citizens. Jorge's close friend, President Aleman, had granted him an oil distribution monopoly in 1952 that raised prices to consumers while netting Pasquel thousands of dollars daily. Aleman's successor as president, Adolfo Ruiz Cortines, inaugurated in December 1952, soon announced that such government-protected monopolies must promptly end. First to be canceled was Pasquel's control of oil distribution, terminated on March 23, 1953. Pasquel was left in mild disgrace, content to manage his other quasi-legal enterprises and to go on the worldwide hunting safaris he so much enjoyed.

Jorge Pasquel died violently on March 7, 1955, in the crash of a private plane; five others aboard also perished. The fatal crash occurred in a rugged mountain region near Valles, 225 miles north of Mexico City. Pasquel thus did not live to see the Mexican League come fitfully into U.S. organized baseball only a month later in April 1955, nor had he played much of a role in the difficult negotiations, planning, and preparation that brought about this finest hour for Mexican professional baseball. Pasquel does deserve muted credit, however, for sparking a livelier interest in baseball among Mexicans, and he was thus not inappropriately elected into the Mexican Baseball Hall of Fame in 1971. Regrettably, he had been unable to build a solid financial and organizational base for the Mexican League during the years he controlled it. That task remained for Dr. Eduardo Quijano Pitman, Arnulfo T. Canales, Federico Miranda, and a succession of other league presidents and club officials, who together have raised today's Mexican League operation and calibre of play to the highest level of professionalism for which it is now justly known throughout the hemisphere.

References

Gunther, John. *Inside Latin America*. New York: Simon and Schuster, 1941.

Honig, Donald. *Baseball When the Grass Was Real—Baseball from the Twenties to the Forties, Told by the Men Who Played It*. New York: Coward, McCann and Geoghegan, 1975.

Rogosin, Donn. *Invisible Men: Life in Baseball's Negro Leagues*. New York: Atheneum Publishers, 1985.

Vaughn, Gerald F. "George Hausmann Recalls The Mexican League of 1946-47" in: *Baseball Research Journal* 19 (1990): 59-63.

Hall of Famers Shine in Puerto Rico

Thomas E. Van Hyning

Winter League baseball in Puerto Rico during the 1950s featured memorable teams, record-breaking performers and future Island and Cooperstown Hall of Famers. My family moved to Puerto Rico in the fall of 1956, about the same time Sandy Koufax joined the Caguas Criollos for the 1956-57 Winter League campaign.

The three-time Cy Young winner formed part of a club with an infield of Luke Easter (1B), Charles Neal (2B), Vic Power (3B), Felix Mantilla (SS). Koufax started Caguas' opening game on October 20, 1956 against the Ponce Lions before 8,635 fans at the Lions' den. He pitched well striking out 11, but lost 2-0.

Koufax, infielder Neal and pitcher Taylor Phillips were released later that winter due to a December 20, 1956 ruling that no Puerto Rico Winter League team could have more than three experienced Major Leaguers, excluding natives, on its active roster. Koufax finished at 3-6, 4.31 ERA with 76 strikeouts and 54 walks in 64.7 innings. He gave Island fans something to remember on December 16th when he shut out the powerful Santurce Crabbers 2-0 on two hits, both of them by 22-year old Roberto Clemente.

Clemente and 19-year old Juan Pizarro were Crabber teammates sold to Caguas in late December 1956. The Crabbers had just undergone an ownership change and were strapped for cash. Clemente, in the midst of winning his only Puerto Rico batting title, finished at .396 with 2 homers and 29 RBIs in sixty-two contests.

The four-time National League batting champion had

an 18-game hitting streak for Santurce at the time of the sale, and then hit in five straight games for Caguas. Luis Arroyo of the San Juan Senators put a halt to the 23-game hit streak when Clemente was collared in four trips in

Thomas E. Van Hyning *is assistant professor of Travel and Tourism at Keystone Junior College in La Plume, Pennsylvania, and also serves as stateside correspondent for the Puerto Rico Winter League Hall of Fame.*

Roberto Clemente

game two of a January 5, 1957 doubleheader. Clemente's average rose to .433 after his 23-game streak, a streak that is still the regular season standard.

While she was in Ponce, Puerto Rico, for the October 20, 1991 first-ever Island Winter League Hall of Fame baseball ceremonies—thirty-five years to the day after Koufax pitched his first game in Ponce—Roberto Clemente's widow, Vera, told me: "Roberto played just as hard in Puerto Rico as he did in the Majors. He felt very strongly about pleasing the local fans and did not want to let them down."

Clemente was one of eight native players inducted into the Winter League Hall of Fame. Vic Power, another inductee, was Clemente's teammate at Caguas in the 1957 and 1958 Winter League seasons. In 1959-60, he bested Roberto for the batting title by hitting .347 to the 25-year old outfielder's .330 mark. Power remembers Clemente playing with a bad back.

"Even though he played hurt, Roberto toiled with pride and was a winner," said Power. "Because of his bad back, I wasn't sure Roberto was going to be the superstar he became with Pittsburgh from 1960 on, but felt he would give his best effort."

Power is justifiably proud of his two Puerto Rico batting and home run titles, and serving as player-manager for Caguas in the 1960 Caribbean Series, the last one with a Cuban team. He also has fond memories of Caguas teammates Koufax and Hank Aaron.

"Koufax came to Puerto Rico to work on his control in 1956," said Power. "He was plagued by wildness, but he had a good work ethic and he worked hard on improving his pitching."

Vic Power reminisced about the other Winter League champs he played on including the 1949-50, 1953-54 and 1957-58 Criollos. He also mentioned the 1950-51 regular season champion Caguas team with a 57-20 record which lost in the finals to Santurce.

The former gold glover then discussed the 1953-54 Caguas squad which featured 19-year old Hank Aaron. "Aaron, Jim Rivera, Bob Buhl, Brooks Lawrence and myself were the key players in that pennant-winning season," said Power. The 1953-54 Criollos (46-34) were a worst-to-first team, having finished last in 1952-53. Aaron and "Jungle Jim" Rivera tied for the league lead in homers with nine while Aaron (.322) and Power (.304) finished third and fourth, respectively, in the batting chase. Bob Buhl (14-3) and Brooks Lawrence (13-7) provided reliable pitching.

Caguas had a close working relationship with the Milwaukee Braves in the 1950s, much like the Santurce Crabbers–New York-San Francisco Giants links during the same decade. This accounted for Aaron joining Caguas in October of 1953 and Willie Mays doing likewise for Santurce a year later. In both cases, personal friendships also helped. Felix Mantilla was a close friend and teammate of Aaron's. Giants owner Horace

Stoneham "delivered" Mays in appreciation for Crabbers owner Pedrin Zorrilla tipping him off to Ruben Gomez and other prospects.

Willie Mays captured the hearts of Puerto Rico's fans with his enthusiasm and hustle. He won the batting title with a .395 mark and led the league with seven triples. The Crabbers had a "Panic Squadron" with Mays in center, Clemente (.344, 38 RBI) in left, Bob Thurman (.323, 60 RBI) in right, along with George Crowe (1B) and Buster Clarkson (3B). Middle infielders Ronnie Samford and Don Zimmer played well as did catcher Harry Chiti. Sam Jones (14-4) and Ruben Gomez (13-4) were the league's top hurlers. The Crabbers' strong bench was bolstered by Luis Olmo (.278).

While Mays and Clemente grabbed most of the headlines, reliable Bob Thurman—a veteran of the Negro Leagues and minors, and the career home run leader in Puerto Rico Winter League history with 120—came through for the Crabbers. He was 2-0 as a pitcher that season and hit more homers than Mays did, fourteen to twelve. Bob Thurman was one of two Americans inducted into the Puerto Rico Hall of Fame on October 20, 1991; the other was Willard Brown.

"We were better than most Major League teams of that era," said Thurman. "Our outfield was second to none."

Brown still holds the record for higest lifetime batting average (.347) in Puerto Rican Winter League history. In second place, with the highest average by a native Puerto Rican, is another inductee, the great batsman of the '30s and '40s Francicso "Poncho" Coimbre, with a .337. Because of his color, Coimbre never had a chance to play in the majors.

Mays got off to a slow start with Santurce and failed to connect for a homer in any of his first thirteen games. He then hit home runs in four straight games and was on his way to a banner season. In a key 7-6 win over Caguas, Mays' two-run homer with Clemente on base in the bottom of the ninth inning gave Ruben Gomez the win. By December 15, 1954, the Crabbers had overtaken Caguas for first place and their record was 25-14. Mays (.423), Clemente (.382) and Thurman (.382) were the league's top three hitters at that date. The Crabbers finished in first place with a 47-25 record, and went on to defeat Caguas four games to one in the finals.

Unlike Hank Aaron the prior winter, Mays was granted permission to play in the 1955 Caribbean Series held in Caracas. In the Crabbers' third game, Mays hit a two-run homer off New York Giants teammate Ramon Monzant of Venezuela with Clemente on base for a 4-2 win. This 11th inning homer broke an 0-12 series slump by Mays and according to Peter Bjarkman, "It remains one of the most dramatic clouts in Caribbean Series history."

In Santurce's next game against Cuba, Mays went 4-for-5 with 3 RBI in a 7-6 win. Clemente and Don Zimmer had important RBI in the victory. Santurce then clinched the Caribbean Series with an 11-3 win over Panama. Mays had three more hits, but was picked off base twice. Clemente and Zimmer continued their solid hitting with three hits apiece. Two of Clemente's hits were triples.

The best native athlete on the 1954-55 Crabbers was Ruben Gomez, the winningest pitcher in Puerto Rico history with 174 Winter League victories over twenty-nine seasons. Ruben also played in the outfield, becoming an everyday player the latter part of the 1956-57 season after Clemente was sold to Caguas. Gomez was so incensed by this sale that he refused to put his uniform on before the December 30, 1956 game at Mayaguez.

Poncho Coimbre, who starred for years in Winter League play.

Luis Alvelo

seventeen strikeouts against Panama in Puerto Rico's first game of the 1958 Caribbean Series. It's a record that has stood the test of time.

"I was a very dominant pitcher in Puerto Rico between the late 1950s and early 1960s," said Pizarro after the 1991 Island Hall of Fame Induction Ceremonies. "The lighting at the various stadiums wasn't always the best and I threw very hard—maybe in the low 90s."

Orlando Cepeda came into his own in the 1957-58 season with a .300 mark, thirteen homers and 45 RBIs for Santurce. The "Baby Bull" broke in with Santurce in 1955-56, the same year Pizarro did.

Gomez was another 1991 Winter League Hall of Fame inductee, but he did not attend the ceremony. Two of his Crabber teammates, Juan Pizarro and Orlando Cepeda, did attend. Pizarro earned 157 Winter League wins over twenty-two seasons, second only to Gomez. His most dominant Winter League season was the MVP one for Caguas in 1957-58 when he went 14-5 with 183 strikeouts and a 1.32 E.R.A. His nine shutouts set a new record as did his nineteen strikeouts against Ponce on November 20, 1957, a 3-hit, 1-0 win.

Ten days after this effort, Juan Pizarro pitched the league's sixth no-hitter in its twenty-year history by defeating Mayaguez 7-0. Pizarro struck out eleven Indians and walked four in this gem. The lefty also won game 3 of the 1958 league finals against Santurce by a 7-4 score. He struck out fifteen Crabbers, but allowed a two-run homer to his friend Orlando Cepeda. The hero of this series was again Roberto Clemente who hit at a .529 clip for Caguas in their four-game sweep over Santurce.

Perhaps Juan Pizarro's crowning achievement was his

After his 1958 Rookie-of-the-Year season with San Francisco, Cepeda won the 1958-59 Winter League batting title at .362. He paced the Crabbers to the league title in the best of nine series with two clutch homers in game five against Caguas, a 9-3 win. Cepeda's homer in game six helped defeat Caguas 9-2, and Santurce went on to win the series, five games to two.

Cepeda, like Clemente, had a .323 lifetime average in Puerto Rican play. He felt the League was a launching pad for his successful Major League career and had some kind words for Willie Mays after the 1991 Island Hall of Fame Ceremony.

"Willie was very supportive and helpful those first seasons in San Francisco," said Cepeda. "Mays and I had a good rapport, and Willie spoke well of Puerto Rico, its fans, and players."

The 1950s were the "Golden Era" of Puerto Rico's Winter League. Such Hall of Famers and legends as Clemente, Pizarro, Cepeda and Ruben Gomez made this designation a reality.

A Russian ace in the Land of the Rising Sun

The Amazing Story of Victor Starffin

Richard Puff

Victor Starffin's life reads like a Hollywood novel and, in a way, so do his pitching statistics: He was the first moundsman in Japanese baseball to notch 200 career wins and nine years later became the first to gather 300 victories. During a six-year period from 1937 to 1942 he amassed 182 wins against only 53 defeats. His highest ERA during that span - 1.70 in 1937!

No pitcher in Japanese baseball history gathered so many records, many of which still stand nearly 40 years later: most consecutive seasons with 30 or more wins (3), most victories in a season (42), and most career shutouts (84). And so many times during Starffin's life, circumstances nearly prevented it all from coming true.

Victor Constantinovich Starffin was born May 1, 1916 in the village of Nizhnii Tagil in the middle of the Russian Urals. His father, Constantin, was a military officer attending Czar Nicholas II. A year after Starffin's birth the Russian Revolution toppled the Czar and many of the ruling elite were exiled including the Starffin family. To escape the battling Red and White armies, the family was carried in a cramped freight train with typhoid patients. Later, they escaped from a town in the hands of the Red army by hiding in a truck transporting corpses. After traveling more than 3,000 miles, the family reached Harbin in Manchuria where they lived for several years while awaiting permission for entry into Japan. The Japanese, however, were only permitting those refugees into the country who had a minimum of 1,500 yen. Luckily, the Starffins had held onto some jewels and family keepsakes which they sold—far below their actual value—to buy

their way to a new life. The exiled family's journey finally was completed in September 1925 when the Starffins reached the northern city of Asahikawa where many Russian refugees were settled.

Victor enrolled in an elementary school where he received his baptism to baseball and soon flashed signs of his enormous natural athletic ability. Of course, he certainly was helped by his six-foot height, which he reached by the time he was 12 years old, to tower over his Japanese teammates. Starffin was taking the mound for his elementary school team and soon began to shut out junior high and adult teams. Before long Starffin became an idol throughout the island of Hokkaido and was pitching for the area's best teams. But then, when all seemed to be going well, tragedy again struck.

In 1933 Starffin's father was accused of murdering a young Russian girl who worked at a tea shop he had recently opened. The elder Starffin was convicted after having confessed to the killing (at first he admitted killing her out of "sexual jealousy," but later accused her of being a Soviet spy) and was sentenced to eight years in prison. At this time, the Japanese All-Star team, which later would become the basis for the country's first professional team, tried to persuade Starffin to join the squad. Area fans, however, refused to let the righthander leave their team. Their fervor was so strong that they even hid Starffin and his mother and assigned bodyguards to safeguard him. Starffin's dedication to his team equalled the fans' devotion. The family was then threatened with deportation to the Soviet Union—a certain death sentence—because they were without a means of support since Constantin Starffin was in prison. After finally agreeing to serve on the national squad, Starffin

Richard Puff *is a SABR Director and was an organizer of SABR 19 in Albany, New York.*

was surreptitiously led away with his mother at 2 a.m. on November 25, 1934 to join the team in Tokyo with the promise that his family would not be deported. Constantin's prison sentence also suddenly was reduced by two years.

Victor Starffin warms up

Three weeks before his departure to join the team, the November 3, 1934 edition of *The New York Times* reported that 100,000 cheering Japanese baseball fans greeted Babe Ruth and his American teammates as they rode down the Ginza in Tokyo. Ruth and his American League barnstormers were in Japan to play a series of games against Japanese competition. The article concluded by saying, "A leading light of the all-stars is expected to be Young Stalin [sic], a 6-foot 2-inch middle school youth, the son of White Russian parents who took refuge in Japan at the time of the Bolshevik revolution. Stalin is the pitching wonder of the northern region." Starffin's lone appearance during the series came November 29 in Kyoto in relief during a 23-5 trouncing by the American All Stars.

Starffin began pitching for the Great-Japan Tokyo Baseball Club, which in December 1934 became the Yomiuri Giants, the country's first professional nine. In February 1935 the club made the trans-Pacific voyage to America to play an extended barnstorming schedule throughout the United States and Canada. A second trip to North America came in 1936. One time during this latter visit, while the team was seated in a restaurant, an unsuspecting waiter approached him to take his order. In his best effort, Starffin, who learned to speak fluent Japanese, proudly blurted out in broken English, "I am a chicken." The remark not only got him a finger-licking meal, but also a new nickname: Chicken.

In 1937, the second year of professional ball in Japan, Starffin burst on the scene with 28 victories. Through 1942, Starffin averaged 30 wins while his earned run average soared no higher than 1.70. In 1939, Starffin took the mound for 68 of the Giants' 96 games and won 42 of them. With a Giant pennant came the MVP award. In 1940, when he dropped to 38 victories, he reeled off 18 wins in succession and won his second consecutive MVP award.

Still Starffin was the number two pitcher on the staff behind Eiji Sawamura. Sawamura had been the ace of the Giants staff since the 1934 American barnstorming tour when he nearly outdueled Earl Whitehill. Sawamura lost 1-0 on a Lou Gehrig home run, but at one point in the game he struck out Charlie Gehringer, Babe Ruth, Jimmie Foxx and Lou Gehrig in succession. An annual award equivalent to the Cy Young Award is given to Japan's outstanding pitcher in memory of Sawamura, who joined the Japanese Army after Pearl Harbor and was killed in battle late in World War II.

By the early 1940s, Starffin seemed to have it all—he was one of the most famous players in all the land and with the notoriety came proportionate financial rewards. And he had a beautiful Russian wife. But then came World War II. For most of the war, Starffin, as a Russian, was continuously questioned about being a spy. He faced constant surveillance and he even had to change his name to Hiroshi Suda. Secretly, he wrote the letter "V" for Victor on the shirt he wore beneath his jersey as his only act of defiance.

In 1944, the Giants banished Starffin from the game, fearful that a foreigner on the team may give the authorities the impetus to ban "the sport of the enemy." Soon the government did just that and the game was halted. Starffin was forced to enter a detention camp in Karuizawa and became bedridden with pleurisy.

With the war over, Starffin was hired as an interpreter with the occupying forces. His wife, however, soon found interests away from her husband and before long she left him. Starffin turned to liquor to ease his pain.

The layoff from the war had taken its toll on Starffin and his fabulous right arm. He continued playing until 1955 but only once—1949—did he return to his former prominence with a 27-17 record. He hung on long enough to win his 300th game in 1955 to become the first in the Japanese league to do so.

The alcohol which earlier had eased the pain of his broken marriage took its greatest toll on January 12, 1957. Soon after leaving a party that night in Tokyo, Starffin's car crashed into the rear of a streetcar. A half hour later he was dead without regaining consciousness.

Police attributed the crash to speeding and driving under the influence of alcohol.

The affable Starffin was later remembered by his admirers in Asahikawa with a huge bronze statue in front of its 25,000-seat municipal stadium, aptly named Victor Starffin Stadium, which was completed in 1983. The park is the only one used in Japanese professional baseball that is named for a former player. Final tributes came when he was elected to the Japanese and the World Baseball Hall of Fame during the 1980s.

A "V" on his shirt: Starffin before the war.

Victor Starffin Year By Year

Year	Team	G	CG	ShO	W	L	IP	Hits	BB	SO	R	ER	ERA
1936	Yomiuri	4	2	0	1	2	24.0	20	8	23	10	7	2.63
1937	Yomiuri	51	23	8	28	11	312.0	216	112	187	88	59	1.70
1938	Yomiuri	48	30	12	33	5	356.1	217	119	222	74	59	1.49
1939	Yomiuri	68	38	10	42	14	458.1	316	167	282	114	85	1.67
1940	Yomiuri	55	41	16	38	12	436.0	242	149	245	67	49	1.01
1941	Yomiuri	20	13	4	15	3	150.0	93	46	58	28	20	1.20
1942	Yomiuri	40	27	8	26	8	306.1	174	121	110	50	38	1.11
1943	Yomiuri	18	11	3	10	5	136.0	75	60	71	22	18	1.19
1944	Yomiuri	7	7	2	6	0	66.0	40	23	17	9	5	0.68
1946	Pacific	5	2	0	1	1	31.2	35	16	11	10	7	1.97
1947	Taiyo	20	16	1	8	10	162.1	142	50	77	59	37	2.04
1948	Kinsei	37	28	3	17	13	198.1	240	83	138	90	72	2.17
1949	Daiei	52	35	9	27	17	376.0	357	23	163	130	109	2.61
1950	Daiei	35	17	2	11	15	234.1	270	52	86	115	103	3.61
1951	Daiei	14	8	0	6	6	100.2	79	24	47	39	30	2.67
1952	Daiei	24	12	1	8	10	150.1	145	45	44	63	51	3.04
1953	Daiei	26	17	3	11	9	201.2	175	46	61	67	60	2.67
1954	Takahashi	29	11	1	8	13	178.1	191	48	52	85	74	3.72
1955	Tombo	33	12	1	7	21	196.2	205	34	56	102	85	3.88
Totals		**586**	**350**	**84**	**303**	**175**	**4075.1**	**3232**	**1226**	**1950**	**1222**	**968**	**2.09**

Sluggers in Paradise

Frank Ardolino

On October 19, 1933, in the depths of the Depression, the ebullient Babe Ruth, the "Mighty Bam," arrived in the Hawaiian Islands for the first time to play a series of games as a member of a local all-star team. The Babe's appearance was the culmination of a series of visits from big league teams to Hawaii which began with the arrival of A. G. Spalding's around-the-world tour of "baseball missionaries" in 1888. The impetus for the big league junkets to Hawaii can be said to have begun in 1849 when the putative founder of baseball in 1845, Alexander Cartwright, Jr., arrived in Honolulu, where he lived until his death in 1892. In 1849, Cartwright left New York for the California gold mines, but he quickly tired of the treasure hunt and decided to sail home via China with a stopover in Honolulu. He disembarked seasick and never left Oahu, except for two mainland business trips within the next two years. He soon promoted the development of baseball in Hawaii by drawing up a diamond at Makiki Field, now renamed Cartwright Field, and by teaching the rudiments of the game to school children. Also, he attended league games in his customary seat of honor, and in a letter to his old Knickerbocker chum Charles Debost, Cartwright explained that "I have in my possession the original ball with which we used to play on Murray Hill. Many is the pleasant chase I have had after it . . . on the sunny plains of Hawaii nei. . . ."

According to A. G. Spalding, Cartwright was instrumental in having his around-the-world tour come to Hawaii in 1888 for two games. Unfortunately, the games never took place because the players arrived on Sunday,

---

Frank Ardolino *is associate professor of English at the University of Hawaii, where he teaches courses on both Shakespeare and sports literature and occasionally publishes critical articles on baseball fiction.*

Alexander Cartwright, all fired up.

November 24, instead of Saturday and the Sunday blue law was invoked. In an effort to bypass the law, 1000 people signed a petition and offered to pay any fines incurred; however, Spalding refused to overrule the blue law, "though . . . the crowd gave vent to its disappointment . . . declaring that they would make an issue of the Sunday question at the next election." That night, despite the prevailing disappointment, the players, who included future Hall of Famers Adrian Anson (1852-1922) and John Montgomery Ward (1860-1925), were treated to a grand luau at the Queen's home. King Kalakaua was a gracious host, encouraging the players to call him "Kally," and revealing that he had wanted the games to go on, but was overruled by the powerful missionary element, which also, as Monte Ward complained, deprived the players of seeing hula dancers.

Within the next decade momentous changes occurred in Hawaii as the monarchy was overthrown in 1893 by a cadre of American businessmen led by Sanford Dole, who became the first governor of the Territory of Hawaii in 1900, two years after it had been annexed by the United States. With the increase of American influence over Hawaii, cultural exchanges became more frequent, and in 1914 arrangements were made to rectify the missed connections of 1888 by having two major league teams play a series of games.

The party of 56 began the tour in Milwaukee on October 17 and ended it in Honolulu with six games in the first two weeks of December, about four months after the outbreak of World War I. Among the twenty-eight players were Bullet Joe Bush, Jeff Tesreau, Grover Cleveland Alexander, Fred Snodgrass, Max Carey, and the ill-fated Ray Chapman, voted the best player of the Hawaiian games. The steamer Manoa brought the All-Nationals and All-Americans on December 1, and the *Honolulu Advertiser* grandly declared that "Today will inaugurate the greatest sporting event in the history of the Hawaiian Islands, for . . . twenty-eight of the world's greatest baseball players will set foot on the . . . Paradise of the Pacific to prepare for the biggest and most wonderful series played anywhere in the world. . . ."

After the first game at Moiliili Field, which was attended by 2300 people, Al Castle spoke at the Ad Club meeting about the growth of baseball in Hawaii, remarking that it was ironic that, as the son of missionaries whose influence prevented the 1888 game, he "is now giving his support to promoting Sunday baseball in Honolulu." The visiting players of 1914 made the islands forget the earlier missed games by splitting six, with the great Alexander pitching some strong games and winning one he didn't pitch with an eight-inning homer. The major leaguers also played games against two local teams, gave lectures and clinics on baseball techniques and history, and, in general, ingratiated themselves with the local populace, who felt that a return visit, albeit with fewer games, would be welcome.

In 1923, another major league visit was made by a team with, among others, Bullet Joe Bush, Waite Hoyt, Casey Stengel, Luke Sewell, George "Highpockets" Kelly, and Emil "Irish" Meusel, who were returning from a tour of the Orient. During this visit, the memory of Alexander Cartwright as a baseball pioneer was honored by his descendants, a contingent of players and Hawaiian dignitaries, many of whom had known Cartwright. They gathered at his gravesite in Nuuanu Cemetery, where Herb Hunter, "America's baseball ambassador to Japan," spoke eloquently of the reasons for the laying of the wreath, inscribed with the words "A Tribute from Organized Baseball," on Cartwright's tomb:

> *Because we believe that baseball is an honorable and characteristic element of American life, we take this opportunity to pay our tribute to its founder, by placing the wreath on his last resting place. May God bless his memory and keep the great American game which he founded true to the highest ideals of American sportsmanship.*

The 1923 visit was important because it provided the first public celebration of Cartwright's role in the development of baseball and his presence in Hawaii. His grandson Bruce, Jr., took part in the ceremony, and twelve years later began his vigorous campaign to convince Hall of Fame officials to honor Alex during the centennial celebration of baseball. As a result of his providing relevant materials, his grandfather was honored in the 1938 ceremonies both in Cooperstown and Hawaii, and in 1939 he was inducted into the Hall of Fame.

In 1931, major league all-stars arrived in late fall en route to Japan where they would play twelve games. The fourteen players, including Rabbit Maranville, Lou Gehrig, Lefty Grove, Frankie Frisch, Al Simmons, and Jimmy Foxx, were accompanied by the well-known sports reporter Fred Lieb, who served as manager and representative of Commissioner Landis. Lieb's job was to guarantee that the players would not engage in the nefarious act of hippodroming or barnstorming antics. Fifteen thousand fans showed up from as far away as Maui and Kauai, creating the largest gate in Hawaiian baseball history. Lefty Grove, who was 31-4 for the year and won two games for the Athletics in their 4-3 defeat of the Cardinals in the World Series, pitched four strong innings. Al Simmons and Lou Gehrig smashed homers, and the big leaguers handily defeated the local team, showing the fans the skills displayed by these "baseball goliaths" in big-league play. After the game, Gehrig was asked whether his famous teammate Babe Ruth would come to Hawaii, and Lou remarked that the Babe would probably never come because he hated sailing.

Although Gehrig asserted that the Babe would not cross the ocean to Hawaii, Ruth did just that two years later, accompanied by his wife Claire and his adopted daughter Julia. When the Ruths arrived on the Lurline on

October 19, they were greeted by 10,000 fans who bedecked them with leis. Babe showed no evidence of seasickness, having participated in shipboard activities, including skeet shooting, with great gusto. The major-league season, in which the Yanks finished second to Washington, had ended three weeks earlier when the Babe pitched and won the last game of the season against the Red Sox with his homerun. At the age of 40 and near the end of his glorious career, Ruth engaged in a whirlwind of activities, bathing his fans in the warm glow of his good-will and energy. He met with Governor Judd and the Japanese consul, went surfing, played superlative golf in exhibition rounds, spoke before business clubs and schoolchildren, wrote a baseball column, sold tickets on the beach, and, finally, played in a series of baseball games, during which he pitched, played first and the outfield, and swung mightily at the pitches of local all-star hurlers, all in the space of two frenetic weeks.

The Babe arrived on Thursday at 10 a.m. and, after a meeting with Governor Judd, journeyed to Nuuanu Cemetery to lay a wreath on Cartwright's grave, adding his stature to the growing recognition of Cartwright's role as baseball pioneer. After this ceremony, he played a round of golf at the Waialae Country Club, where he scored a 75. His prodigious drives awed his gallery and moved a local sports reporter to exclaim that "Honolulu has seen golfdom's greatest stars in action . . . but not a longer ball has ever been hit on the 'rock' than the drives which . . . Ruth sent screaming down the Kahala fairway."

Ruth received a truly royal ovation at the Royal Hawaiian Hotel from the 200 members and guests of the Representatives Club. Secretary of Hawaii Raymond C. Brown hailed Ruth as visiting royalty: "It has been my privilege to welcome to the Territory kings and heirs to many thrones of the world and today I feel that the greatest honor of them all is mine when I welcome another king to Hawaii, the King of Swat. . . ." Ruth shed tears over the size and impact of the greeting from his island fans, told the audience that he had extended his tour to November 4, and said Hawaii had proved so attractive to his family in their short time there that he and his wife intended to return every winter if possible.

On Saturday, Ruth visited the St. Louis School and told the assembled boys that if they played straight with the brothers, they would be the lads' best friends: "I know because I attended a school very much like this, and found that the brothers were square shooters." In Babe's baseball column, "Never Be a Quitter," he advised young athletes that "If you are fair to your leader, your team mates, your opponents and the men who serve in the difficult work of arbitrators then you are fair to yourselves and also to baseball."

Sunday October 22 dawned and all Honolulu was abuzz with news of the great Babe, whose appearance on the ball field, it was hoped, would help Hawaiian tourism. The Babe predicted over the loudspeaker that he would hit a dozen balls over the right field bleachers about 400 feet away, but a stiff breeze blowing in proved a deterrent to his intentions. His team won 5-2, as Babe played the outfield, first base, and pitched a few innings. He had three hits, including a normal-sized homer, and two RBIs. During the game, the Babe wore three ilima orange and ginger leis, a gift from women admirers which he refused to take off despite the Honolulu heat. The stands were filled with dignitaries and the polyglot races that make up Hawaii, and they demonstrated vociferously their admiration for this "overgrown kid, a genial giant . . . with the fun-loving, good-natured mind of an unspoiled child. . . ."

The next day the Babe played another game for 4,000 school children who received a half day off to see the Bambino for a quarter. Ruth swung lustily trying to knock one over the right field bleachers, but he failed, although he did hit one 450 feet in practice. At the conclusion of the game, he was off for two more games on the island of Hawaii, becoming the first major leaguer to visit there. Ruth loved everything about his barnstorming junket, except surfing, because "the water made his legs stiff."

The Babe returned to Hawaii the following year, not as a one-man ambassador of baseball, but as playing manager of a contingent of fourteen American League stars en route to Japan under the direction of Connie Mack, who reportedly was considering making Ruth manager of his team, the Athletics, the following year. Nine thousand fans saw the big leaguers, including Lefty Gomez, Charlie Gehringer, Lou Gehrig, Moe Berg, Earl Averill, and Jimmy Foxx, beat the local team 8-1. Gomez pitched a strong four innings, Lou hit one out, and the Babe hit a one-bouncer off the center field fence and "like a portly old gentleman passing a contribution box in church, toddled down to second base."

Although "a portly old gentleman" of forty-one, Ruth nevertheless took Japan by storm, playing every inning of the seventeen games and hitting thirteen homers. Ruth's appearance in baseball-mad Tokyo was instrumental in the creation of the first professional Japanese league in 1936. After the Japanese series was over, Babe continued on a trip around the world with his wife and daughter, but he never returned to his beloved Hawaii nor did he become a manager. Seven years after Ruth visited Hawaii, the Japanese attacked Pearl Harbor, and major league stars like Joe DiMaggio, Joe Gordon, Phil Rizzuto, and Bill Dickey came to Honolulu not on barnstorming tours but in uniform to play on military teams. But that, as they say, is another story.

California's Quirky Spurs

R. Scott Mackey

The wind barely rustles the palm trees on the golf course beyond right field as the theme song from "Magnum P.I." fades out and the voice of public address announcer Buddy Meacham booms in to welcome one and all to Salinas Municipal Stadium, home field of the Salinas Spurs.

Seconds later Meacham, a bearded 250-pound cross between a ZZ Top guitarist and a Hell's Angel, is singing sweetly about "the dawn's early light." A newspaper delivery man by day, and P.A. announcer by night, Meacham is a bona fide baseball junkie who sings the National Anthem as well as anybody this side of Pavarotti. He is just one of the cast of colorful characters who make the Salinas Spurs perhaps the most unusual professional baseball team in the United States.

The Spurs are an independent member of the California League, a Class A minor league that ranks above rookie ball and little else in the world of American Organized Baseball. And while they may play in California, the Spurs are not your typical American baseball team. First off, there's the owner, 34-year-old Don Nomura who jets in from Tokyo, Japan, to catch an occasional game. Then there's the ex-political staffer who runs the show, and the ex-corporate attorney turned radio play-by-play man. But what really sets this team off from any other team in America is the players. Half are Americans on their way down the professional ladder; half are Japanese climbing Japan's professional baseball hierarchy. The Japanese speak no English; the Americans speak no Japanese.

R. Scott Mackey *is a Sacramento-based freelance writer whose book-length history of the 1920's Pacific Coast League will be released during 1992 by McFarland Publishers.*

Somehow they communicate. Somehow they get along. Somehow this quirky operation seems to work.

Billy and Ralph—Before a mid-season game against the league's only other independent team, the Reno Silver Sox, a visitor runs a gauntlet of Japanese players sitting on wooden benches, smoking, outside the clubhouse. They look at the American intruder; one player, between puffs on a Marlboro, murmurs something in Japanese that sets the row of players into hoots. Inside the clubhouse a dozen American players pull on their uniforms and exchange verbal barbs. Two Japanese players point and laugh along with the Americans at a practical joke involving a jockstrap.

A few minutes later the players mosey on out to the field, followed by a reporter and photographer, both eager to find out what the hell this team is all about.

Six-foot-two catcher Hideyuki Yasuda is called Ralph by the American players because it's easier to say. Ralph saunters about the dugout area, half-shy, half-smirking; he seems both cocky and deferential as he sizes up his interviewer with an up-and-down glance. Even though he is one of the best players on the Spurs, one who could be a legitimate prospect for a major league team, Ralph does not like to talk about himself or baseball with a stranger. He's asked about the difference between American and Japanese baseball.

"Very pretty girls," Ralph says in Japanese. Doubting translator Michael Okamura's skills, as well as his doleful skepticism each time a question is proffered, the inquisitor repeats himself.

"McDonalds," Ralph says.

Two other Japanese players—Hideyuke Mifune (a.k.a.

"Billy") and Ryo Kawano say the same thing, in the same order: pretty girls, McDonalds. Based on their nonstop smoking before the game, cigarettes would rank next on the list and then maybe baseball. However, risking another question to a Michael Okamura translation doesn't seem to be worth the effort.

With gametime still twenty minutes away, five Japanese players cluster around a giant telephoto lens to view, up close and personal, the local female talent in the bleachers. These guys are having a blast. And who can blame them? Each Japanese player—unlike his American counterparts—receives a salary of $40,000 to $60,000 a year from his Japanese parent ballclub. All that money, and California Girls, too.

A few feet away, fellow Spurs Todd Cruz and Jim Eppard, two ex-major leaguers, warm up, game faces on. Cruz is 36 and seven years removed from his last stop in "The Show." He holds onto his dream to return to the majors while making less than $5,000 a season. First baseman Eppard, 31, joined the team earlier in the week, released by the Toronto Blue Jay organization because he couldn't hit for power. For both men, Salinas is their lady or their tiger; baseball death or salvation, depending whether the demi-gods of the diamonds—the major league scouts—will grant them another chance.

In the eyes of Cruz and Eppard are visions of bush league towns worse than Salinas. They've been to the summit of baseball for little more than a cup of coffee; today they'd settle for just one more slurp. But in a league full of 20-year old phenoms, a 36-year old shortstop's future is dim.

Eppard and Cruz are driven; Ralph and Billy just want to have fun. It is not a question of race or nationality, but of desire—or desperation—to reach a dream. The Spurs offer players like Eppard and Cruz a chance to dream, just as they offer the Japanese players a chance to enjoy.

The Owner—Whatever the players' goals may be, they can thank Nomura for the chance to reach them. The Salinas Spurs ballclub is his baby. An ex-Japanese minor leaguer, Nomura looks more like a UCLA student than the international businessman that he is. In fact, he lives in Westwood about half the year. He does, he admits, pretty well in real estate, but baseball is his love.

Nomura's goal is not to infiltrate and conquer American baseball; rather, it is the opposite. He wants to export the best parts of American baseball back to Japan.

"I hated the Japanese baseball system by my fourth year," he says without an accent. "They run it like a boot camp over there. Nine hours a day. The good thing about the Spurs is that we don't run it like a Japanese team. We run it the American way. Individual skills. Playing games. I'm convinced that playing—not practicing—is the way you get good at baseball. We've brought our players over here to learn the American way of baseball and to take it back with them."

The Japanese players are young and are seen as the most promising youngsters in the systems of the Yakult Swallows and Daiei Hawks—the two Japanese major league teams supplying Salinas with players. The Japanese teams hope the exposure to American baseball will hasten the players' development and broaden their skills.

"I don't think this is a trend," Nomura says about Japanese baseball coming to America. He names a couple of other minor league teams owned by a Japanese corporation, but they, he says, are staffed with players from Major League franchises. Besides, he says, "Japanese baseball is way behind American baseball in quality."

1991 was Nomura's first year as sole owner of the Spurs. He bought out partner and minor league legend Joe Buzas after the 1990 season. Though he and Buzas had been partners for two years, the two did not share the same management philosophy. Nomura felt that Buzas preferred to squeeze every dollar he could out of the fans, while he sought to make the ballpark more comfortable and enjoyable, rewarding fans for coming.

After several reigns of owners who seemed to hold their interests just slightly above a Shiite terrorist's, the Salinas fans seem to appreciate Nomura's style.

"The operation is a thousand percent better," says Richard Ortiz, vice president of the Spurs booster club, an honor which entitles him to bring a keg of beer to each Sunday home game. "This year it's good vibrations as far as I'm concerned."

Booster Club President Dale Hooper concurs: "This year the owner is willing to spend money to make it enjoyable at the ballpark."

From a sampling of fans it's clear they like the added promotions and improved security at the park. Most of all, they like the team, Japanese and American, which will finish eight games better than the 1990 ballclub. The Spurs' third-place, 32-36 record in the second half of the season is the team's best in years. This new, improved version of the Salinas Spurs managed to draw 66,079 fans in 1991—double the 1990 mark.

The General Manager—A large part of the credit for making the team more competitive, and for attracting the fans, should go to Kevin Haughian, the thirty-two year old general manager who has rediscovered baseball after four years in state politics. 1991 was Haughian's first year running the Spurs.

Haughian looks more like John McEnroe than John McEnroe does. Two hours before game time, he wanders through the stands picking up hot dog wrappers and worrying about whether he was perhaps too rough on the drunks in the stands giving the barnyard chant the night before. Welcome to minor league management. Not that Haughian minds. "I knew I would never be a big success in politics," says Haughian, a staffer for California State Assemblyman Rusty Areias. "In Sacramento there are a lot of people who are passionate about politics. You need to love what you're doing if you want to be better than average. I found politics more frustrating than fulfilling. In baseball, I don't mind working 100 hours a week."

Most of that time has been spent putting together promotions, improving concessions and comfort at the part, getting players, and organizing a community outreach program with schools, Little League and other youth groups. Except for the occasional lack of communication with the Japanese players, Haughian says there's no difference running a team of half Japanese than there is running any other minor league club.

This is Haughian's second stint with the Spurs. When he left as assistant general manager in 1985 to get a "real job" he thought it was for good. A trip to Ireland two years ago with his father, however, changed his mind. "Basically, he told me that life moves quickly and that you better do what you like or you will regret it. It's great to be back in baseball. I don't know a lot of people who flat out love their jobs. I took a major cut in pay to do this, but I feel lucky."

Another guy who just took a major cut in pay is John Sandler, the "Voice of the Spurs." While the Salinas-Reno game he's announcing is not exactly "The Game of the Week" on network television, Sandler delivers his play-by-play with the smooth intensity of a Vin Scully, and more skill than a half-dozen major league announcers.

Not bad for a corporate attorney who gave up a six-figure salary for a minimum-wage dream. Still in his early thirties, Sandler hopes to climb through the minors on his way to the big time.

"My friends who are attorneys think this is the greatest thing in the world. The people who aren't attorneys think I'm crazy," says Sandler, still ebullient after a three-hour broadcast.

In addition to his enthusiastic handling of play-by-play duties, Sandler, like his role-model Scully, is an able pitchman. One of his spots is for the Salinas Tallow Company, which, among other services, "removes large fallen animals . . . and fat and grease from kitchens." Sandler has fun with his material, whether it's difficult Japanese names, less-than-great baseball, or large fallen animals.

The truth is it's not difficult to have fun watching the Salinas Spurs. They look good in sweeping their mid-season series with Reno, and they also offer the genuine good times of Minor League Baseball USA. Every other inning or so, a kid trots up to the press box to pick up a box of Nestle's Crunch, the prize for having the winning ticket stub. A bingo game continues through nine innings . . . on the field a couple of kids and adults toss baseballs through a wooden catcher's mitt for free food . . . Meacham leads a rousing chorus of Take Me Out to the Ballgame in the bottom of the seventh inning . . . and, a few moments later, two kids are spinning themselves silly around a bat in hopes of winning brunch at the Ramada Inn. Some of the players and principals may be Japanese, but this is American minor league baseball all the way.

The Skipper—Manager Heidi Koga speaks baseball, as well as Japanese, English and Spanish. After four decades of experience—including 20 years in the front office of the Daiei Hawks—Koga knows baseball more than Bo does.

He invites a visitor into his "office," nothing more than a bathroom-sized cubicle in which Koga and his three assistants change clothes and prepare for the game. An army surplus desk, vintage 1955, is cluttered with stat sheets, coke cans and a couple of barbecue ribs courtesy of the Spurs booster club. A dog-eared English-Japanese/Japanese-English dictionary sits on the hot corner of the desk.

Though he is warm and gracious in the clubhouse, Koga is aggressive on the field. Sandler has taken to calling him "Go Go Koga" for his active running game. "I like to run to put pressure on the other team," he says in an accent so thick about every third word drops in a muddy clump. "I don't know if you could say my style is Japanese or American style of baseball. I try to teach the American way if I can."

Koga knows both styles well, having played and coached in Japan, as well as a year in the States during the 1960s. "In Japanese baseball there are too many coaches. Players are told too much what to do. American players are very independent and do things their own way. In Japan, the players have too much to think about. The American way is better."

How does it work? How can players of different cultures, who are playing the game for different salaries and different reasons get along?

"At first I was worried about how the Japanese and American players would get along," Koga says. "But the players don't seem to view each other as Japanese players or American players—we are not Yakult Swallows or Daiei Hawks, just Salinas Spurs." A couple of days with the team seems to confirm Koga's assessment. If the Americans are jealous or envious, prejudiced or fearful of the Japanese, it's not noticeable. In the locker room and on the field, the players somehow get along.

"I love my teammates—all of them," says pitcher Carlos Carrusco. "Communication is half the fun on this team. But you know what? If you know baseball, you can get along. I mean if two strangers met on the street and didn't speak the same language it would be tough to communicate. Here we've got baseball in common. Baseball's kind of a universal language."

Later, a Japanese coach shows an American catcher the proper way to catch a curveball, the way to frame it so that the umpire is more likely to call it a strike. It's a fairly complex concept. Yet with a combination of sign language and head nods the two figure it out. The next inning the catcher executes the new technique properly.

Baseball, the universal language. Carrusco is right. Here in Salinas, Michael Okamura doesn't need to translate. Baseball itself communicates loud and clear.

Where Do They All Come From?

William Humber

From a Canadian perspective the 1980s will long be remembered for the rise and fall of the Montreal Expos, the conclusion of Fergie Jenkins' Hall of Fame career, and the arrival of the Toronto Blue Jays as one of the major league's dominant franchises. All these successes, however, have not contributed to a significant increase in the number of Canadian-born players.

On average one finds about five Canadians at any one time occupying major league rosters. The figure with odd moments of negligible variation hasn't changed much this entire century. In their study for the *Minnesota Review of Baseball* (Vol. 10, No. 1, 1991), writers Carl Ojala and Michael Gadwood calculated a total participation of 154 Canadians over the life of major league baseball, commencing with the New Brunswick-born Bill Phillips who played with Cleveland in 1879. (Phillips, like many other Canadian players, however, remains somewhat suspect. He had a Canadian birthplace but an early move with his family to Chicago seems to account for his baseball skills.) In any case, Canada leads all foreign countries in providing big leaguers, although it's being overtaken rapidly by the Dominican Republic (see p. 87).

The golden age of the Canadian ballplayer and particularly those from southwestern Ontario belongs to the 19th century, a period when virtually all ballplayers hailed from the northeastern region of North America. Canadian baseball had its genesis in the 1830s, brought by Americans seeking quicker access to the midwest on the Niagara-to-Detroit route through southwestern Ontario.

William Humber *is Canada's foremost baseball historian, coordinator of Continuing Education classes at Toronto's Seneca College, and author of the classic* Cheering for the Home Team: The Story of Baseball in Canada.

Until 1872 Canadian teams were all home grown. The game's more relaxed amateur focus prevented the importation of American professionals. This hot house atmosphere allowed young Canadians the chance to develop their skills and confidence. Too many embarrassments like Woodstock, Ontario's loss by 64 runs to the Brooklyn Atlantics at a Rochester tournament in 1864 might have irreparably damaged the enthusiasm of this first generation of Canadian ballplayers.

In Guelph, Ontario, young men like Jimmy Nichols, a policeman and former cricket player, Billy Sunley, a tinsmith, Eph Stephenson, a clergyman, and Bill Smith, a jeweller were evidence of the game's egalitarian and popular structure. By 1872 Guelph dominated Ontario baseball and on a memorable July afternoon led by Smith's clutch hitting, and Sunley's 16-hit pitching job, they defeated Baltimore, at the time third in the National Association, by one run. That same year Ottawa hired two American pros and the eventual submersion of the Canadian game into that being played south of the border was inevitable.

By 1877 the best teams like the London Tecumsehs and Guelph Maple Leafs, members of the International Association's inaugural season, were dominated by American professionals. Manager Richard Southam and substitute Tom Gillean were London's only Canadians but their presence was notable. Southam was a member of a family that would establish a Canadian publishing empire and promote the game through their newspapers' pages. Gillean, a local jeweller, would become one of the National League's first paid umpires in 1879, at five dollars a game.

A second generation of Canadian ballplayers who as

children had watched and learned from the local heroes of the 1860s and 70s would swell major league ranks in the 1880s. There are unfortunately no statistics revealing the size of this baseball enthusiasm in southwestern Ontario in the 19th century but the last two decades of the century witnessed incredible participation borne out by the number of major league players, minor league teams, and amateur club formations. Our evidence is often anecdotal, like the death notice of Joseph Gibson of Ingersoll, Ontario. Born in 1842, Gibson was a prominent amateur in the 1860s. As a postmaster and fighter in the cause of temperance and prohibition he became one of his town's leading citizens. Yet his happiest moments were said to be playing baseball with his six sons in the park adjoining his home.

It was no different in the Southam household, referred to above, where uncles Bill and Richard would teach their nephew George "Moon" Gibson some of the game's finer points, which he eventually practiced on the diamonds of Pittsburgh as first a catcher and then a field boss in the early part of the 20th century.

In the village of Orono, Ontario, northeast of Toronto, young Wyman Andrus (1858-1935) was a star athlete in school sports and a keen follower of local baseball. By the mid 1870s nearby teams, the Bowmanville Royal Oaks and the Newcastle Beavers, led by the scholarly William Ware Tamblyn, were among the best amateur teams in Canada. During the 1880s Andrus earned his way through Trinity Medical College in Toronto by playing professional baseball in the summer months. Ever the itinerant ballplayer, he played in that decade in Indianapolis in 1883, St. Louis and Minneapolis in 1884, Hamilton, Ontario, in 1885-86, Portland, Maine, in 1887, Hamilton again the next year, Buffalo in 1889-90, and finally Manchester, New Hampshire, in 1891.

Recent research suggests Andrus left Hamilton late in the 1885 season and was conscripted for Providence's National League lineup on September 15. (*The Sporting Life*'s boxscore says that Wally Andrews played that game but newspaper accounts, then as now, often sacrificed accuracy in service to a deadline.) A brief blip on the major league scoresheet, Andrus eventually graduated from medical school and practiced in Miles City, Montana, where he served as mayor for twelve years as well.

Itinerancy likewise marked the career of Jonas Knight. Born in Port Stanley, Ontario, in 1859, Knight played in Philadelphia and Cincinnati in the 1880s but also made stops in London, Hamilton, Syracuse, Binghamton, and eventually his final home, St. Thomas, Ontario. Fred O'Neill from London (1865-1892) played briefly for New York's American Association team in 1887, sandwiched in between stops in Hamilton, Denver, Kalamazoo and Port Huron among other locales. Daniel O'Connor from Guelph (1868-1942), played for Louisville's 1890 American Association team, but spent most of his time in places like Iona, Elkhart, Guelph, and Hamilton. Michael Jones

from Hamilton (1864-1894) also played a few games in Louisville, but the rest of his minor league career was served in Canadian cities. William Hunter, born in St. Thomas in 1859, played in Louisville in 1884 after stops in Toledo and Saginaw. Stephen Dunn from London made St. Paul's Union League team for 32 at bats in 1884 but then drifted from Buffalo to Rochester and eventually Port Huron. Charles Collins from Dundas, Ontario, tasted major league ball in 1884 and '85 but played mostly as an amateur in Ontario. Fred Wood from Hamilton (1863-1933) had brief stays in Detroit and Buffalo in the mid 1880s. Joe Webber from Hamilton (1861-1921) made Indianapolis' 1884 American Association lineup, as did William Watkins from Brantford (1858-1937). George Walker from Hamilton pitched for Baltimore in 1888. Billy Reid from London (1857-1940) played amateur ball in London and Toronto and finally made the bigtime with Baltimore in 1883.

During this period three of the magical figures of Canadian sports became well known in the baseball households of America—Robert Emslie, James Edward "Tip" O'Neill, and Art Irwin.

Emslie's 60-year career as a player, umpire and league official was to earn him eventual entry on a special Honour Roll developed by the Hall of Fame in Cooperstown. Born in Guelph, Ontario, in 1859 Emslie watched

Robert Emslie

Sunley and Nichols play for the local team in the 1860s and when his family moved to London he would often skip school for the allure of the ball diamond. Despairing of Bob's academic future the family sent him to learn the pharmaceutical business from his brother in Kansas in 1874. Here he hooked on with the local Waterville club which played games in Atchison, Kansas, and St. Joseph,

Missouri. The grasshopper plague, however, put his brother out of business and Emslie returned to London, where he picks up the story,

> After returning to London, I started to learn the jewelry business, but I never finished my trade, owing to too much thought of baseball. In the spring of 1878, I pitched my first baseball game on a Good Friday, against the Tecumseh club of London, a professional club that included such well-known players as Fred Goldsmith, Juice Latham, Mike Dinneen, Bucky Ledwith, Harry Spence, and Joe Hornung. The club I pitched for was all young boys from London, all amateurs. They beat us in ten innings, 3-2. The winning run was scored on an error by our second baseman, with two men gone.

Emslie played semi-pro ball for several years in Ontario before joining a team in Camden, New Jersey in 1882. From there he went to Baltimore of the American Association, winning 32 games in 1884. By next season his arm had gone dead and his promising career was finished by 1887. In that year, however, he umpired a Dominion Day doubleheader between Toronto and Hamilton and was an instant success. By 1891 he was umpiring Western League games. In mid August he received a telegram from Nicholas Young, president of the National League. "When Milwaukee jumps to the American Association," it said, "You jump to Cincinnati in the National League."

Emslie remained in the NL until retiring in 1924. He would later umpire spring training games and serve the league in an administrative capacity. He would be forever tagged with the sobriquet "Blind Bob" by John McGraw, in part because of his support of Hank O'Day's ruling that Fred Merkle had failed to touch second base in the 1908 game that eventually cost the Giants a pennant.

The greatest Canadian-born player of the 19th century, however, was both a skilled pitcher and a great batter. James Edward "Tip" O'Neill—born in Springfield, Ontario, in 1861—grew up in Woodstock, Ontario, home of Canada's first significant team, the Young Canadians. Commencing in 1877 he pitched several years for his home town team. In keeping with the itinerant life of that day's ballplayer he left town in the early 1880s to pursue a professional career with the barnstorming Hiawathas, sponsored by a tobacco company out of Detroit. In the off season O'Neill honed his pitching skills in a large building adjoining the family's O'Neill House hotel in Woodstock (this hotel, now known as the Oxford, is still part of the Woodstock scene).

O'Neill's arm failed him in his inaugural National League season with the Metropolitans in 1883 but his natural batting ability won him a position with St. Louis of the American Association in 1884. O'Neill's splendid career with Chris Von Der Ahe's team was highlighted by seven consecutive plus-.300 seasons, including a .435 av-

Tip O'Neill

William Humber

erage of 1887 which had actually once been recorded as .492 owing to the inclusion of bases on balls in hit totals. Several more such seasons would have made O'Neill a Hall of Fame candidate; as it is he resides among a select group of very good but just missing stars.

In his day, however, O'Neill was one of the greatest of colorful baseball personalities. In St. Louis his portrait adorned a large banner affixed to the team's train. When he came to bat, one story suggests, a dozen maidens in flowing robes sounded a fanfare on silver trumpets. His fame and name were well known for years and children with the last name of O'Neill often became Tip; such at least was the case for a famous 20th-century Speaker of the House from Massachusetts.

But O'Neill was also a man narrowly bound by the nasty prejudices of the day. In 1887 he presented a petition on behalf of his teammates objecting to an exhibition game with the Cuban Giants. "We the undersigned," it read, "do not agree to play against negroes tomorrow. We will cheerfully play against white people at any time, and think by refusing to play, we are only doing what is right..." The flamboyant O'Neill slightly redeemed himself in later years by assuming the presidency of Montreal's Eastern League team in 1898 where he was tireless in his support of baseball in the Canadian city until his death on the last day of 1915.

A third prominent member might be added to this cast of 19th century baseball achievers. However Toronto-born Art Irwin grew up in the Boston area so his claim to Canadian identity is suspect, though he later assumed an important place on the Toronto sporting scene as part owner of the minor league Toronto Maple Leafs.

Irwin was an acclaimed shortstop, the New York *Clipper* once noting that "His fielding in the Worcester–Cincinnati contest of August 31, 1880, was phenomenal, he accepting all of the fifteen chances offered him, and assisting no fewer than thirteen times." The account may suggest nothing extraordinary except that in those days players went without gloves, a condition Irwin did much to rectify a few seasons later as a member of the Providence Grays. A hard hit ball broke two of his left-hand fingers and Irwin, risking the inevitable call of sissy, bought a buckskin glove several sizes too big, added some padding, and fit his two broken digits into one of the glove's roomy spaces.

Irwin played when others may have sat and Providence eventually won the National League pennant and followed with a championship over the New York Metropolitans.

Arthur Irwin

William Humber

Within two years most ballplayers had adopted the "Irwin Glove". Irwin was a true innovator, helping to lead the player revolt of 1890, introducing professional baseball into Cuba, managing Washington on three separate occasions, scouting for New York, and even umpiring. Always seeking a challenge, he also wrote a successful players' guide, "Practical Ballplaying".

Irwin gained a variety of nicknames including Foxy, Doc, Artful Arthur, and Cutrate Irwin, the latter owing to his willingness to take less pay than other applicants because of a compulsion to try new jobs. One of the truly fascinating characters of early baseball, his life's end was filled with similar oddity. Apparently depressed about his inability to maintain two marriages at the same time, he jumped overboard while sailing between New York and Boston. That at least is the official story and one the various Baseball Encyclopedias support with their reference to his burial place as simply, Atlantic Ocean.

The 1890s likewise saw more Canadians reach the big leagues and by now the numbers were swelling to include players from the Maritimes and Quebec. As in southwestern Ontario, these were often second-generation Canadian ballplayers who had had a chance to watch competitive baseball in their small towns as youngsters.

In 1894, however, the Alien Contract Labour Act was introduced in the United States and its impact was to put a roadblock in the way of young Canadians seeking employment south of the border. This decade also witnessed significant development in the sport of hockey which would eventually kill off lacrosse and seriously erode baseball's pool of potential players and organizers. The impact of these developments is difficult to chart. Suffice to say that the golden age of Canadian baseball players of the late 19th century would not occur again.

This is not to suggest that baseball went into immediate decline. The gradual spread of baseball throughout the United States widened the source of capable talent without weakening the game's appeal in its former strongholds. The northeastern American States' status as the leading supplier of baseball players was eroded and eventually supplanted by first the midwest and then California. This shifting player source has continued to expand in the 20th century with the inclusion of black players and the growth of baseball in Latin America.

In truth the record of 20th century baseball in Canada is far from shabby. Besides the aforementioned George Gibson, prominent ballplayers have been drawn from across the country, including Fredericton's boisterous Larry McLean, Saskatchewan's Terry Puhl and Larry Walker from British Columbia. And while some Canadians like George Selkirk and Jeff Heath probably owe their advance to training in the United States, others like Ron Taylor and Ferguson Jenkins are classic demonstrations that weather and location are not inhibiting factors for major league success. Ron Taylor's high school, North Toronto Collegiate Institute, was known for training scholars and fans but it didn't even have a baseball team. Jenkins' amateur teams only played a twenty- or thirty-game schedule each year.

Since 1889 all but one of Canada's ten provinces have provided native sons to major league baseball. In 1991, besides Larry Walker, British Columbia was represented by Kevin Reimer (Rangers) and Steve Wilson (Dodgers, Cubs), Ontario by Rob Ducey (Blue Jays) and Kirk McCaskill (Angels), Denis Boucher hailed from Quebec (Blue Jays, Indians), New Brunswick was represented by Rheal Cormier (Cardinals), and Nova Scotia by Vince Horsman (Jays, Athletics). It was, if anything, a banner year soured only by the Dodgers' release of Newfoundlander Tom Humber from their organization. The author can only regret the failure of a provincial representative from Canada's youngest province to finally crack the major league barrier. He regrets as well the absence of so fine a last name in a big league boxscore.

Lefty O'Doul and the Development of Japanese Baseball

Richard Leutzinger

Lefty O'Doul was not so much a star as he was a comet. He blazed a brilliant path through the National League from 1928-34, left a scattering of batting records in his vapor trail, and then disappeared back to the minor leagues, whence he had come.

He might have been recognized as one of the great hitters of all time, had he not squandered five years of his career trying to be a pitcher and four more after that, at a relatively advanced age, learning to play the outfield. As a consequence, O'Doul didn't begin his major league career in earnest until he was 31 years old.

He then had time to bat only 3,264 times, not enough to qualify him for official career records, where 4,000 is needed to be listed with the likes of Ty Cobb, Rogers Hornsby and Shoeless Joe Jackson, the only three players with higher lifetime averages than O'Doul.

Lefty O'Doul batted .349 over his eleven seasons, including those as a pitcher with the Yankees and Red Sox, won two batting championships while playing for the Phillies and Dodgers, and in 1929 had one of the best years any batter ever had. He set a National League record with 254 basehits, a modern NL record of 330 hits and walks combined, and batted .398, the highest this century by a National League outfielder. He also drove in 122 runs, hit 32 home runs and struck out only 19 times. No one has ever hit so many homers and struck out so few times in one season.

There was another side to O'Doul's career, however, separate from what he enjoyed as a major league ball-

player, equally impressive, as different as east from west, and not altogether unrelated. O'Doul went to Japan at least twenty times—in the early days by trans-Pacific steamer—as a player, manager, batting instructor, negotiator and goodwill ambassador. He had an influence on every aspect of Japanese baseball, at every level from schoolboy play to major league competition.

Lefty was later to be dubbed by sportswriters in his hometown of San Francisco "The Father of Baseball in Japan," and many have interpreted this over the years to mean that O'Doul actually started baseball in Japan. He did not. Nevertheless, his contributions to the birth and growth of professional baseball in Japan are so numerous that he is as well known to Japanese baseball fans as to their American counterparts.

Baseball was introduced to Japan before O'Doul was even born. It goes all the way back, in fact, to 1873, when a Christian missionary named Horace Wilson taught the game to university students in Tokyo. Christianity never really caught on with the Japanese, but they took an immediate liking to baseball and it has grown steadily in popularity ever since. The Yomiuri Giants of Japan's Central League regularly play before more than 3,000,000 spectators a year, although they play only sixty-five home games, 16 less than major league teams in North America. One year the Giants finished in last place and still drew 2.8 million, a figure which only a handful of American or National league teams have ever reached.

The first game between Japanese and American teams was played in 1896, when a Tokyo school nine challenged the American Athletic Club of Yokohama. Much to the surprise and embarrassment of the Americans, the Japanese team won, 29-4. A rematch was arranged, to be

Richard Leutzinger *lives in Pacific Grove, California, and is author of a forthcoming book on the underrated and under-appreciated baseball life of San Francisco slugger and statesman, Lefty O'Doul.*

played two weeks later. This time the Americans cheated by recruiting a number of players from U.S. battleships moored nearby. Once again the Japanese won by a lop-sided margin.

In 1905, a Waseda University team made a trip to California to play a series of games against American college teams. Waseda's game against Stanford University was to be the first in which Japanese players wore spiked shoes, and they arrived in Palo Alto with the spikes attached to their shoes backwards. Local cobblers had to be found to make some quick alterations before the game could be played.

The New York Giants and Chicago White Sox played three games in Japan during their round-the-world tour in 1913, and then in the '20s, American all-star and Negro League teams began to visit Japan on a regular basis. Three Japanese professional teams were even formed in the early '20s, but all soon expired due to lack of competition and a major earthquake in 1923. By 1930, baseball had become so popular that it began to rival sumo wrestling as the national pastime.

O'Doul was a member of an all-star team which arrived in Japan in October 1931, following a two-week crossing of the Pacific on a Japanese luxury liner. The American all-stars swept the seventeen games they played against university teams, commercial league clubs and a Japanese all-star team. Small wonder they won every game: among O'Doul's teammates were Lou Gehrig, Lefty Grove, Mickey Cochrane, Frankie Frisch, Rabbit Maranville, George Kelly and Al Simmons, all future Hall of Famers.

Not all the wins came easily, though. Gehrig was hit by a pitch during a 2-0 win over Keio University in the seventh game of the tour, suffered two broken bones in his right hand, and was unable to play during the remainder of the trip. Little did he know that these would be the only games he'd miss because of injury in 15 years, while playing 2,130 games in a row for the New York Yankees.

One day after Gehrig was injured, O'Doul was knocked out of the line-up with an injury of his own. He had been having a marvelous time up until then, having won all the deck games on the ship coming over—fastest runner around the ship, highest jumper, longest jumper. He had beaten all the others at cards and throwing dice. Once ashore, he'd established himself as the best golfer of the group. And through the first seven baseball games, he was batting an incredible .600 against Japanese pitching, far better than any of his teammates.

The eighth game was marked by intense bench jockeying, which went unnoticed by most of the Waseda University players, since few knew enough English to understand. One who did understand, though, was the Waseda second baseman, who had been nicknamed Nosey by Maranville. Nosey directed a few uncomplimentary epithets of his own at the Americans.

As O'Doul left the dugout before one of his at-bats, he told his teammates: "I'm going to bunt and force Nosey to cover first base. We'll have some fun." O'Doul laid down a bunt, just inside the first base line, which was fielded by the Waseda first baseman. Nosey ran over from his position to take the throw, arriving at first base at precisely the same time as O'Doul, who was racing up the line full-speed. The two collided at a 90-degree angle and the surprised O'Doul was sent flying ten feet into foul territory. When he landed, in a painful heap, he had two broken ribs.

The Japanese second baseman held onto the ball for the putout, said something in Japanese to O'Doul, and returned to his position. O'Doul didn't understand what Nosey has said, but his Japanese teammates did, and all responded with larger than life smiles. O'Doul was finished with baseball and golf for the rest of his stay in Japan.

Aside from the injuries to Gehrig and O'Doul, the 1931 tour was a resounding success. All the games were played before capacity crowds, some in stadiums that held up to 75,000 people, and the total attendance was 450,000 for seventeen games. Everybody made more money than expected. And newspaper circulation soared, which was important because the whole tour had been underwritten by wealthy industrialist and publisher Matsutaro Shoriki, as a promotion for his newspapers. Nevertheless, Shoriki was the only person to express any disappointment about the tour. He had wanted Babe Ruth to be part of the American team, and although the Babe had been invited, he had been unable to come. He reportedly was busy making a movie in California.

O'Doul became acquainted with both Shoriki and his righthand man, Sotaro Suzuki, while in Japan. Before going home, they contracted with him to become their liaison with Ruth, with instructions to bring him to Japan the following year. Lefty did not have an easy time convincing his old pal from Yankee days and had to get Mrs. Ruth to help persuade him. It took three years for O'Doul to accomplish his mission. Finally, in 1934, Ruth relented and came.

When the ship carrying the Bambino and the 1934 American all-star team arrived in Yokohama, it was met by a huge crowd. No one could be sure at the time whether everyone had come out to see Ruth or the entire team, which also included future Hall of Famers Gehrig, Charlie Gehringer, Earl Averill, Connie Mack, Lefty Gomez and Jimmy Foxx. It became apparent soon enough, though, that Ruth was the main attraction.

The team was paraded down the Ginza in Tokyo in open cars, with the Babe's in front. Fans crowded so tightly around his car that the whole cavalcade came to a dead stop. Newspapers reported that more than a million people had come out to see Ruth. Gehringer, in an interview years later with Donald Honig, author of *Baseball, When the Grass Was Real*, remembered the reception well. "It seemed like all Tokyo was out, waving and yell-

Lefty O'Doul with the New York Giants in 1932

Gehrig and Foxx in succession, before finally losing, 1-0. Sawamura became a national hero overnight. Sadly, he was later killed during World War II at the age of 26.

The Japanese were awed by the size and power of some of the Americans, particularly Ruth, Gehrig and Foxx. "They just couldn't believe anybody could hit a ball so far," Gehringer recalled. "Of course, the Japanese were so much smaller than our guys. I remember a few games Ruth played first base—Gehrig was in the outfield—and whenever one of the Japanese got to first, Ruth would stand on the bag to make him look smaller. The fans loved it. They loved everything he did. His magic was unbelievable."

By the time Ruth finally made his triumphant visit to Japan in 1934, O'Doul and Shoriki had become close friends. It was not surprising, then, that when Shoriki started laying plans to establish a professional baseball league in Japan, Suzuki and O'Doul were his closest and most trusted advisors.

Shoriki named his own team, the first of eight formed, The Great Japan Tokyo Baseball Club. O'Doul just about gagged when he heard that name and convinced Shoriki that something easier to say and write might be better. He suggested Tokyo Giants. Shoriki agreed, but being a great publicity seeker, later changed the team's name to Yomiuri Giants. Yomiuri is not the name of a Japanese city you've never heard of; it is the name of Shoriki's largest newspaper, *Yomiuri Shimbun.*

In 1935, Shoriki had a baseball team but no one to play. With O'Doul's assistance, he arranged to send it to the United States on a 110-game barnstorming tour. The Giants won seventy-five games, playing mostly against minor league teams, and the tour was a sensation in the Japanese press, particularly Shoriki's *Yomiuri Shimbun*, which printed a play-by-play account of every game. Within a year, Japan had seven pro baseball teams and was ready to begin league play.

To get his Giants ready for their first season of league play, Shoriki sent the team to California to take spring training with the San Francisco Seals of the Pacific Coast League, who not coincidentally were by then being managed by O'Doul. The two squads trained together for three weeks and played a series of exhibition games against one another. In one noteworthy contest, Eiji Sawamura pitched a three-hit shutout and struck out ten at Seals Stadium in San Francisco.

O'Doul's first visit to Japan in 1931 had been primarily as a player, but by batting a barely believable .600 against Japanese pitchers on that tour, he had established a credibility that would serve him for all future visits.

He returned in 1932, along with Washington Senators catcher Moe Berg and Chicago White Sox pitcher Ted Lyons, to coach Big Six University League players in Tokyo. Berg, like O'Doul, quickly fell in love with Japan. At least, he gave that impression. He even learned to speak Japanese. However, it was revealed years later that

ing," he said. "We could hardly get our cars through, the streets were so jammed. What was interesting was that they knew who we all were. You'd think being so many miles away and being [of] such a different culture, the whole thing would have been strange to them. But apparently they'd been following big league baseball for years and gee, they knew us all. Especially Ruth, of course. They made a terrific fuss over him, and he loved it."

The Americans had played before large crowds before, but never before as many as the 100,000 who pushed and shoved their way into Meiji Stadium in Tokyo for one game. Being a natural-born showman, Ruth reacted beautifully to the crowd.

The game was played during a torrential rainstorm. Ruth said if the fans were willing to sit through a downpour to see the game, the least he could do was play the whole nine innings. In the first inning, a fan came out of the stands and handed Ruth his umbrella. The game was halted briefly while Ruth and the fan exchanged courteous bows. The Babe played the entire game, except when he was batting, holding the umbrella.

The Americans won all eighteen games they played on this tour, with Ruth hitting thirteen home runs, and were able to clown their way through almost every contest, winning by comfortable margins. However, everyone got serious for at least one game when an 18-year old high school pitcher, Eiji Sawamura, almost shut out the Americans, fanning Ruth three times and Gehringer, Ruth,

Berg secretly took photos of Tokyo from the roof of St. Luke's International Hospital, which were used to help plan U.S. bombing raids during World War II.

O'Doul concentrated on teaching during nearly all of his visits to Japan from 1932 on, up into the 1950s. He found the Japanese extremely receptive to his lessons.

"I like the people," he once said in an interview. "See, I like people who you're not wasting your time on, trying to help them. The American kid knows more than the coach. Teaching Japanese and Americans is like day and night."

There were several years, of course, when O'Doul was unable to visit Japan. He was notified by wire, more or less at the last moment, to cancel his plans to bring a ballclub over in 1937, due to a "conflict" in China. He remained locked out from then until after World War II ended in 1945.

O'Doul didn't wait to be invited back when the war ended. He travelled to Japan on his own early in 1946 to start groundwork for the resumption of relations between Japanese and American ballplayers. "I knew if we brought a baseball team over there it would cement friendship between these people and us," he explained. It's doubtful he anticipated that an American baseball team would have such a profound effect on the Japanese as it had, though.

What O'Doul accomplished during his first post-war tour of Japan with a team in 1949 transcended everything he ever did on a baseball field. It transcended baseball.

Pro baseball had become so popular in Japan that it almost survived without interruption through World War II, despite being an invention and the national pastime of the enemy. It wasn't until October of 1944 that play finally was suspended. Some 10,000 geisha houses and other amusement centers had been shut down a year earlier, which must indicate something about Japanese priorities.

When O'Doul, then manager of the San Francisco Seals, arrived for a six-week tour in 1949, he found the Japanese starving for baseball. General Douglas MacArthur, commander of U.S. occupation forces in Japan, had encouraged the rebirth of the game and had ordered the clearing of the Yomiuri Giants stadium, which had been turned into an ammunition dump. The Seals gave dozens of clinics and played ten games, four against American service teams and six against Japanese clubs, and drew over half a million spectators. Their visit also raised more than $100,000 for Japanese charities.

O'Doul had found the entire country submerged in a deep dark depression when he arrived. "Jeez, it was terrible," he said in his interview with Lawrence Ritter, author of *The Glory of Their Times*. "The people were so depressed. You know, when I was there years ago their cry was always *banzai, banzai* (bravo, bravo). But in '49 they were so depressed that when I hollered *banzai* at them, they didn't even respond." When he left six weeks later, he said, "all of Japan was *banzai*-ing again."

O'Doul and his team of minor leaguers in just forty-odd days had restored the nation's morale, broken the post-war tension in Japanese-American relations and laid a new foundation for friendship between the two countries. "All the diplomats put together would not have been able to do that," MacArthur said later. "This is the greatest piece of diplomacy ever."

Emperor Hirohito was so grateful that he summoned O'Doul, Seals president Paul Fagan and vice president Charlie Graham to the Imperial Palace to thank them personally for all they had done.

O'Doul had a huge influence on the game of baseball in Japan, not only before the war and in 1949, but for years after. He and Joe DiMaggio travelled together to Japan several times during the fifties to coach Japanese players. And he took his first post-war team of big leaguers to Japan in 1951, to play sixteen games against all-star teams from the Central and Pacific Leagues. The team, appropriately called "O'Doul's All-Stars," included Joe and Dom DiMaggio, American League batting champion Ferris Fain of the Philadelphia Athletics, Yankee rookie second baseman Billy Martin, and pitchers Ed Lopat of the Yankees, Mel Parnell of the Red Sox and Bobby Shantz of the Athletics.

Dom DiMaggio, in particular, has fond memories of the tour because he had been so disappointed when the 1937 trip was canceled. "I made Lefty promise he'd take me when the opportunity arose again," he recalled, forty years later. "He called me during the 1951 season and I said: 'You remembered!' And he said: 'Of course, I did'."

The Japanese were dominated by the Americans, as usual, although they did win one game. Ten different American teams had played in Japan since 1908 and they had a combined record of more than 150 wins and only three losses by the conclusion of the 1951 tour.

The Japanese couldn't understand why they weren't making more progress towards parity with the Americans, considering their great enthusiasm for learning. O'Doul felt the Japanese were being retarded in their development because there were no minor leagues in Japan. All the professional teams were stocked with players who came straight from high school, college or from amateur industrial league teams.

During his earliest post-war visits, O'Doul began selling the Japanese on the idea that they could raise the level of their play significantly by establishing farm teams. It took him a few years to convince a majority of club owners and general managers of this, but his idea eventually was brought to fruition in 1954 when the first Japanese minor league was formed.

O'Doul was also the man behind another overseas trip by the Yomiuri Giants, when they held spring training in California in 1953. This time, they shared a training camp at Santa Maria with the New York Giants and, before returning home, won six of eighteen games against major and minor league competition.

O'Doul's influence on Japanese baseball was so far-reaching that he even determined what uniforms players would wear. To this day, the Yomiuri Giants wear uniforms nearly identical to that worn by O'Doul when he played for the New York Giants in 1933-34, complete with "Giants" in the same type black and orange lettering across their shirts. Only the letters on their caps are different. Several other Japanese teams wear pinstripes, a style which became popular following the 1949 visit of O'Doul's Seals, who also wore them.

Periodic efforts have been made to get O'Doul elected to Japan's Baseball Hall of Fame, but so far these have failed, although he did receive votes in1969 and 1979.

O'Doul's diplomatic achievements were of enough lasting significance that Japanese and Americans were still fully aware of what he had done a generation later. After O'Doul died of a heart attack in San Francisco in 1969—on December 7th, of all days—Japanese Consul General Seichi Shima led a delegation of his countrymen to the funeral. "No single man did more to reestablish faith and friendship between our great nations than did Lefty O'Doul," said Monsignor Vincent Breen, directing his eulogy at Japanese and Americans alike.

O'Doul's death reminded Pulitzer Prize winning sports columnist Red Smith of another incident in his long and warm relationship with the Japanese.

"In a Catholic mission in Tokyo, the kids were preparing for confirmation," he wrote in a column published shortly after O'Doul died. "They were told they had the privilege of adding a new name to that received at baptism, but little Toshi couldn't think of a saint's name he wanted to adopt.

"'Why don't you choose Francis?' suggested the nun who was his teacher. 'For St. Francis de Sales.'

"'Ah, so,' Toshi said.

"A few days later the bishop was about to administer the sacrament.

"'And what is your confirmation name?' he asked.

"Toshi's face lit up.

"'San Francisco Seals,' he said."

With Joe DiMaggio at a presentation during the "O'Doul's All-Stars" visit in 1951

Sadaharu Oh's Place in Baseball's Pantheon

Frederick Ivor-Campbell

From June 1, 1974, when *The New York Times* introduced Sadaharu Oh to the American baseball public by reporting his 600th career home run—through Oh's retirement as a player after the 1980 season with the unapproachable total of 868 home runs (154 more than Babe Ruth, and, in 467 fewer games, 113 more than Hank Aaron)—Oh has been discussed in the American press (and therefore perceived by American fans) almost exclusively as a hitter of home runs.

The Japanese press and public knew more than this one dimension of Oh, but even in Japan it was Oh's home runs that were the focus of fan adulation. On the perennially champion Yomiuri Giants of Tokyo, for whom he played his entire professional career (1959-1980), Oh was not considered the team's best or most popular player: Shigeo Nagashima—who burst on the scene a year ahead of Oh to lead the Central League in homers and RBIs—was throughout his career regarded as a finer player than Oh, and is still remembered in Japan as that country's most popular player ever. It was not until after 1974, when Oh's home run output had passed 600 (and Nagashima had retired to manage the Giants) that Oh began to emerge from Nagashima's shadow.

But if Oh trailed Nagashima in the fans' affection, he was Nagashima's equal or superior at the plate. Although it was home runs that fueled his popularity, Oh was hardly a one-dimensional hitter. True, his most impressive statistics relate to home runs: his Japanese season record of 55 in 1964, his fifteen Central League home run

Frederick Ivor-Campbell *is a former university English professor and noted authority on nineteenth-century baseball, as well as author of chapters on team histories, post-season play, and the All-Star Game for* Total Baseball.

championships (including an amazing thirteen in a row), and of course his career record 868. But Oh also led the league five times in batting average, thirteen times in RBIs, and fifteen times in runs scored. He won back-to-back triple crowns in 1973 and '74, a feat unequalled in Japanese (and American) major league ball. And despite the fact that for much of his career he preceded the dangerous Nagashima in the batting order, for nineteen of his twenty-two seasons he led his league in bases on balls, including sixteen seasons as leader in intentional walks. Oh was a remarkably durable player who rarely missed a game. Eleven times he led the league in games played, and wound up his career with 328 more games than Babe Ruth, despite his shorter 130-game seasons.

But while Oh ranks among the greatest batsmen—perhaps as *the* greatest—in the history of Japanese baseball, can he be compared with the greats of the American major leagues? Comparisons between Japanese and American baseball records are difficult. Conventional wisdom—Japanese as well as American—says that the quality of play in Japan's professional leagues is about equal to the best American triple-A ball. Compounding the difficulty of comparison is the fact that Japanese ballfields are somewhat smaller than American fields. Tokyo's Korakuen Stadium, where Oh played his home games, for example, measured only 295 feet down the foul lines and 394 feet to center.

But the same kinds of problems arise when we attempt comparisons between the generations, or between ball parks, in American baseball. Were the major league pitchers of the 1920s as good as those of the sixties? Would Ruth have overwhelmed in the '80s as he did in the '20s? What if Ruth had played for Cincinnati, with its right field foul line which varied in length during Ruth's heyday between 377 and 400 feet. (The right field foul pole at Ruth's home Yankee Stadium was 296 feet away, compared to 295 feet at Oh's home field.) What if Aaron had played out his latter years somewhere other than Atlanta with its home-run-conducive altitude?

All in all, it seems as reasonable to accept records made in Japan as to accept those made in 1974 Atlanta or 1927 New York. For the sake of comparing Oh's career hitting with that of America's best, let us assume the equivalence of American and Japanese baseball.

In terms of productivity, the greatest American hitters are Babe Ruth and Ted Williams. (Hank Aaron leads the American pack in home runs by a comfortable margin, but in slugging percentage he ranks only twelfth, and in on-base percentage he is nowhere near the top hundred. In over-all production—slugging plus OBP—he ranks eighteenth.) As a slugger, Ruth, at .690, holds an imposing 56 point lead over second-place Williams. Williams, though, ranks number one in on-base percentage, at .483, nine points ahead of Ruth. In over-all production, Ruth scores 1,163, Williams 1,116. Lou Gehrig ranks third, at 1,080. (These rankings remain the same even when production is adjusted for the differences in ball parks. Since sabermetricians have not yet, to my knowledge, calculated the ballpark factor for Japanese baseball, I have used the raw production figures in this study.)

How would Oh rank among these giants? If he had played in the American major leagues and had put up the same numbers he did in Japan, he would find himself near the top. In on-base percentage, Oh's estimated* .453 would rank him fifth behind Williams, Ruth (.474), John McGraw (.465) and Billy Hamilton (.455); Gehrig (.447) would follow Oh in sixth place. Oh's 2,504 bases on balls would rank an overwhelming first, and he would reign with Ruth (2,056) and Williams (2,019) as the only three major league batters to walk more than two thousand times. In walks-per-game, while Oh remains in first place, he just edges Williams, .8845 to .8809.

Although Oh's .63373 career slugging average would rank him third, he would wind up in a virtual tie with second-place Williams (.63379). Just one more single stretched into a double would have nudged Oh past Ted. Oh's 1,315 extra-base hits trail Ruth's 1,356 and lead Williams's 1,117. But Williams, who lost several peak seasons to military service and played in 539 fewer games than Oh, leads Oh in extra base hits per game .49 to .47. Ruth is way ahead of them both in EBH/G, with .54.

Oh's production total of 1,087 (or 1,084 if we discount his estimated HBP's) would rank third all-time, behind Ruth's 1,163 and Williams's 1,116, and just ahead of Gehrig's 1,080.

Granted, the smaller dimensions of the Japanese ball field contributed to Oh's amazing home run total. But if the smaller Japanese playing fields increased his home runs, they also limited his doubles and triples. Oh surpassed Williams's home run total by 347, although he played in only 539 more games than Williams. (Had Williams played in as many games as Oh, he would have hit about 644 homers.) Yet the career slugging averages of the two players are all but identical, as we have seen, and Williams holds a slight edge in extra-base hits per game. For while Oh homered with historic effect, he doubled and tripled far less often than Williams (or Ruth, or Aaron). Where Williams's doubles (525) equalled his home runs (521), Oh homered more than *twice* as often as he doubled (868-422), and Williams in his shorter career nearly tripled Oh's output of triples (71-25).

Sadaharu Oh

With Aaron, we see an intriguing alternation of Williams-like and Oh-like home run/double ratios. In the twelve years Aaron played for the Milwaukee Braves, his doubles (391) closely matched his home runs (398). But after the Braves moved to Atlanta, where the higher elevation produced an effect in Fulton County Stadium similar to Japan's closer fences, Aaron's home run production over nine years (335) outpaced his doubles (209) by 62 percent. Then, when he returned to Milwaukee for two final seasons, his doubles (24) and homers (22) once again evened out. Ruth, who played most of his home games in parks with short foul lines but distant center fields, struck a happy medium between Williams and Oh in double/home run ratio: he doubled 71 percent as often as he homered.

It seems reasonable to conclude that, while the shorter distances to the Japanese fences permitted a number of Oh's shots to sail out for home runs that in American parks would have gone for fly outs, many of Oh's home run shots would have gone to the walls and into the corners of American parks for doubles and triples. While we may not be able to say with confidence that Oh is a greater *home run* hitter than Ruth or Aaron, there seems little doubt that he deserves to be ranked among the three or four most *productive* hitters ever.

Since I don't have Oh's hit-by-pitch stats, I have raised his OBP (which, using at bats and walks only, is .450) three points, the same amount that HBP raises both Ruth's and Williams's OBP. I follow the Total Baseball *calculations of OBP, which ignores sacrifice flies. —F. I-C.*

"If it hadn't been for baseball, it would have been unbearable"

Baseball Behind Barbed Wire

Jay Feldman

In May 1942, Kenichi Zenimura looked out over the barren landscape of the Fresno Assembly Center, and he knew exactly what needed to be done. "Every time my dad went someplace, if there was no baseball park, he'd make one," says Howard Zenimura, 63.

From the second decade of this century, baseball was the most popular recreation in the Japanese-American community, and at five feet tall and 105 pounds, Kenichi Zenimura, "the dean of Nisei baseball," was the most influential figure in the sport. Born in Hiroshima in 1900, "Zeni," as he was affectionately called, was introduced to baseball as a boy when his family moved to Hawaii. In 1920, he settled in Fresno and played shortstop for the town team; in '24, he organized the first tour of a California team to Japan.

By the 1930s every community had a Nisei (second-generation) team, ardently supported by the Issei (first-generation) immigrants. "The Issei were crazy about baseball," says Pete Mitsui, 76, who played for the San Fernando Aces in the thirties and forties. "It was all community-oriented. The communities didn't intermingle like they do now, you see, and the ballclub was an important part of the community identity, so they really wanted us to do well."

"There were tremendous rivalries between towns," adds Hugo Nishimoto, 73, who played for and then managed the Newcastle team. "The Issei used to bet a lot of money on those games. If we won, they would take us out to a big dinner."

Jay Feldman *writes prolifically about baseball for popular magazines, has organized unique "Baseball for Peace" ballplaying tours to Nicaragua, and still plays in an "over-30 hardball league" in California.*

The outbreak of war changed everything. On February 19, 1942, President Franklin D. Roosevelt signed Executive Order 9066, which would quickly lead to the evacuation and internment of virtually the entire Japanese-American populations of California, Oregon and Washington, of which approximately two-thirds (77,000) were American citizens.

Most families were given little more than a week to get ready. People sold cars, furniture, refrigerators, and other large articles for a fraction of their worth, taking only money and whatever possessions they could carry with them. The majority of the evacuees were sent to temporary "assembly centers" like that in Fresno—mostly converted county fairgrounds—while the government hastily prepared ten permanent camps.

The transition was abrupt and shattering. For a people whose culture stressed personal decorum and hygiene, and placed a premium on privacy, the indignities of camp life represented an acute aberration. Living quarters—barracks arranged in blocks—were severely cramped. Meals were served in large mess halls; toilets and bathhouses were communal.

One of the first problems facing the internees was to establish some sense of normalcy in the face of totally disrupted patterns of life. Cultural, recreational and work activities took on tremendous importance. There were schools for the children, and many adults were employed within camp by the government at standard G.I. wages.

Baseball played a major role in the effort to create a degree of continuity. "At the Fresno Assembly Center, there was nothing there but the fairgrounds, but Zeni had everything for a baseball diamond planned in his mind," recalls Herb "Moon" Kurima, 77, who managed and pitched for the Florin Athletic Club. "He lined up tractors, lumber, carpenters, and we started work on the grounds. Within a week, everything was ready."

Two leagues were formed—a six-team "A" division, and an eight-club "B" circuit. Many of the better draft-age players were already in the Armed Forces, so Kurima and the other managers had to patch together teams from the available talent—aging veterans and inexperienced high-school kids. Through a friend in Sacramento, Kurima sent for his team's uniforms and equipment, which he'd had the foresight to collect and put in storage before the evacuation.

Behind Kurima, whose blazing fastball and pinpoint control had made him one of the dominant pitchers in pre-war Nisei baseball, the Florin club quickly established itself as the team to beat, and Kurima, who was still recovering from injuries incurred in a near-fatal auto accident in April 1941, found himself the target of the other managers' dirty tricks.

"Every time Florin had a game against some strong team like Hanford or Bowles, these guys would call a meeting in the afternoon," says Kurima. "It was 100 degrees, and on a game day, I needed to take a rest, but they would hold a meeting to try and tire me out."

Meetings notwithstanding, Kurima won ten games, as Florin thoroughly dominated the A league, going undefeated in 13 games and, in a contest played before 3,000 spectators (more than half the center's total population), whipped a highly favored, Zenimura-managed all-star team, 7-2, behind Kurima's six-hit pitching.

The lower division title was captured by the Fresno B club, which included the 15-year-old Howard Zenimura and his 13-year-old brother Harvey—both of whom would later play Japanese big-league ball for the Hiroshima Carp in the fifties—and George "Hats" Omachi, now a scout for the Houston Astros.

In October 1942, the inhabitants of the assembly centers were again uprooted and assigned to one of the ten permanent camps geographically scattered through seven states (California, Arizona, Utah, South Dakota, Wyoming, Colorado, and Arkansas). At every camp, despite characteristically remote locations and inhospitable terrain, one of the first tasks undertaken after resettlement was the building of baseball diamonds.

Most of the group from the Fresno Assembly Center went to Jerome, located on Arkansas swampland. "I was on the clean-up committee, so I was one of the last to leave the Fresno Assembly Center," relates Omachi, 68. "I stayed behind about a month or six weeks. By the time I got to Jerome, they already had a diamond."

At Tule Lake, located on dry lake bottom in northeastern California, volunteers cleared the rocks and seashells from one area, while Bill Matsumoto, head of the warehouse division, used the food-delivery trucks to haul in dirt from the camp farm.

At Manzanar, in the desert near Death Valley, the teams took turns going up to the hills in a dump truck for

Kenichi Zenimura flanked by Lou Gehrig and Babe Ruth

decomposed granite, and San Fernando Aces catcher Berry Tamura, who worked for the camp fire department, saw to it that the field was well watered down by conducting frequent fire drills on the diamond.

Nothing compared, however, with the field that Zenimura built in the Arizona desert at Gila River. "As soon as we got to camp my father started looking for a place to build the diamond," recalls Howard Zenimura. "Right near our block was an open space, so we started digging out the sagebrush with shovels, and pretty soon people came by to ask us what we were doing. We told them we were building a ballpark, and then everybody was out there with their shovels clearing that place. When it was all cleared we got a bulldozer and leveled it.

"The fence that surrounded the camp was built of 4x4s strung with barbed wire, so we just took out every other 4x4 till we had enough to build a frame for the backstop. Then we took these long pads that they used to wet down and spread over cement to keep it from drying too fast, and we hung those over the frame to provide a cushion for passed balls, which was very nice. The only catch was, first thing when we went out, we'd have to pick up all the pads and check—you didn't want to go in after a passed ball and find a rattlesnake."

Next they worked on the mound and the infield, scraping the top layer and hand-straining out the rocks and pebbles. They diverted water from a nearby irrigation ditch and flooded the infield to harden and pack it down.

A grandstand was the next project. "We needed lumber," says Harvey Zenimura, now 61. "We were in Block 28 and the lumber yard was way across the other side of the camp. We'd go out there in the middle of the night and get the lumber, lug it all the way out in the sagebrush, bury it in the desert, and go pick it up later as we needed it. They probably knew what was going on, but nobody said anything."

The graded bleachers had four or five rows, and Zenimura went so far as to delineate individual seats on the planks. "My dad marked the benches with paint," laughs Harvey, who was all-Japan with the Carp in 1955-56. "He drew lines and put numbers. Anybody that donated a lot of money would get a good seat."

Beyond first and third base, dugouts were excavated so the fans could enjoy good sight lines. More of the cement-curing pads covered the dugouts and bleachers, to provide some shade against the desert sun. The pebbles strained from the infield were spread below the bleachers and on the dugout floors to keep down the dust. For an outfield fence, they planted castor beans at ten-foot intervals and dug a ditch behind them to deliver water. Finally, clumps of Bermuda grass were planted in the outfield, and some plumber friends ran a line from the end of Block 28 to the ballpark for a portable sprinkler system.

Thirty-two teams competed in Gila, where the climate allowed for year-round play. At every game, a collection was taken up, and Zenimura used the proceeds to have baseball equipment shipped from a Fresno sporting-goods dealer. In a 1962 interview, he claimed to have ordered about $2,000 worth of equipment from Fresno every month!

Given the popularity of baseball in the pre-war Japanese-American community, its prominence in the camps is hardly surprising; while there was organized competition in many sports, including basketball, football, boxing, and softball, none were pursued with the passion and ardor devoted to baseball.

The same creativity that was tapped for the construction of ballfields was used to provide uniforms. "We ordered jerseys from Sears Roebuck, and one of the fellows stenciled in the name," relates the gravel-voiced Nishimoto, who managed the Placer Hillmen to a Tule Lake camp championship in 1943. "But the pants were potato sacks that came from the farm. They were heavy cotton, bleached white. Two or three of the ladies sewed them up for us, and they looked real professional, too." Another Tule Lake team, the Wakabas, removed the canvas covers from the government-issue mattresses, and

George "Hats" Omachi takes a cut while Moon Kurima waits on deck. Jerome, Arkansas, internment camp, 1943.

had custom shirts and pants made.

The Issei continued to be a major force behind the scenes—financially and otherwise. "I went to learn sumo wrestling," says Florin's Yosh Tsukamoto, 70. "I got holy hell from the backers. They didn't want me to get hurt. So then I went to learn how to box. One of the guys wanted to put on an exhibition, and about half a dozen Florin guys were in it. When I came to the ring, I saw my dad standing over there. Boy, we all caught hell from the parents. That ended that. Stick to baseball."

As before the war, betting on ballgames was common among the Issei. Berry Tamura, 74, remembers three old men who attended every game at Manzanar and bet so much money that none trusted either of the others to keep the cash, so every inning, a different member of the trio would hold the stakes.

At the time, the San Fernando Aces were enjoying a winning streak that would lead to the 1943 camp championship. "We were scheduled to play the weakest team in the league, the Sacramento Solons," says the angular Tamura, a retired gardener whose voice rises and falls emphatically when he tells a story. "Well, one of the old men who always bet on us was very happy, and he told everyone he would pay three to one. What he didn't know was that the Solons had recruited a pitcher from Japan named Horimoto, and he was hotter than a firecracker that day. We couldn't touch him, and we lost. And that old man had to pay three to one. He was white; he wouldn't eat anything. He looked like he'd been kicked by a horse."

In mid-1943, thousands of camp residents were once again displaced as a result of a loyalty questionnaire administered to all internees. The two key questions involved willingness to swear allegiance to the United States, forswear allegiance to Japan, and serve in the U.S. Armed Forces. All who answered no to those questions were transferred to Tule Lake; any Tule Lake residents deemed loyal were relocated to other camps.

The loyalty test was designed to identify and isolate the pro-Japan elements, but it also caused substantial anguish for many others. "My father had been classified '4C-Enemy Alien'," says Isao Fujimoto, 56, who was nine years old when his family moved from Heart Mountain (Wyoming) to Tule Lake. "He was not allowed to become a U.S. citizen, so he couldn't renounce his allegiance to the Japanese government, because if he did, he would have had no citizenship at all. So he was sent to Tule Lake; my family chose to stick together, and we all went."

Many stayed at Tule Lake for similar reasons. Says Nishimoto, "My wife's father was there, and he was an old man, and my mother and stepfather were there, living in the next barrack, and I didn't want to leave them there alone, so we stayed. There were a lot of people there who were not disloyal, but because of family, they stayed in Tule Lake."

Many individuals wrestled with the loyalty test as a matter of conscience, and answered no on principle. "It was a difficult decision," explains Matsumoto, 72, who left Tule Lake and went to Amache, in Colorado. "Here your folks are sitting behind barbed wire, and they're asking if you'd go fight. It was hard."

For Berry Tamura, who had been drafted before evacuation, the loyalty questions were absurd. "I was all ready to go in the army," he says, recalling the irony. "I had my physical and everything, but before the time came, we had to go to Manzanar. As soon as we got there, they reclassified us as aliens. So when the question came up, I said the hell with it. I really shouldn't have felt that way about it, but you know how kids are."

Berry was assigned to Tule Lake, and the whole Tamura family went with him, enduring the undeserved stigma of disloyalty—a stigma which, in a culture that venerates allegiance, carried a heavy personal weight and, to this day, still causes concern. "We went to Tule Lake as a *family*," says Berry's brother Jim, 67, a soft-spoken man, making the point with quiet emphasis.

With its original population mix, Tule Lake had been a tense environment from the beginning. One large segment of the camp—from in and around California's Sacramento Valley—was dark-complected from farming in the intense Valley sun; the other portion of the population consisted of people from Oregon and Washington.

"It was a strange mixture and we didn't hit it off too well socially," says Matsumoto. "They'd call us black Californians, or something, and a fight would start. So we weren't on very good terms. More than one time we got chased out of the ballpark because the fans got so carried away. The cardinal rule that we broke was that we would talk to the fans. There would be a close play, and one of them would say, 'He was out,' and one of us would say something like, 'No he wasn't, you dumbbell,' which would start a fight. They would come after you with bats. There were times when we just had to go home—run like hell."

With segregation, the population of Tule Lake swelled. Now, in addition to the strained relations among the original inhabitants, there was also the enormous tension between the pro-Japan faction and the loyal American group, all of which made for a highly volatile milieu. Leading the pro-Japan bloc were the Kibei-Nisei who had been born in the U.S. but educated in Japan—who were not only strongly partisan to the Rising Sun, but particularly rabid baseball fans.

The eyes of the outside world were now on the segregated camp. On May 2, 1944, under the headline 'Tulelake [sic] Turns Out For Baseball Season," the following article appeared on page three of the *San Francisco Chronicle*:

> Baseball season opened at the Tulelake internment camp on the heels of ceremonies celebrating the birthday of the Emperor of Japan

over the weekend, the War Relocation Authority announced yesterday.

Ceremonies Saturday were brief and the day passed without incident, according to the WRA. The Tulelake baseball convention was opened by Project Director Ray Best, who threw out the first ball for the opening game. More than half the 17,000 residents of the center were present for the game, it was announced.

There were 15 "major-league" and 23 "minor-league" teams for the 1944 season. There were block teams (mostly B-level), home-town clubs, and squads from the other camps which formed after the move to Tule Lake. The newcomers from Jerome, Manzanar and Poston (Arizona) all fielded A-league clubs named for the camps they'd left behind.

Not surprisingly, baseball became more competitive after segregation, and the tensions which plagued the camp spilled over onto the diamond. In a crucial play-off game between Poston and Manzanar, the pressure came to a head and exploded.

As usual for any game involving the Manzanar team, there was a better-than-average turnout. "Our fans had an organized rooting section led by Kibeis," says Berry Tamura. "They had the flags, just like you see in Japanese stadiums today. We sure drew the crowds; they all wanted to see our cheerleading team."

The Manzanar fans also included a prominent group of burly fishermen from the harbor community of San Pedro who had a well-deserved reputation as a hot-headed bunch, always ready to mix things up.

With Jim Tamura pitching for Manzanar, the score was knotted at 5-5 after nine innings. In the top of the fourteenth, Poston broke through for three runs. In the Manzanar half, with a runner on second and two out, shortstop George Tamura—younger brother of Jim and Berry—got a hit, advancing the runner to third. The next batter belted a fly ball into the gap in left field.

Nishimoto was umpiring at first base. "The leftfielder went up and jumped," he relates, "and the ball was deflected off his glove, but the centerfielder, who was backing him up, caught it. Red Tanaka, the third-base umpire, and I both raised our hands, 'Out!' Oh, boy! The Manzanar fans couldn't take it, and they started storming out on the field."

The Manzanar rooters claimed the ball was trapped. George Tamura, 64, describes the ensuing melee: "This fellow who was a real close friend of ours, he went after the whole Poston team himself, right into their dugout. He got hit over the head with a chair. I saw his dad going in there, pulling him out with a bloody head. That really started it. All these big bruisers came out of the stands with fire in their eyes. We were in the infield, and we held everybody back."

In the pandemonium, the umpires and the Poston centerfielder had to be escorted back to their blocks. "After things settled down a bit, the player who claimed he caught the ball, he came to our block with his father and mother and apologized to my friend's family," continues George. "After that he quit baseball. Later on, we asked our friend why he went into the dugout like that, and he told us he felt sorry for Jim, that Jim was pitching such a good game, he hated to see him get robbed of a win."

The incident is briefly mentioned in *Baseball: Tule Lake Center 1944*, a 74-page, camp-published book about the '44 season: "True rabidness of the local diamond fandom was unveiled during this colorful brawl which saw differences of opinion voiced by the spectators and fists fly between a few of the more rabid baseball followers. This incident gained center-wide recognition as well as the attention of out-of-town newspapers."

On the less tempestuous side, it should be noted that the four Tomooka brothers led the Guadelupe team—which had transferred basically intact from Gila—to the Taiseiyo (Pacific) League Championship, and went on to take three straight from the Tule Lake Nippons, winners of the Taiheiyo (Atlantic) Division title, for the overall camp crown.

After the war, the Japanese-American community faced rebuilding from scratch. "Until about 1950, life was very hard," says Fujimoto, who teaches applied behavioral science at the University of California at Davis, "and baseball continued to play an important role—not only as a recreational outlet for the younger people, but in allowing a lot of the older people to come back together. They could take a Sunday afternoon and go to a ballgame.

"My experience playing and watching baseball in camp helped me get resettled because I knew so much about the game. I was in seventh grade when I got out of camp. I met a lot of kids my own age who played, but they didn't know strategy. They didn't know how to warm up; they didn't know how to do infield practice. That was all stuff I knew very well. The school I went to had a team, and the principal saw right away that I knew quite a bit, and he put me on the team. I was a shrimp, a foot shorter than a lot of these kids, but I was able to make the team because of what I knew about baseball from camp."

In August 1988 President Reagan signed a Congressional bill granting a redress payment of $20,000 to every living survivor of the internment camps. In October 1990, 48 years after FDR issued the internment order, the first payments were made.

More than forty years after the closing of the camps, many internees point to baseball as one of the few bright spots of a dark time. Matsumoto: "I think baseball was the main salvation against the loneliness of the camps. More than anything else, it got people together. If it hadn't been for baseball, it would have been unbearable."

Minneapolis Millers versus Havana Sugar Kings

Stew Thornley

It was a minor-league series with major-league drama. The Junior World Series, a post-season meeting between the champions of the American Association and International League that was played off and on from the early 1900s into the 1970s, over the years produced its share of highlights and strange events. But few Junior Series were more exciting—and none more bizarre—than the 1959 affair between the Minneapolis Millers of the American Association and the International League's Havana Sugar Kings.

Not only were two contests, including the decisive seventh game, decided in the last of the ninth inning, with another two going extra innings, but it was the only Junior Series in which the submachine guns outnumbered the bats.

The Millers, a Boston Red Sox farm team managed by Gene Mauch, were the defending Junior World Series champions and were making their third appearance in the minor-league classic in the last five years. Minneapolis was bolstered by the recent addition of a young second baseman named Carl Yastrzemski, who had joined the team during the Association playoffs.

Havana, on the other hand, had finished the previous season at the bottom of the International League standings. In 1959, though, they rose to third during the regular season and then upset Columbus and Richmond in the playoffs for a berth in the Junior Series.

Managed by Preston Gomez, the Sugar Kings' roster

was comprised of a mixture of Latin and North American players, several of whom would go on to respectable careers in the major leagues, including pitchers Mike Cuellar and Luis Arroyo and infielders Leo Cardenas, Elio Chacon, and Cookie Rojas.

Cuba in 1959 was no longer a Caribbean paradise. The recent years of revolutions and upheavals had turned the country into a battle-scarred island. Even the baseball diamond was not immune from the increased tensions following the overthrow of dictator Fulgencio Batista at the beginning of the year.

Shortly after midnight the morning of July 26th, while the Sugar Kings and Rochester Red Wings were in the 11th inning of a game at Gran Stadium, demonstrations began in the streets of Havana, marking the anniversary of the 1953 attack on the Moncada army garrison in Santiago de Cuba by a band of rebels led by Fidel Castro, an event viewed as the conception of the eventual revolution.

During the course of this observance, a wild burst of gunfire broke out, and a pair of stray bullets found their way inside the ball park, striking Rochester's Frank Verdi, who was coaching third base at the time, as well as Havana shortstop Leo Cardenas.

Neither Verdi nor Cardenas was seriously injured, but the incident nearly ended professional baseball in Cuba. The Red Wings left the country immediately, refusing to play the final game of the series, and they and other International League teams expressed fear and reluctance at returning to Cuba.

But baseball in Havana survived, in part because of the efforts and intervention of Fidel Castro, who by this time was premier of Cuba, having taken control of the govern-

Stew Thornley *is the author of several books on Minnesota sports history, including* On to Nicollet: The Glory and Fame of the Minneapolis Millers, *for which he received a 1988 SABR-Macmillan Baseball Research Award.*

ment after Batista had fled the country.

Castro was a great fan of the sport. He had played baseball at the University of Havana in the late 1940s and had even pitched in an exhibition game at Gran Stadium only two nights before the shootings.

And while the political turmoil continued, it could not obliterate the fanatical baseball interest that peaked when the Sugar Kings reached the Junior World Series. "There is no more violence in Havana," said team owner Bobby Maduro. "The fans have only baseball to think about now."

The series opened at Metropolitan Stadium in Bloomington, Minnesota. The first three games were to be played in the Millers' home park, but a premature blast of wintry weather brought an early close to their end of the series.

Only 2,486 fans showed up on Sunday, September 27 to watch Havana take the opener, 5-2, in a game played in a steady drizzle. Even though they were more than 1,500 miles from home, the Sugar Kings had the most vocal rooting section at the stadium. Cuban natives living in the Minneapolis area staked out spots in the box seats behind the Havana dugout. Equipped with maracas and Cuban flags, the fans cheered wildly, particularly during the Sugar Kings' four-run rally in the third inning.

As the weather grew colder the next day, the attendance dwindled to 1,062 for Game Two. The Millers' bats were hot, however, and they used the long ball to battle back from 2-0 and 5-2 deficits. Roy Smalley—the brother-in-law of manager Gene Mauch (and the father of the Roy Smalley who later played in this same stadium for the Minnesota Twins)—connected for a two-run homer to tie the game in the second inning, and home runs by Lu Clinton and Red Robbins retied the game in the last of the eighth. When Ed Sadowski opened the Minneapolis ninth with another home run, the Millers had pulled out a 6-5 win.

The Havana players appeared more bothered by the frigid temperatures than they were by the Miller rallies. They consumed large quantities of hot coffee during the game, and a newspaper photo the next day showed a trio of Sugar Kings huddled around a fire they had built in a wastebasket in the dugout.

On September 29, the thermometer reading plummeted even further. When the rain drops began turning to snow crystals, not only was that evening's game called off, but the decision was made by the minor-league commission to shift the balance of the series to Havana. The weather in Cuba was more conducive to baseball, and the reception that both the Sugar Kings and Millers received from the Havana fans was equally warm.

Upon their arrival, the teams received a gala civic welcome that included a parade from the airport to city hall. "This is a national event," proclaimed Bobby Maduro.

Fidel Castro concurred, and attended each of the games played at Gran Stadium, even calling off a meeting

Gene Mauch, right, was the Millers' playing manager

© 1992 STAR TRIBUNE/Minneapolis-St.Paul

of Cuba's cabinet so he and other high government officials could attend one of the contests.

As Castro made his entrances onto the field through the centerfield gate, the fans chanted his name and waved white handkerchiefs, giving the appearance of a snowstorm despite the 90-degree temperatures. The premier sat in different sections of the stadium during the series, and at one point even found a spot on the Havana bench.

In a home plate ceremony preceding the first game played in Havana, Castro addressed the 25,000 fans in attendance: "I came here to see our team beat Minneapolis, not as premier but as just a baseball fan. I want to see our club win the Little World Series. After the triumph of the revolution, we should also win the Little World Series."

The premier shook hands with the players from each team before settling into his box seat to watch the game.

The pomp at the plate, however, wasn't enough to make the Millers forget the strife that surrounded them. Everywhere they went in the city—from their quarters at the Havana Hilton to the ball park—they were greeted by the sight of Castro's bearded troopers. Nearly 3,000 soldiers were at the stadium during the game, many lining the field and others stationing themselves in the dugouts, their rifles and bayonets clearly evident.

"Young people not more than 14 or 15 years old were in the dugout with us, waving their guns around like toys," recalled Millers' pitcher Ted Bowsfield. "Every once in a while, we could hear shots being fired outside the stadium, and we never knew what was going on."

Gene Mauch reports that the soldiers were not above trying to intimidate the Minneapolis players. As Miller centerfielder Tom Umphlett entered the dugout after

The Millers' Carl Yastrzemski hooks second base.

making a catch to end an inning, a soldier made a slicing motion across his throat. Umphlett and the other players clearly understood the message.

"Our players were truly fearful of what might happen if we won," said Mauch. "But we still tried our hardest, figuring we'd take our chances if we did win."

The atmosphere, however, was still unnerving to the Millers. They couldn't hold a 2-0 lead in Game Three as Havana scored two runs in the last of the eighth to tie it and another in the last of the tenth to win it.

Carl Yastrzemski, who hit a 400-foot home run in the game, said the Millers found no relief away from the stadium. "We had been warned not to leave the hotel between games," he said in his autobiography, *Yaz.* "It was like a revolution in the streets, even though it wasn't violent. But with the guns and the noise it was just scary."

The Millers' relief corps was unable to hold another late-inning lead in the fourth game. This time, Havana tied the count, 3-3, on a run-scoring single by Dan Morejon in the bottom of the ninth. Morejon then drove in the winning run with another single in the 11th and the Sugar Kings were within one game of the championship.

On the verge of extinction, though, the Millers battled back. Ignoring Castro's troopers, they won the next two games to tie the series and force the seventh and deciding game.

At this point, Castro decided to get into the act. After entering the stadium prior to Game Seven, he made his way around the warning track to get to his box seat. According to the Millers' Lefty Locklin, as Castro passed the Minneapolis bullpen, he paused, looked at the players, patted the large revolver on his hip, and said, "Tonight, we win."

The Millers had other ideas, however. Joe Macko led off the fourth inning with a home run, and, when Lu Clinton did the same to start the sixth, Minneapolis was ahead, 2-0.

The lead held until the eighth when Elio Chacon opened the inning with a single. One out later, Dan Morejon nicked the right-field foul line with a ball that bounced into the stands for a ground-rule double. Ray Shearer looked at a called third strike for the second out, but pinch-hitter Larry Novak brought Castro and likely all of Havana to its feet with a single to center that brought in the tying runs.

In the last of the ninth, Havana put runners at first and second with two out. The pesky Morejon then stepped to the plate and lined the first pitch into center field to bring in Raul Sanchez, who slid home ahead of Umphlett's throw with the winning run.

The entire city celebrated the Sugar Kings' Junior World Series championship. As for the Millers, they went home disappointed, but relieved. "In some ways," recalls Ted Bowsfield, "nobody minded losing the game in that country and under those conditions. We were just happy to get it over and to get out of town with our hides."

Soviet Baseball: History and Prospects

Kim Steven Juhase and Blair A. Ruble

Amongst the ruins of Perestroika and of the Union of Soviet Socialist Republics, the game of baseball is attempting to survive. Like many ideas it was imposed from on high by the Soviet Government on a mostly disinterested public. Its survival will depend on whether what little the Soviet public has seen of baseball will create strong enough roots for it to continue without strong central government support and in the midst of an economy in complete disarray.

The recent surge of baseball interest in the Soviet Union is directly related to baseball being made an Olympic sport. However, the Russians have long played a traditional game called lapta which some Russians have claimed is the direct ancestor of baseball, and were even playing baseball for a short time during the 1930's.

Lapta, which can be traced back to the reign of Ivan the Terrible, is usually played between two teams of between 5 and 15 players each on a field that is 70-80 meters (77-87 yards) long and 30-40 meters (33-44 yards) wide. A 8-10 centimeter (3-4 inches) diameter soft ball is used which is hit with a stick (called lapta) some 70-80 centimeters (27-31 inches) in length and 3-3.5 centimeters (1.2-1.4 inches) in diameter. The batter attempts to hit the ball, which is pitched underhand by a player on the opposing team, as far as possible. While the ball is in flight, the batter runs from one end of the field to the other as many times as possible. The other side tries to get to the ball and return it to a teammate who can tag the runner. If the

Kim Steven Juhase *is an attorney-at-law in New York City and Executive Editor of the* New York International Law Review. **Blair A. Ruble** *is Executive Director of the Kennan Institute for Advanced Russian Studies in Washington, D.C.*

ball is caught in the air, or if the runner is hit by a ball thrown at him by the opposing team, the team switches sides. Each run counts as a point and the team that collects the most points in a fixed time period wins.

Even though the game resembles rounders much more than it does baseball, this has not stopped some Russians from claiming that it was the origin of the American Game. As recently as 1987, on July 4, no less, an S. Shachin in an article in the Soviet paper *Izvestia* claimed that lapta was brought to America by the first Russian settlers in the early 1800's, adopted by the Americans as baseball, "and has now returned to us in a different form and with a strange, foreign name." Even the Soviet Government, however, no longer backs this claim. Lapta is not widely played anymore and is universally considered a children's game.

The first real baseball was played during the inter-war years when thousands of Americans voluntarily went to the Soviet Union to work in the factories and to help the Great Socialist Experiment. As can be expected, whenever there is a group of Americans together for a period of time anywhere in the world, they will eventually play baseball. In the spring of 1933, the American workers residing in Moscow, Leningrad (now St. Petersburg), and Petrozavodsk introduced the game to the Soviet public. The Moscow "Anglo-American" team staged an exhibition game at that city's Dynamo Stadium which attracted 25,000 spectators according to the *Moscow News*. That paper also reported that the State Central Institute of Physical Culture in Moscow had made baseball part of its curriculum. In 1934, the Supreme Council of Physical Culture reported that native baseball teams had sprung up in Petrozavodsk, Kondopoga, Leningrad, Gorki and

Erevan. In Erevan, the local Armenian youths reportedly learned the game in the early '30s from Americans who worked on the Transcaucasia railroad and who left them all of their baseball equipment.

The first inter-city baseball game ever played in the Soviet Union was held on June 6, 1934 between the Americans who worked at the Gorki Auto Plant and the Moscow Foreign Worker's Club in Dynamo Stadium. Moscow beat Gorki 16-5. By July 1934, the *Moscow News* could report that a list of popular sports in the U.S.S.R. would include baseball. Uniforms were being made by the Central Sports Equipment Laboratory at the Institute of Physical Culture, and other equipment was being produced at the Dynamo Sports Goods Factories in Moscow and Leningrad. Baseball was slated to be taken up by the Stalin (AMO) Auto Plant in Moscow in 1935, one of the two largest factories in Moscow. Teams of Soviet players were formed. The Moscow baseball team, with an appropriation of 8,000 rubles, was to have two out-of-town trips to Gorki and Petrozavodsk. However, after the beginning of 1935, there is no further mention of baseball in the Soviet press and in fact there is no evidence of baseball being played since then in the U.S.S.R., until the 1980's. What happened? One could surmise that the Soviet's sudden interest in the American game of baseball, besides being related to a large contingent of Americans in their midst, may be directly related to the United States' recognition of the Soviet Union in November of 1933. After 1935, Russia was engulfed in the turmoil of the Communist purges and show trials. Nazi Germany was an immediate threat and the country was preparing for war. The central authorities apparently saw no need to continue to support a foreign sport that did not directly contribute toward building a strong armed force as would parachute jumping, a frequently referred-to popular sport. During the war, which devastated the country, there was little sport of any kind. After World War II, when the Cold War set in, the Soviet newspapers labelled baseball as a "bad imperialist game." Playing the American-as-apple-pie game of baseball in the Soviet Union in the 1950's would be the equivalent of raising the Communist flag in the deep South during the same time period. This hostility and ignorance toward baseball continued well into the 1980's.

The reintroduction of baseball in the U.S.S.R. is directly related to the decision in 1984 by the Olympic Committee to make baseball a gold medal sport starting with the 1992 Olympics. Since the Soviets did not want to forfeit the chance of obtaining additional gold medals, in 1985 the Central Sports Committee decided to encourage baseball on an organized basis. Once the informal ban on the game was removed, some Russian students immediately took up the new sport. They had developed their interest either through seeing the Cuban and Nicaraguan students play pick-up games at the universities in their country, or through travels abroad. It is not therefore surprising that the first organized Russian baseball teams arose at the universities.

At first the university students would play informal games with the Cuban and Nicaraguan students and their instructors were mostly Cuban. However, socialist camaraderie went only so far. Fidel Castro, the *Los Angeles Times* reported, once told the President of the International and U.S. Baseball Federation "We will help the Soviets to beat you, but never teach them enough to beat us". As Perestroika and Glasnost took hold in the Soviet Union, the Russian baseball players had a chance to travel abroad and interact with players from other countries, especially those from the United States.

One of the best of the early teams was from D.I. Mendelayev College of Chemical Technology. They won the Soviets' first international game in the Summer of 1987 when they beat a Czechoslovakian team in Tbilisi, Georgia. On June 1, 1988, the first baseball game with a visiting American team in the U.S.S.R. was played in Moscow by the Johns Hopkins University Blue Jays who faced the Mendelayev team. The first run and hit by the Russians were made by Aleksei Koshevoy. He scored on two stolen bases and a wild pitch. This trip was reciprocated in October of 1988, when the Mendelayev club became the first Soviet baseball team to visit the United States. They came for a three-game, two-week tour. And they were predictably slaughtered. The first game was played on October 12, 1988 against the same Johns Hopkins University team that had visited Moscow. The Soviets lost 16-0 in a no-hitter and committed six errors in the first inning alone. They continued to lose the next two games by large scores. This, however, did not dampen their enthusiasm for the game. Vadim Kulakov, the team's 22-year old catcher, worshipped Gary Carter so much that he wore his number 8 and curled his hair like Carter. He told *The New York Times* that he considered that his real age was one, since that was how long he had been playing the game. "The game", he told the paper, "once you begin to see how much is in it, how everything changes every second, is like no other. It is as though it is from another planet."

Unfortunately, emphasis and financial support has been directed almost solely to the national team of Olympic hopefuls. In 1986, the All-Union Baseball, Softball and Russian Lapta Federation was formed. The following year they organized a national squad. In order to encourage participation, the Red Army offered to release from military duty any serviceman who volunteered to play for the national team. In 1988, team members received a weekly salary of 238 rubles ($368) which at that time was more than the average Soviet worker might earn. Although the national team does receive financial help from the government, most of the support, instruction and equipment has come from the United States. In February 1988, Soviet coaches Alexander Ardatov and Guela Chikhradze, visited the U.S. for three weeks as guests of the U.S.

Baseball Federation to learn about baseball. They visited major league spring training camps and also some colleges and high schools. The first, and so far only baseball stadium in the Soviet Union, a 1,000 seat, $3.2 million field was built with funds donated by Dr. Shigeyshi Matsumae, president of Tokai University in Japan. Most of the equipment the team uses has been donated by American manufacturers or by American corporations in return for sponsorship rights when the national team travels to the U.S. When the national team toured the United States in April 1989, they were sponsored by Taco Bell. The players' uniforms were paid for by Taco Bell and had Taco Bell patches on the sleeves, and all the team's other equipment came from the United States. The players made numerous publicity stops at Taco Bells along the way, sometimes chanting for the T.V. cameras "Da, Da, Taco Bell."

The national team did poorly against the U.S. College teams they played. They played their first U.S. game against the U.S. Naval Academy on April 11, 1989 and lost 21-1. At the end of their three-week, ten-game tour they displayed an 0-11 record. The next year they participated in the Goodwill Games in Seattle, Washington and lost all five games they played against the U.S., Mexican, Japanese and Puerto Rican teams by a combined score of 67-5, making 20 errors in the process.

The national team had been making some progress before the attempted coup on August 18, 1991. In 1990, the team won the Group B European Baseball Championships beating such teams as Switzerland, Poland, Czechoslovakia, Yugoslavia and West Germany. This gave them the right to participate in the August 1991 Group A European Baseball Championships in Italy which would determine the European team to play in the Olympics. However, the Soviets lost to France in their first game and were thus promptly eliminated from the 1992 Olympics.

Baseball, like so much else in the Soviet Union is following two separate paths. In determining the future of the game in that country, each path must be considered separately. The first level is the national team training for the Olympics, and it faces severe challenges like many other Soviet institutions. It has been split by nationalism. Two top pitchers from the Soviet Republic of Georgia quit

after regional flare-ups. Before Lithuania became a separate republic, a star pitcher from that area had to quit because he refused to wear the national team uniform stating they would kill him in Lithuania if he wore it. Since the Central Government is disintegrating no one knows who will provide financial support for the national team. In addition, no one on the team has been playing baseball for more than five years and all team members started playing in their teens or later. To be competitive in baseball, one must usually start playing it when less than ten years old, a fact that even the Russian coaches admit. It is thus unlikely that any Soviet baseball team will play in the Olympics until the next century.

The prospects on the grassroots level are much brighter. It is here that the future of Russian baseball rests. In an interview for this article held in November, 1991, Khalik Feiskhanov, head coach of the Moscow State University team stated that those Soviets who see the game really like it. "More and more children and adults are coming out to play and watch baseball and get some exercise. People like it because anyone can play at any age and make a field anyplace. Everything points to baseball growing and developing."

The major problem, which he and all other Soviet coaches quickly point out is the lack of equipment. "Youth programs are stunted because of this," he told us. Another major problem is the shortage of press coverage. The major sport in the U.S.S.R. is soccer. Baseball, with about 13,500 players nationwide playing before an average of a few hundred fans, is not deemed newsworthy enough. Mr. Feiskhanov decries the lack of publicity. "We need to get more people to hear about baseball in Moscow, come to see a game, and get to understand the athletic-intellectual combination required for the sport."

The Soviets have joined the Little League movement and Mr. Feiskhanov is working on a plan to have American Little Leaguers and six coaches visit Moscow for a joint two-week summer camp.

Baseball as an organized sport in the Soviet Union can only survive if their youngsters are willing to try it and stick with it. The enthusiasm of the players is there. It is up to the Soviet Government or the government of the successor republics to provide a stable environment in order to allow the game to grow.

This article was completed only weeks before the disintegration of the Soviet Union, which accounts for references throughout to the U.S.S.R. —Editor

Taiwan Little Leaguers Grow into Big Leaguers

John B. Holway

Whatever becomes of all those Taiwan Little Leaguers who dominate the world's best twelve-year-old players? They grow up to play in the Olympics, in Japan, and now in the world's newest professional league.

Take crew-cut Lee Jee-ming, a second baseman on the 1971 Little League champs. He played center field on the 1984 Olympic squad that won a bronze medal, narrowly losing to Will Clark, Mark McGwire, Shane Mack, and the U.S. team, 2-1, at Los Angeles. Today, wearing his age — "33" — on the back of his imperial yellow uniform, Lee is the most popular player on the most popular team, the Elephants, in the four-team Taiwan league.

"Lee is the league status symbol," says American Mathis "Matt" Huff, who goes by the name "Ma," or Horse, in the box scores of the Dragons. In 1987 Matt hit .417, highest pro average in the entire United States, as his Pioneer League team, Salt Lake City, won a record 29 straight. Their autographed ball now reposes next to Babe Ruth's jersey at Cooperstown.

Taiwan is a tough league, Huff observes. In 1990 the Dragons defeated the Tokyo Giants, 4-1, although the Giants beat a Taiwanese league all-star team three times. The Dragons boast five Olympic veterans. Huff claims that two are major league caliber.

Pitcher Hwong Ping-yong, the "Golden Arm," is one of these—if his manager, a former star pitcher of the Korean leagues, doesn't pitch his arm off. Hwong, featured in a 1991 *Sports Illustrated* cover story, had "incredible numbers" in the 1990 inaugural season, Huff reports. He was

20-8 overall in the 90-game season and ran up 246 innings pitched. Last year he hurt his arm but still hurled 210 innings despite the injury, led the league in ERA (1.89), and tied for the lead in victories at 13-9. Hwong has seven pitches, says Alan Wu, editor of Taipeh's *Pro Baseball* magazine, including a sinker, slider, curve, and wicked change of pace.

Center fielder Lin Yi-Tzung, the base stealing champ, "has the best set of tools," according to Huff. Lin is another veteran of the 1984 Taiwanese Olympic squad. "He's got it all—the speed, a great arm, and he's Taiwan's most consistent hitter." Lin batted .335 and .292 in the league's first two years.

Another top prospect is pitcher Kevin Tu of the Lions (11-3, 2.34 ERA). Tu and Hwong "would give it a good shot," Huff says. "They've got good control, command of their curve balls, and they hit their spots."

Wu, on the other hand, sees the top prospect as being Gwaw-lee Jien-fu, a flamethrower who turned down a Los Angeles Dodger contract in order to pitch in the 1992 Olympics. He's got a good fastball and control, but his main problem is holding his weight down, Wu has observed.

"They've got pitchers here who could definitely pitch in the States, without a doubt," nods shortstop Darrell Brown of the Elephants. Brown, 36, has played for the major league Twins and Tigers, and hit .322 in the Mexican League in 1990, according to SABR's Bob Hoie. Brown's not sure if position players could stand the rigors of a 162-game schedule, however, since they play only three games a week in Taiwan.

The scouts keep snooping, hoping to find another Sadaharu Oh, the Tokyo-born Chinese (Wong Tzung-chi in

John B. Holway *is the nation's best-known author of books on Negro League history and winner of the prestigious 1988* Spitball Magazine *"Casey Award" for his landmark* Blackball Stars.

Chinese), who remains the world home run champion. Will he be 13-year-old Fong Shung, the bespectacled pitcher-shortstop who mashed five home runs in the 1991 Little League world series in Williamsport? One mighty wallop flew far over the center-field fence and into the fans half-way up the hill behind it.

The Taiwan league itself opened with four teams—Elephants, Dragons, Lions and Tigers—and plans to expand to six teams in 1994. A unique feature of this newest of the world's pro baseball circuits is that there are no home teams. The clubs travel together from city to city, playing every other team once each from Thursday night through Sunday.

But everybody's favorite team seems to be the Elephants, who have perhaps the wildest fans since the old Brooklyn Dodgers. Two broken ribs to key players dropped the Elephants into last place in the second half of the 1991 split season. But such ill fortune didn't subdue their fans. Elephant games are always sellouts. The parks hold about 20,000, and attendance is respectable for every game—6,000 is perhaps an average crowd.

"There are cheer leaders, drums, horns, whistles, portable loud speakers," Huff says. "It's quite a show. It's also obnoxious right above the dugout!" They're good fans according to Huff, but they don't seem to understand the Americans' aggressive style. When Huff barreled into the Elephants' catcher, knocking him down and out, Matt was shelled with beer bottles, batteries, water bottles, whatever was loose and could be hurled onto the field. "It was a scary scene for a few minutes," reports the beleaguered American player.

Last year Elephant fans even once stormed the field, picked up rakes and began attacking the opposing team, in this case the Tigers. A woman reporter was struck upon the head and hospitalized during the fray. The Tigers players themselves fought back with bats and other stray equipment. On yet another occasion the fans pelted the Dragons' bus and even the police seemed afraid to intervene. The league is now moving to stop such violent displays, having recently instituted a new rule which suspends guilty players without pay.

In 1995 Taiwan baseball will surprisingly celebrate its proud 100th birthday. The diamond sport was introduced to the land by Japan, which controlled Taiwan between 1895 and 1945. Even today the four pro managers read and speak Japanese, which they learned in the nation's public schools.

Elephants manager Tzung Jee-En—70, diminutive, white-haired, his face creased like Casey Stengel's—could have come from a Hollywood casting office. He's spent fifty years in baseball, he claims, and once produced eleven high school champions in thirteen seasons. Taiwan's high school players are every bit as good as the fabled Little Leaguers by Tzung's reasoning.

Tzung currently has five foreign players on his pro squad, from the Twins, Pirates, and Angels organizations.

One, Panamanian Freddie Pibuccio, finished second in batting last season with a respectable .318 average. Tzung has even taken his teams to the States twice for games against U.S. pro clubs.

In 1984 Harvard-educated Yen Shiao-chong took over as head of Taiwan's Amateur Baseball Association. Yen spent money liberally once in his new post. He brought in U.S. coaches and introduced a running, breaking-ball style of play. He even took a team to the United States for training, and he brought a Chinese battery back from Japan, where they had been playing several seasons with the Nankai Hawks. A few more Chinese players also returned from Japan last year. "The league has shown so much improvement from 1991," says Huff. "The pitching has improved 200 percent. There's not a weak pitcher on our staff anymore."

One ace the Chinese hope to lure home from Japan is Gwaw Tai-yuen, a right-hander with a 95-mph fastball who struck out a dozen Americans in the 1984 Olympic match-up. He lost to Will Clark, Mark McGwire and company by the tight score of 2-1.

Chinese coaches, like the Japanese in previous years, overwork their aces, and Huff worries that, as with the Japanese, many top Taiwan hurlers will likely burn out early. To guard against just such an eventuality, a new rule of the league now prohibits managers from using a pitcher more than once every three days.

Hong Ton-son, owner of the Brother Hotel Company, the Elephants' parent company, has recently donated large sums of money to the nation's little leagues. Five years ago those leagues numbered only 20 to 30, and now they total almost 400 spread throughout the country.

This author watched the Taiwan team win its 15th world championship in 23 years at Williamsport, Pennsylvania, during the past summer season. The Chinese youngsters all insisted that they practice only one and a half hours daily, although Lee Jee-ming admits freely that it is more like three or four hours in reality—perhaps eight hours right before a big tournament. U.S. officials complain that the Taiwan boys are marched to and from the field in a Prussian military formation, but I saw no sign of anything like that. They were surprisingly normal kids, more interested in playing Nintendo than in talking baseball with any persistent reporter.

But the suspicions persist. "We've visited Taiwan looking for ringers and other irregularities," one little league official told me. "Yet we can't seem to find any clear violations." However, little league officials did object that Taiwan teams represent schools rather than towns or neighborhoods, and a single Taiwan school may well have more boys in residence than a good-sized American town. Taiwanese officials have promised to bring this practice to an immediate end and the action—if carried out—may well make the Little League World Series far more competitive in upcoming years.

But, says Jong Jung-long, coach of the 1991 Taiwanese

world champs, the Chinese simply work harder than the spoiled American players. And this goes for the pro level too, contends Huff. A Taiwanese baseball year spans ten and a half months, February through November, including two and a half months of marine boot camp hell euphemistically known as spring training. "It's probably the longest spring training in pro baseball history," complains Huff. Spring training in the States is also intense, but it lasts little more than four or five weeks.

The brief off-season is far too short for the individual body to rest, Huff contends, and nagging seasonal injuries don't have a chance to heal. Matt's own average dropped from .332 in 1990 to .234 in 1991, and his home run totals from 16 to 12. Yet he still helped the Dragons with the first half-season championship.

They clashed with the Lions, the second-half pennant-race winners, in a seven-game playoff. Ma homered in game one, as Hwong won 5-2. The Lions beat America's Joe Strong (13-10) in game two. But Strong (8-1 at California League Reno in 1989, according to Hoie) came back to win game three, 3-2.

The turning point of the 1991 playoffs came in the fourth game. Hwong took a 2-1 lead into the ninth, but the Lions tied it on a home run in the final frame and won with two out in the 14th, 3-2. Hwong himself went all the way to suffer the crucial loss. Strong lost game five to give the Lions a three-to-two lead in the series. But Hwong took a must-win sixth game with a 2-0 shutout. However, the Dragons eventually blew a 4-0 lead in game seven, as Hwong came in once more in relief with but one day's rest and was battered in a stinging 13-5 loss.

Is there another Sadaharu Oh waiting to be discovered somewhere within the environs of Taipeh? The Tigers' Ling Choong-chew, a compactly built right-hander, who looks a bit like Oh at bat, is the defending home run champ with 16 and may yet inherent Oh's mantle. The 1992 Olympics may reveal more such stars on their way up the professional baseball ladder as well. Will the next super-star be Fong Shung, who crushed several 1991 home runs the likes of which had never been seen before at the Little League world series? He'll be 21 in 2000, ready for Olympic action. And after that, perhaps for the major leagues. But then, we'll have to wait to see *which* major league he chooses.

Are future major league stars playing in the Far East's new professional leagues? This action's from Korea's circuit.

The Babies of International Baseball

Kevin Brooks

When the Soviet Union dropped out of the 11th Annual AAA World Youth Baseball Tournament three days before play was scheduled to begin in Brandon, Manitoba, Canada, the Nigerian National Team mourned; the Soviet Union was the only team the Nigerians had a chance of defeating. Nigerian assistant coach Ben Ofuani was confident that his team could have overcome the relatively small edge in "experience" that the Soviets possessed. Baseball was introduced to Nigeria eighteen months before the World Youth Tournament (July 26-August 4, 1991), putting the Nigerians about six months behind the Russians. The battle of the "Babies" of baseball did not materialize, leaving Nigeria alone to "play with the big kids": the U.S.A., Cuba, Taiwan, Australia, Mexico, Brazil, and Canada. The Nigerians remained hopeful that they might upset one of the two other baseball "infants"—Netherlands and Italy—but the "generation gap" was too large to overcome.

The tournament's loss of the Soviets, and all the subsequent Nigerian losses, resulted in fanfare and media attention that grew steadily over the ten days of competition. Fans were drawn to the African team's charisma and class. The Nigerian Youth Team enthusiastically pounded on their bongo drums before each game, a sharp contrast to the American and Canadian players "playing it cool" in front of the major league scouts. Nigerian center fielder Toba Elegbe assured me that baseball is a fast, exciting game that often unfolds much too quickly, like the beat of the drums. Every successful play by the Nigerian team produced more drumming and cheering. A 6-4-3 double play in the Nigerian's first game, against Mexico, produced pandemonium. The 32-0 final losing score was secondary to the successes met on the field.

In nine games, the Nigerians scored only six runs, gave up 189, and committed 78 errors. Every game they competed in was cut short by the "10 up after 7 innings" mercy rule. The daily beatings dampened the Nigerians' spirits at times, particularly against teams that showed little regard for the Nigerians' inexperience. A low point in enthusiasm was reached on a scorching hot afternoon against the Australians. The Australians, eventual fourth-place finishers, continually took two bases on wild pitches and passed balls, despite being up by more than 20 runs. Nigerian Head Coach Mike Milmoe worked on blocking drills between innings with his catcher Deji Adekunle, and some improvement was evident. But the Australians continued to apply pressure, never giving Adekunle or his teammates a chance to catch their breath. The heat and the humiliation kept the drums silent that game.

The Nigerian spirit was resilient, however. Before the team's second-to-last game, against Canada, catcher Adekunle said, "Even though we are losing we still keep trying. Someday, Nigeria is going to be a good team. We're really encouraged here to keep trying. It's been really fun to be here. It makes us all happy that the people here like us and want us to keep up with baseball. It doesn't matter if we haven't won. The coach tells us that baseball is for fun, not winning or losing."

Nigeria faced Italy, also winless, in their last game of the tournament, and 1,500 people turned out to see the match-up. These fans saw the potential that the rough-hewn Nigerian ballclub possesses, as well as the hurdles

---

Kevin Brooks *now resides in Calgary, Alberta, Canada, and was an official host to the Nigerian youth baseball team in Winnipeg, just prior to the 1991 World Youth Championships in Brandon, Manitoba.*

they still have to overcome. Solomon Asaju excited his team early with an infield single in the first against the Italians. Coach Milmoe had emphasized short, compact swings to put the ball in play. Asaju, like most of his team-mates, was very fleet afoot. His single against Italy was hit into the hole between short and third, and he easily beat the throw. "If these guys ever learn how to read a pitcher, they will steal ten out of ten bases," said Milmoe. "Going on their speed alone, they have stolen six of seven." The problem, of course, was not being able to steal first.

Team speed usually means good team defense, but with the Nigerians, there was never any guarantee that a ball tracked down would result in an out. No fly balls were dropped against the Italians, but Asaju, playing left field, and Robert Onwukwe playing right, made every fly ball look like an adventure. Asaju repeatedly would charge in hard then have to make a last minute adjustment, often jumping up for the ball because he had raced in too far. Center fielder Toba Elegbe showed more refinement, however, drifting easily under all fly balls hit his way.

Nigeria's starting pitcher against the Italians, Caesar Ofoedu, was another example of potential only partially fulfilled. A tall, lanky left-hander, Ofoedu would start his full windup with a short drop step, pivot sharply, then coil. Text-book mechanics, so far. But when Ofoedu threw the ball, he kept his left elbow, fully extended, almost completely locked. His pitches more closely resembled the gentle arch of an Abdul-Jabbar skyhook than the hard flash of a Koufax fastball. The potential velocity suggested by the early stages of Ofoedu's delivery still needed to be coaxed and coached out of him.

If learning how to pitch is not difficult enough for a 17-year old who has never played baseball, baseball also demands that the pitcher become an infielder at certain times. Caesar Ofoedu's inability to make that quick transition led to an eight-run inning for the Italians, the only inning in the game in which the Nigerian's inexperience got the better of them. With the bases loaded and nobody out, Ofoedu fielded a ball hit sharply back to him. Rather than instinctively throwing the ball home, Ofoedu looked at third base, then second, and finally at first. Suddenly rushing, he threw the ball into right field. Two runs scored, and there were now runners on second and third. Two more errors that inning accounted for most of the eight runs scored. In no other inning did the Nigerians allow the Italians more than two runs, and in no other inning did they make more than one error. The Nigerians seemed to be within one inning of being competitive, being respectable, but it may take years to make up that one inning.

The Nigerians played one more game before heading home. An exhibition game was arranged between a Brandon Youth Team and the Nigerians following the official tournament. Spectators brought used baseball equipment for admission, and the equipment was handed over to the Nigerian team. The Nigerian coaches and players went home with bags of equipment and souvenirs, and considerable hope for the future of baseball in Nigeria. But even without the warm reception the team received in Brandon, the trip across the Atlantic would have been a success. For the Nigerian Team, and for baseball in Nigeria, the real accomplishment was fielding a team, and making it all the way to Brandon. Everything else was pure gravy.

Baseball has become a sport of interest in Nigeria primarily because of the involvement of one man, Major General Ishola Williams. A few years ago, General Williams became interested in European Handball, and now Nigeria is a country with outstanding handball teams. Many of the baseball players are skilled at handball, and one of the coaches was on the National Handball Team.

The people, and more specifically the athletes, of Nigeria have faith in General Williams. Willaims has earned a reputation for knowing how to get things done, and he gets the right people involved in his projects.

One of the "right people" is Ben Ofuani, assistant coach. Ofuani is extremely serious about making baseball an important sport in Nigeria, and across all of Africa. He has been involved with the Nigerian baseball program since its inception.

An extreme desire to improve and succeed seems to motivate Ofuani's passion for baseball. He recognizes how much fun the game is, and reports that the families of the players are closely involved with the national program, creating a small baseball community in Nigeria. But the drive for improvement, for eventual "perfection," seems to take precedence over the game's recreational features. The military influence of General Williams and Coach Ofuani (a Navy Officer) was stamped on the team, most obviously in their regimented calisthenic warm-ups and in the occasional harsh criticism Ofuani directed toward his players. In a pre-tournament exhibition game, he yelled out, matter-of-factly, "You fucked up, you fucked up," when his left fielder misplayed a single, resulting in a two-base error.

The influence of Nigeria's armed forces on baseball may seem to suggest that baseball is heavily funded by, and supported by, the government of Nigeria, but in fact, Williams' success comes from the fact that he has the power to circumvent regular bureaucratic route. Ofuani insisted that if baseball is to survive in Nigeria, it will have to stay out of corrupt government hands. Coach Milmoe, an American hired by the Nigerians, suspected that despite the work of Williams and Ofuani, some of the money meant for the Nigerian Team had been misappropriated by government officials.

Actually playing the game of baseball in Nigeria may be almost as difficult as avoiding the bureaucratic nightmares. Ofuani claims that at the present time, one group, in one part of Nigeria, might have a bat and some gloves, but no ball, while another group will have a ball, but nothing else. The Nigerian Youth Team brought a home-made bat with them. Its shape was regular, but the wood was very red and very dense, weighing close to 45 ounces. No one in Nigeria has been able to produce a playable ball yet. And if gloves could be found anywhere, their cost would be equivalent to a worker's average monthly salary.

It is hard to imagine how a country without equipment, and without any proper fields, could hold a National Championship, but the first one was indeed held in December of 1990. A makeshift field was put together, and from play in that tournament, sixty players were selected to try out for the National Team. Without experienced coaches, however, and no legitimate place to play, the team made limited progress until Mike Milmoe arrived to coach full time.

Milmoe, 23 years old and a recent graduate from Cornell University, enthusiastically took up the challenge. He brought some aluminum bats with him, some baseballs, and a bunch of used gloves. But equipment alone was not going to make the team. "On the field, when I had my first practice on April 26, if I had told them to put their glove on their foot and hit the baseball with their heads, they would have done it. That's how little they knew about baseball." Milmoe spent the first two weeks simply playing catch.

Language was not a complete barrier between Milmoe and his players. All of the players spoke some English— some better than others. Milmoe enforced an "English only" rule on the field so he could keep track of what his players were saying. The team was not shy speaking English on the field; each inning began with a chorus of "None Out," often started by the pitcher. Nicknames were assigned: the team became "The Nigerian Nightmares," and most notably among players, Chuks Nwandu became "Chuckles."

Milmoe knew his players were not going to be good, but he didn't realize how sick he was going to get—not of the job, but on the job. After making reasonable progress through May and June, Milmoe contracted malaria early in July, three weeks before the tournament. Medical complications led to liver failure, and he had to be flown home to the States. The Nigerians were on their own again, and they were not sure if they would see their coach again.

The Nigerian Team headed south rather than north after arriving in New York. They spent ten days in Dodgertown (Vero Beach, Florida) prior to the tournament in Brandon, but Milmoe still could not join them. The IBA (International Baseball Association, based in Indianapolis) provided instruction for the Nigerian Team during their stay at Dodgertown, but the lack of coaching continuity slowed the team's progress.

The Nigerian coaches and officials were very careful with their own money, and the players' money—no player was allowed to carry any cash on him—but Florida proved to be a hot shopping stop. Every player had a Florida t-shirt or sweat-shirt of some shape and color, and most of the players seemed to have found a good deal on

cameras that went "clunk" instead of "click" when they pressed the shutter release. Many players wore their snug fitting LA Dodger caps rather than their flimsy, ill-formed Nigerian baseball caps, even while sitting in the dug-outs in Brandon.

From Florida, the team flew to Minneapolis, a trip which apparently drained most of the Nigerian team's funds. Rather than flying to Winnipeg, Manitoba (the closest International Airport to Brandon), the Nigerians bought 23 tickets on a regularly scheduled commercial bus-line. They left Minneapolis at 2:00 a.m. on a Monday morning—eight hours after their flight had arrived—and pulled into Winnipeg at 3:00 p.m.

The Nigerian Team was billeted in Winnipeg for two nights, staying with families of ball players their own age. The host committee in Brandon paid for food and accommodations while teams were participating in the tournament, but teams had to pay for their own accommodations if they wanted to arrive before July 24th. Since the Nigerians were travelling by commercial bus, they obviously could not afford the $550/day price tag of staying in Brandon.

The Nigerians split their squad while in Winnipeg, and played two exhibition games against the teams that were hosting them. Losses in both of these games foreshadowed the difficulties the Nigerians were going to encounter in Brandon.

Headaches also foreshadowed future difficulties. Many of the players began to complain of headaches the evening of their arrival in Winnipeg. Although the days in Manitoba at the end of July are still quite hot, the nights often start to cool down. The first few nights the Nigerians spent in Manitoba, the temperature dropped below 10 Celsius (50 Fahrenheit). The cold and the hard travelling schedule seemed to be catching up with the players. When the team arrived in Brandon on Wednesday, five players, four of them outfielders, were checked into a local hospital—with malaria. News of the players' condition produced a scare in Brandon, but of course the parasite that causes malaria had simply remained dormant in the bodies of the Nigerian players until their immune systems could no longer fight it off.

Ironically, it was also on the same Wednesday that Mike Milmoe "re-appeared". The reunion of coach and players was a joyful one, as the players mobbed Milmoe in the middle of a shopping mall, but once reunited on the field, Milmoe could see they had slipped back into some bad habits. Milmoe and his players did what they could to get back "on top of their game," but the Nigerian Youth Team of 1991 will be remembered for its charisma, not its ballplaying talent.

Even if the Nigerians had been able to avoid their difficulties in travelling, and the sickness they soon encountered, they would still not have been able to close the gap in playing ability between themselves and the other teams in the tournament. Recognizing that ability gap, and acknowledging the financial commitment necessary in starting a sport completely foreign to their country, the Nigerians are continuing to promote baseball. The first baseball-only diamond will be completed in November, one month before the 2nd Annual Nigerian National Baseball Championships. Two more diamonds are reportedly in the planning stage.

Nigeria will also be sending another Youth Team to North America in 1992 for the "Merit Cup," a tournament for countries just developing baseball. It is possible that other African countries will be attending that tournament; the IBA is currently sponsoring clinics in Zambia, Zimbabwe, and Angola. Tunisia has long been a member of the IBA, but has not shown the same desire the Nigerians have to compete internationally. South Africa, an IBA member 25 years ago, has just applied to re-enter the Association. Although these countries represent only a small fraction of the African population, they are, or can be, united by the African Baseball and Softball Association. Friday Ichidé, a Nigerian, has been named the Executive Director of that Association.

The "Babies of International Baseball" are obviously looking to grow up quickly. They will have to—for the time being—grow on their own; coach Mike Milmoe returned to upstate New York after the tournament, his assignment completed. The will to succeed and improve is present in the Good People of Nigerian Baseball—General Williams and Ben Ofuani being the two key figures—and the love of baseball that is so much a part of the North American baseball ethos is vividly present in the enthusiasms of the young Nigerian baseball players. Even if it takes years for the them to master the game's difficult skills, the spirit they have shown will long sustain baseball in Nigeria.

Minoso By Any Other Name

Richard C. Lindberg

In one brilliant moment a "Cuban Comet" streaked across the Chicago baseball horizon. The stunning debut of Saturnino Orestes "Minnie" Minoso on May 1, 1951, turned the page on a grim, disquieting period of Chicago White Sox history—the "wandering in the desert years" bridging the 1920 Black Sox Scandal and the "Go-Go Era" of the glorious 1950s. Minnie Minoso, whose entire career represents one man's triumph over the barriers of language, color, and ethnicity in a nation pockmarked by racial divisiveness, became the very symbol of a style of play that lay dormant in Major League baseball since the heyday of the "Gas House Gang" in the 1930s. Minoso, more than anyone on that spirited '51 club, keyed the running offense which revolved around the base hit and stolen base. The color barrier, which Minnie had so effectively shattered, became a non-issue to Chicago fans who coined the famous "Go! Go!" chant that season in order to encourage his base running derring-do. The road to Chicago had been a perilous one, but Minoso's quiet determination and boundless enthusiasm for the game he first played in El Perico, Matanzas, Cuba, mandated that one day he would realize his dreams. "I never look for anything," he recalls. "I do my duty and offer my friendship to everyone. I respect everyone. If they respect me and what I offer, that's good enough."

Minnie Minoso is not one who reflects bitterly on past misfortunes. But the facts show that he came from an impoverished rural background in the Cuban sugar fields.

Richard C. Lindberg is a Chicago-based freelance writer who specializes in baseball of the nineteenth century and has published three volumes on the history of the Chicago White Sox, the team he serves as official historian.

His father lost it all in the Great Depression, and at the age of 14 Minnie was planting, fertilizing, and harvesting sugar cane in the broiling Cuban sun alongside men three times his age. His name in those days was Orestes Arrieta, since the sons take the maiden name of their mother in Cuba.

At the age of twelve Minnie was managing a kid's baseball team which used equipment discarded by the old fellows who played sandlot ball in the Matanzas Province. By the time he was fourteen Orestes had resolved to become a professional ballplayer for one of the Negro League teams in the U.S. But first he gained some valuable experience by hooking up with a factory team in Havana, the Ambrosia Candy Company operated by Rene Midesten. In his first season playing for the Ambrosia nine, Minoso (his brother's name actually, but the long-time residents of Perico began calling him that during the years he played sandlot ball), batted .364—which earned him the princely sum of $2 per game plus an additional $8 a week working in Rene's garage.

The big money offers came much later, after Minnie had established himself as a star for the Marianao club of the Cuban League, owned by former Cincinnati Red outfielder Armando Marsans. Here he found himself playing in the same stadiums where the stars of his boyhood once graced the diamond: Martin Dihigo, Robert Ortiz, Silvio Garcia, and Beto Avila. In his rookie season of 1945, Minoso batted .300 and was awarded a new contract calling for $200 a month. That year, he was named the Cuban League "Rookie of the Year," and was seemingly headed for a rich and rewarding career—with the Tampico club of the Mexican League. Jorge Pasquel, the wily entrepreneur who had floated large cash bonuses before dozens of Major Leaguers in the U.S. to come play in Mexico, offered Minnie more money than he had ever seen in his entire life if he were willing to short-circuit his dream of Negro League stardom and come to Mexico to play for Tampico. In the back of Pasquel's big black Cadillac, Minoso came face to face with a thick wad of bills. "How much do you want?" Pasquel asked. "I say no, I go to the United States," Minnie replied, as he eyeballed $1,000. Pasquel reminded him that there was much discrimination in the U.S. against blacks, and it was doubly hard for Cubans. "I say look—everywhere you go there is discrimination." Jorge Pasquel upped his offer to a guaranteed $30,000 for three full years, and further agreed to deposit the sum in a Cuban bank. Minnie was dubious. "I say the money is not everything. I say compared to what you have over there... this is only one penny." The next year, 1946, Minoso agreed to terms with the New York Cubans of the Negro League. He was paid $150 a month—which was later increased to $300—plus $5.00 a day in meal and hotel money. Learning to speak English was not such an easy thing to do. Most of the time Minnie carried with him a Spanish-English dictionary which he studied every chance he had. Later, with the Cleveland Indians and Chicago White Sox, Minoso relied on Luke Easter, Chico Carrasquel and Luis Aloma to help him negotiate his way in the American culture. In 1948 Minnie played his final season with the Cubans. Along with Jose "Pantalon" Santiago, Minoso was given a tryout with the St. Louis Cardinals, but the Redbirds were not entirely pleased with Minnie's style of play at third base. He had to wait until the tail-end of the 1948 season before his big break finally came.

"Reindeer" Bill Killefer was scouting for Bill Veeck's Cleveland Indians when he was sent to take a closer look at Minnie and a pitcher named Santiago. A deal was reached with the owner of the Cubans, whereby Minoso's contract was sold to the Cleveland club for $25,000. The color line had already been broken by Jackie Robinson and Larry Doby, so the American League moguls began lining up for the top Negro talent. Killefer and Joe Vosmik, who was also scouting for the Tribe, called Minnie the "fastest thing on legs." With the Dayton team of the Central League, Minoso batted a splashy .525 in just eleven games. He broke the color line in that city, much to the dismay of several fans who canceled their season tickets. Minnie admits that a couple of his teammates were "abusive," and a rival manager once unleashed a little black dog on the field as a means of badgering and tormenting him, but to this day he remains upbeat about the racial issue. "My business is to concentrate on what I do here," meaning the game between the lines. "To me my answer was to get on base or hit one out."

On the day of Minnie's arrival in Chicago, Manager Paul Richards assembled his team in the clubhouse and asked his charges if they had any problem with the fact that a black man from Cuba was about to don the White Sox pinstripes. No-one said a word. No-one even moved. Chico Carrasquel later confided to Minnie that even if he'd had an unbearable itch on the top of his head, he would have tied himself to the chair rather than be singled out by Richards for lifting his hand. That night, Chicago's color line was broken in spectacular fashion when Minnie smoked a bullpen home run off Yankee hurler Vic Raschi in his first at bat. Mickey Mantle provided an interesting footnote to the evening's drama by hitting his first career roundtripper as well, off right-hander Randy Gumpert.

Paul Richards, the lean tall Texan who was known in his day as the "Wizard of Waxahachie" was an expert handler of pitchers, and was also surprisingly sensitive to the racial tensions within baseball. From the very first day, Richards took Minnie under his wing and attempted to shield him from the torrent of abuse that came his way from grizzled old veterans like Jimmy Dykes, who never fully accepted the presence of men of color on a Major League baseball diamond. The Philadelphia A's manager rode Minnie unmercifully—but not in Chicago. Dykes was still a big hero to White Sox fans. He had guided the franchise through the lean Depression years and World War II. Because he understood the dangers of negative publicity in a town where he was so dearly loved, Dykes saved his bench-jockey antics for the home town fans in Philly. Once he ordered his pitcher Mario Fricano to "hit that black so-and-so in the head." Sensing danger, Richards asked Minnie if he wanted to bypass the next series in Philadelphia and catch up with the team in New York. Minoso was never one to shy away from the pitched ball—or from Jimmy Dykes. "So I say to Richards, 'if you take me out of the game now, maybe next time they will kill me.'" He played that day, and all the days yet to come.

Minoso was a star-caliber player who bravely faced the second-class treatment shown black players during those painful years before the Civil Rights movement unfolded. In March 1953, for example, the White Sox were scheduled to play a spring training game in Memphis' Russwood Field. Minnie and his teammate Connie Johnson, who with first baseman Bob Boyd and catcher Sam Hairston were the first American-born blacks to play for the White Sox, were banned from the field—a Jim Crow edict dating back to the era of Mayor Edward Hull Crump. Legal statutes were the only way to keep the "Cuban Comet," as Richards liked to call Minoso, out of the lineup.

How Minnie acquired his more famous moniker is another great fable. The nickname "Minnie" was given to him by a South Side dentist named Dr. Robinson. "What the devil," Minnie protested, "that's a female name!" Indeed it was. Minnie was the name of Dr. Robinson's secretary. But it had a nice alliteration to it, and the fans and sportswriters picked up on it until Minoso acquiesced to public opinion and adopted the name legally through the U.S. courts.

It took fines and threats to keep Minnie out of the lineup even when he was injured. He once played ten days with a broken bone in his foot. Then an errant pitch from Frank Lary struck him in the jaw, loosening all his teeth. It took eleven stitches to close the wound, but Minnie insisted on finishing the inning as a base runner before undergoing treatment. "Hit or get hit!" That was his motto, and for six consecutive years between 1956-61, he paced the junior circuit in being struck by the pitched ball—a Major League record.

This was the essence of Orestes Minoso, a gregarious personality who had a kind word for everyone, certainly the most popular player in club history. But it was one of the sad ironies of the game that at the precise moment of the White Sox' greatest triumph, the man who helped them turn the corner on their troubled past should find himself on the wrong side of the aisle when all was said and done. On December 4, 1957, Chuck Comiskey and John Rigney traded Minnie to the Cleveland Indians for Early Wynn and Al Smith. Frank Lane, who had taken over the duties of General Manager for the Tribe predicted that he "had just traded the Sox into a pennant," and in some ways he was correct. Wynn stabilized the pitching staff and was a key factor in the '59 title drive. Minnie spent two years along the shores of Lake Erie, and was in the lineup for Cleveland the night the Sox clinched the pennant. In one of the little known sidelights to that memorable season, Minnie was to have been the main man in a multi-player swap between Cleveland and Chicago midway through the year. However, Providence intervened unfavorably. Minnie went on a hitting tear at the least opportune moment. Within the span of a week he raised his average from .292 to .306, and had driven in a flock of RBIs. "If I trade him now, they'll lynch me!" Lane grumbled to Bill Veeck. The deal would have to wait until the winter meetings. Minnie missed out on the '59 World Series but he has no regrets. He was awarded an honorary World Series ring by the ebullient Veeck, which he continues to wear with pride to this day.

Nineteen-fifty-nine was a pivotal year for Minoso in more ways than one. The Cuban revolution spearheaded by Fidel Castro brought sweeping changes to his native island and deeply affected the Minoso family. Minnie is reluctant to talk about it, because in this life, money is but a small part of the equation. But the fact remains that his vast holdings were seized by the government. An incalculable fortune was lost in a heartbeat. "I come from the ranch," Minoso explains. "I had one pair of shoes, but I had dignity because my mother and father gave me the idea that money wasn't everything."

Minnie returned to his homeland for the last time in 1960-61. It was customary for him to play winter ball on the island every year, and as the president of the Cuban Baseball Players' Association, Minnie was an important link to the host government which had taken an exceedingly dim view of players shuttling back and forth between Cuba and the U.S. He left Cerro Stadium in Havana for good in 1961, closing out a sensitive chapter in his life. Though he is free to return to Cuba at his pleasure, Minoso has chosen not to do so. He has not seen his brother and sister in thirty years, but remains stoic about the whole matter. "I started a family here," he explains.

Minnie made a grand entrance in the Spring of 1961. He drove into the White Sox training facility in Sarasota, Florida in a pink Cadillac with the Cuban and American flags mounted proudly on the bumper. During the roughest months of the Cold War, Orestes Minoso wanted it understood that he was an American first and foremost, but he also maintained a warm affection for the land of his forebears—a land he would never see again, but where his fans remembered him with fondness and adulation. A popular song recorded in 1953 by the Enrique Gorrin orchestra was still given wide play on the Cuban radio stations. It was titled "Minoso At Bat," and it was performed to a lively cha-cha beat.

Minnie's best days were behind him when he reported to the Sox camp in 1961. He was a ten-year veteran who was approaching his thirty-ninth birthday. At season's end the house cleaning began in earnest. Art Allyn wanted to unload the veterans—and the big salaries in one fell swoop. Minnie was traded to the St. Louis Cardinals for Joe Cunningham, and afterwards became a man without a home. He drifted from St. Louis to Washington and back to Chicago for a brief final go-around in 1964.

In 1976, after playing for nearly a decade in the Mexican League, Minoso came back to Chicago to coach for his old mentor Paul Richards, in what many people referred to as a last hurrah for the "over-the-hill gang" —Veeck, Richards and Minoso. But Minnie at age 54 proved there was still life in his bat by delivering a single against California Angels hurler Frank Tanana in a late season contest at Comiskey Park. Sadly however, there is a whole generation of fans that has come of age not knowing what an intimidating presence Minnie Minoso was in his prime. They may think of him as a face on a baseball card, or as a tragic-comic figure who played his part in another one of Bill Veeck's misguided stunts. If that is the case, it is a sad legacy for a man who is a legitimate candidate for Hall of Fame consideration.

Minnie's infectious enthusiasm for baseball is catching. His charm never fails to rub off on the hundreds of youth groups, senior citizens, and business and civic associations he speaks to each year in his capacity as the White Sox community relations "ambassador." Minnie Minoso is one of a kind—in every way the embodiment of the White Sox and the city of Chicago: the team and the town he so dearly loves.

Cuban Blacks in the Majors Before Jackie Robinson

Peter C. Bjarkman

"For awhile I thought that Hi Bithorn, a Puerto Rican who pitched for the Cubs, 1942-43 and 1946, and for the White Sox in 1947, might be entitled to be called the first black player to appear in a big league uniform."—Fred Lieb, **Baseball As I Have Known It**

Perhaps the greatest difference between Jackie Robinson—acknowledged pioneer of baseball's integration—and Hiram Bithorn—forgotten journeyman pitcher for the lowly wartime Chicago Cubs—was in the "color" of their linguistic inflections, the distinctive rhythms of their speech patterns. There was perhaps little enough to set apart the shading of their skin tones or the heritage of their respective racial gene pools. There was, of course, the matter of considerable baseball playing talent to boot. Yet to baseball's rough-hewn country ballplayer stock and its gentlemanly establishment of owners (the great majority of whom were still bigoted Southerners at the close of World War II)—as well as to its hoards of paying patrons—one man (Robinson) remained anathema, an upstart descendant of slave stock who dared challenge baseball's long cherished "gentlemen's agreement." The other (Bithorn) was merely a quaint distraction, another quirky "foreigner" of suspicious appearance and discordant language who lurked on the fringes of the sport and who could not be taken seriously. And therein lies one of baseball's darkest untold tales.

Peter C. Bjarkman *is author of fifteen baseball books and editor of Meckler's two-volume scholarly* Encyclopedia of Major League Baseball Team Histories *and of the popular short-story anthology* Baseball & the Game of Life.

It is a revealing if somewhat whimsical indictment of our American national character that we Yanks like our national history tainted with a strong dose of patriotic myth. In the arena of societal history and politics, certainly, this axiom has held fast for generations of American school children and for serious adult readers as well. A recent generation nurtured on World War II and weaned with the four-decade Cold War has eagerly adopted Esther Forbes's fanciful *Johnny Tremain*, for example, as their most vivid image of the Revolutionary War era (despite this novel's spurious historical treatment and thinly veiled flag-waving thesis: that colonial patriots had genuinely found an American ideal worth fighting and dying for). More recently, social historian Michael Kammen has argued deftly with his *Mystic Chords of Memory* (1991) that in reality almost all American popular history is but a depoliticized version of events and as such always carries a doctrinaire message—our popular history texts offer "revisionist history" written with a clear and heavy-handed social lesson in mind, "history" which is the meek servant of didactic purpose and never the true reflection of documented reality. And it is in precisely this respect, perhaps, that our national character is most ironically reflected in our passions for our national game of baseball.

Baseball fans are undisputably the most historically aware of all sports fans—our undiminished love for the game of our childhood feeds as much upon the memory of past events and past heroes as it does upon the thrill of contemporary contests. And yet the most cherished historical memories sustaining the game for its collective fandom (Ruth's gigantic home run blows or Walter Johnson's blazing fastball) are often embellished fictions—at the very least elaborately woven legends tapping the very roots of fiction. What fan does not know, for example, that Doubleday invented baseball in the pastures of nineteenth-century Cooperstown; that Jackie Robinson broke the odious color barrier as big league baseball's first 20th-century ballplayer of the Negro race; that Fred Merkle's boneheaded failure to touch second base directly cost the Giants a 1908 pennant; that Merkle's ill-fated teammate Fred Snodgrass soon outdid his fellow bonehead by personally losing the 1912 World Series with his ninth-inning dropped fly ball; that Joe Jackson and his 1919 White Sox cronies nearly ruined the nation's sporting spirit by successfully conspiring with gamblers to throw that season's World Series against the Cincinnati ballclub; and that Joe DiMaggio stroked clean base hits in 56 straight games of the 1941 season for baseball's greatest consecutive batting run? And what careful and astute historian of the game should not also know that each and every one of these sacred baseball legends is, in bare fact, not exactly true? Each is, instead, an embellished myth, and each contains at least one significant historical distortion. Several—most especially Jackie Robinson's fortuitous role in integration and Joe Jackson's onerous role in the Black Sox Series—are patently incorrect as they are almost always reported.

It is the Jackie Robinson legend, in particular, that is glossed over with the rosy hue of romanticism and muddled with the inaccuracies of sloppy journalism. The idea that Robinson was a sole crusader who boldly set the very first black foot on a professional baseball diamond—that with his dashing style of play Robinson single-handedly swept aside all final vestiges of prejudice and racial hatred on America's athletic fields—is as firmly ingrained in the popular psyche as, say, the notion that Abner Doubleday concocted the rules of baseball out of thin air in 1839 in the pastures of Cooperstown, or that Babe Ruth indeed did point to the exact spot in the bleachers where he would seconds latter deposit a memorable 1932 World Series roundtripper, or that Fred Merkle irrationally threw away a Giants' pennant victory in 1908 with a thoughtless bonehead play. Ruth did not point; Merkle neither committed an atrocity of judgement nor lost a pennant of his own accord, and Robinson was assuredly *not* the first Negro big league ballplayer! This is not to belittle the magnitude of the Rickey-Robinson experiment in Brooklyn in 1947, nor to discount Robinson's legitimate Hall-of-Fame career, nor to suggest for a single moment that Robinson was not *perceived* by his peers and by fans as a racial pioneer and thus subjected to unimaginable pressures, harassment and abuse. It is simply to suggest—and this is quite a different matter—that the circumstances and events of Robinson's debut in the National League in 1947 have from the first been muddled, and that futhermore the full story of baseball's gradual and fitful racial integration has never been accurately told or popularly accepted.

Much has recently been accomplished by a handful of serious scholars of black baseball to help set the record straight regarding Branch Rickey's plan for integrating major league baseball at the close of the nation's second great world war. Most controversial in the Robinson story is the motive and methods of Branch Rickey's altruistic integration plan. And nowhere are this story and other aspects of the integration saga more accurately and entertainingly told than in Jules Tygiel's landmark study, *Baseball's Great Experiment—Jackie Robinson and His Legacy* (1983). Tygiel recounts in exacting detail how Rickey's moves not only opened big league fields to black players, but also had devastating effects on the Negro leagues themselves, and thus the black communities which had long sustained Negro baseball (just as black baseball had in equal part long sustained those communities). In Tygiel's view, something quite vital and distinctively American died with the passing of black baseball. The Negro Leagues had once represented a thriving $2 million empire, one controlled by blacks, employing blacks, and providing crucial forms of cultural identification for millions of fans. After Robinson, more blacks were playing in the big leagues and none would have it any other way; yet fewer blacks were making their living at baseball, and black communities had lost an important life force that could *never ever* be replaced. And Tygiel, along with prolific baseball chronicler John Thorn, has recently presented persuasive new evidence that Rickey in fact intended originally to bring three or more blacks to the big leagues simultaneously—a plan stymied by a convoluted course of events which Tygiel and Thorn have now unraveled (see "Signing Jackie Robinson," in *The National Pastime*, Number 10, 1990). It was thus apparently only an accident of history that Robinson held the spotlight of racial integration so exclusively to himself.

But there is still another side of the Jackie Robinson legend that to this day remains under-reported and thus largely imbalanced. This is the persistent notion that Robinson was unquestionably the first black man to don the uniform of a big league ball club. The notion is, of course, false on at least several counts. Any devotee of baseball history worth his weight in dusty volumes of Putnam team histories knows that a Negro catcher named Walker out of Oberlin College in Ohio was the regular backstop with the Toledo ballclub when it first gained admittance to the American Association (then a big-league circuit) in 1884; Fleet Walker also formed a colored tandem with pitcher George Stovey of the International League Newark club in 1887, the very season when Chicago manager Cap Anson (already well on his way to instituting the "gentlemen's agreement" that would bar "coloreds" from the senior circuit) staged a boycott of a scheduled exhibition match with the Newark team and its dark-skinned battery. Moses Fleetwood Walker was, for over sixty years, the proper answer to a pair of obscure trivia questions: Who was the first black major leaguer? And who was the last?

Reams have been written, as well, about the odd plight of Cuban ballplayers between the two great wars, especially by such eloquent spokespersons of "colored baseball history" as John Holway, Jules Tygiel, Jerry Malloy and Rob Ruck. While fair-skinned hurler Adolfo Luque was able to pass through the unwritten racial barrier to become the first true Latin big league star—appearing in the 1919 and 1933 World Series, compiling 27 victories in a fabulous 1923 campaign, and gaining nearly 200 career wins over twenty seasons with the Reds and Giants—dark-skinned legend Martin Dihigo (born a decade and a half later and raised only fifty miles from the home of Havana-born Luque) was doomed by race to a barnstorming career that would lead him through winter league seasons stretching across three decades and into the baseball halls of fame in his native Cuba and in the distant nation of Mexico as well (Bjarkman 1990). Like Martin Dihigo, numerous other bronzed Cuban stars were unacceptable to major league teams, whose managers often salivated when they saw the likes of Cristobal Torriente, Poncho Coimbre and Jose Mendez performing during barnstorming off-season games with Caribbean and black league all-star contingents.

Meanwhile another scenario was being played out in the clubhouses and front offices of some of baseball's less successful and less glamorous big league ballclubs. Readers of Paul Hemphill's entertaining novel *Long Gone* (1979) will recall the bold gamble of fictional Sally League manager Stud Cantrell who bolsters his weak-hitting Graceville Oilers club with slugging Negro catcher Joe Brown and passes off the unacceptable black as Jose Guitterez Brown, just off the banana boat from Venezuela. To management and fans starved for winning baseball, a little flirtation with the "gentlemen's agreement" might indeed be okay, provided that the swarthy ballplayer in question could pass as a "foreigner" and hit well enough to distract attention from the hue of his skin. On more than one occasion (as with Bill Veeck's midget in St. Louis, for example) baseball reality has followed meekly a full step behind baseball fiction. The history of the national pastime between the close of the dead-ball era and the demise of the "gentlemen's agreement" is replete with more than one incident of big league management passing off dark-skinned Latinos as "Cubans" or "Castillans."

First came the once celebrated and now largely forgotten saga of two olive-skinned flychasers discovered in the backwaters of the Eastern League by Cincinnati manager Clark Griffith in 1911. Armando Marsans and Rafael Almeida enjoyed short-lived yet historically important careers for the Cincinnati Reds of the immediate pre-World War I period. The Reds had stumbled upon the duo when manager Clark Griffith offered a tryout to a touted Cuban (Almeida) playing with the Class B New Britain (Connecticut League) team in the spring of 1911. Almeida spoke almost no English and thus brought along a teammate as interpreter; the teammate (Marsans) impressed Griffith even more than the original invitee, and soon both were ensconced in the outfield back in Cincinnati (Oleksak and Oleksak, 1991, 25).

Almeida would hit only .270 over three short seasons of National League play, while Marsans stretched out his own career until 1918, compiling only a .269 lifetime average but bashing the ball at a .317 clip during a stellar 1912 season. Yet both were the center of controversy resulting from their prominent olive-colored skin, and a worried Cincinnati management was soon forced to send off to Cuban officials for documents to certify that the two imports were of Castillian and not Negro heritage. Lonnie Wheeler and John Baskin report that even manager Griffith experienced mild concern when hearing of club president Garry Herrmann's original plans to sign up the Cuban prospects ("We will not pay any Hans Wagner price for a pair of dark-skinned islanders"); and when Herrmann went to pick up the imports upon their arrival at the Cincinnati train station, he himself suffered near heart-seizure when a couple of brown Pullman porters disembarked moments ahead of the expected ballplayers (Wheeler and Baskin, 1988, 174-175). Soon enough, however, Cincinnati newspapers were boasting that the two dark-skinned Cubans were "two of the purest bars of Castillian soap ever floated to these shores"—once the needed documentation had arrived. Writing in the very season of Robinson's cataclysmic debut, Lee Allen, dean of Cincinnati baseball historians, puts the whole matter in perspective by suggesting the tensions surrounding the Cubans' arrival in town: "Today [1947] it is almost impossible to realize what a furor the signing of two Cubans caused in 1911" (Allen, 1948, 96). Yet Lee Allen was writing his baseball history in a far different age and makes little speculation about what it was that so disturbed the league's fans about these "foreigners"— certain weighty sociological questions simply didn't yet get asked in popular-press sports books.

If Marsans and Almeida had once caused something of a loud uproar in the conservative midwestern backwater town of Cincinnati, there was soon to be similar upheaval on the professional diamond of the nation's capital as well. Racial questions soon greeted the brief major league appearances of two additional Cubans of the same era— outfielder Jacinto "Jack" Calvo and pitcher Jose Acosta. Calvo appeared briefly with the Washington Senators in 1913 and again in 1920 (33 G, .161 BA, 1 HR); Acosta hurled for the same ballclub, as well as for the Chicago White Sox, between 1920 and 1922 (10-10, 4.51 ERA). While Almeida and Marsans were apparently light-skinned enough to find brief acceptance in the majors (though not without comment and controversy), Calvo and Costa in turn were dark enough to play as well in the professional Negro Leagues. Both teamed on the Long

Beach Cubans and New Jersey Cubans for Negro League play between big-league stints, and in one 1920 winter season exhibition in Cuba Acosta is reported to have fanned the mighty Babe Ruth three times.Thus this second pair of swarthy Cubans became the only two pre-Robinson players to appear in both segregated white and ostracized black major leagues. If the appearance of Calvo and Acosta in full-fledged Negro league play has to give one pause concerning the percentage of Negro blood they each carried in their veins, one has also to speculate about the status of Acosta's brother, Merito Acosta, who also appeared briefly (175 games between 1913 and 1918) in the outfield of both the Washington Senators and Philadelphia Athletics.

Jack Calvo and Jose Acosta were not the only dusky-skinned Washington Senators to walk perilously on a racial tightrope across the American League during the decades after ragtime and Shoeless Joe Jackson and before wartime rations and one-armed Pete Gray. They were followed a decade later on the same Washington ballclub (which was now flooding its roster with low-salaried and often little-talented Cubans and Latinos) by a Venezuelan pitcher who stirred every bit as much doubt and as much consternation around the cities of the junior circuit. Venezuelan hurler Alejandro "Patron" Carrasquel was signed on for Griffith's Senators by superscout Joe Cambria and passed only tolerably well for a white player from 1939 down through 1945, winning 50 games overall for the cellar-dwelling Nats ballclub. Seemingly the nation's capital was a slightly less-hostile environment for border-line "whites" than the heartlands of Cincinnati. Yet Carrasquel was nonetheless heckled for his dark complexion (as was even Dolf Luque) by fans and opponents alike, and when he tried to avoid attention by Anglicizing his name to Alex Alexandra, the beat writers around the league never flagged from calling him simply "Carrasquel the Venezuelan"!

If the cataclysms of World War II would eventually throw open the big-league doors to the nation's black athletes, it would be the damnable war that would crack those same doors for racially questionable Cuban athletes even sooner. Clark Griffith for one continued his policies of penny pinching in Washington, policies which were based upon the Cuban scouting of former Baltimore laundryman Joe Cambria, who Washington baseball historian Morris Bealle carpingly claimed "would do even better if he could get over his predilection for Cubanolas" (Bealle 1947, 162). In the two decades following 1935, Griffith and Cambria imported a full 31 native Cubans onto the diamond in Washington for usually brief big-league appearances, and in spring 1940 Cambria reportedly trucked so many Cubans into camp that Griffith "had to find a special farm for them in Williamsport, Pa." (Bealle 1947, 163). (For more detailed treatment of the Senators' Cuban Era, which Bealle compares to the "daffiness era in Brooklyn" see Bjarkman 1991, Volume 1, 501-509.) The

thin pool of wartime baseball talent made Cuban athletes all the more attractive, of course—for one thing they were not subject to the military draft, for another they demanded small wages—and a floodtide (18 between 1940 and 1945) appeared in the uniforms of league clubs during the first half of the 1940s. At least two of these imports were, like Calvo and Carrasquel in Washington during previous decades, of highly dubious racial stock. Tommy de la Cruz (1944) apparently stirred as much ballpark undercurrent in Cincinnati as Marsans and Almeida years earlier, though the patriotic spirit of wartime America kept most of the strongest disapproval out of the press. And up in Chicago there was the case of Hi Bithorn (1942) from the island nation of Puerto Rico.

Tommy de la Cruz was a hurler of distinctly mediocre talents who would experience the triumphs and traumas of a single abnormal big league season in Cincinnati's Crosley Field during the war-interrupted season of 1944. As baseball's oldest and most traditional franchise, Cincinnati's Redlegs are known widely to baseball historians for their unmatched string of rare diamond firsts—such pioneering moments as the nation's first professional team (1869), first uniformed manager (1869), first fielder's and catcher's mitts (1869 and 1890), first National League left-handed pitcher (1877), inaugural farm system (1887), first Ladies Day (1886), first big league night game (1935), first all-synthetic playing surface (Riverfront Stadium in 1970), and dozens more (Bjarkman 1991, Volume 2). Yet the most explosive "first" in club annals remains buried from sight by the selective view of history. The wartime summer of 1944 in Cincinnati is today enthusiastically remembered for a rare if unimportant pitching debut—the two-thirds of an inning hurled by 15-year-old high schooler Joe Nuxhall, baseball's youngest performer ever. Another mound debut of that same summer has surprising received almost no commentary, by contrast, despite its unparalleled groundbreaking nature. Ebony-hued Cuban righthander Tommy de la Cruz took the hill for manager Bill McKecknie's Reds 34 times that summer during his single big-league campaign and fashioned a record of nine-and-nine in 191 innings of mid-summer work. The Reds steadfastly insisted that their Cuban journeyman was merely "Hispanic" and not black, yet enough doubt existed among rival club owners that young de la Cruz was never to be invited back for a second season's swing around the league (he showed up the following summer in Jorge Pasquel's rebel Mexican League as one of the handful of big-leaguers Pasquel was able to lure "south of the border" in his own effort to compete with the big boys up north). That race and not mound talent was a motivating force in the release of Tommy de la Cruz is perhaps cued by the fact that the pitching-thin Cincinnati club (despite wartime returnees) could boast only three 10-game winners during the following campaign.

It should be noted here that if Tommy de la Cruz did

not receive proper recognition as "baseball's first black" pioneer, he only set an unfortunate precedent that would die hard in backwater Cincinnati. A full decade and a half later ex-University of Toledo basketballer Tom Harmon would appear on Opening Day of 1960 as a token pinch hitter and thus claim the distinction in popular histories (and thus in the memories of local fans) as the first black Cincinnati Reds player. Ironically, Harmon was preceded (by exactly one batter) by another pinch hitter who better deserved this history-making accolade. Saturnino Escalera—native of Santurce, Puerto Rico—launched his own one-year big-league career with a pinch-hit single only moments *before* Harmon, who followed him in the lineup by tamely popping out. Nino Escalera was labeled by local writers at the time as merely "a Puerto Rican" import, despite the fact that his Latino skin was equally as dusky-toned as Harmon's.

A bold claim for Tommy de la Cruz as baseball's true first 20th-century black was recently made before a national television audience by the producers of a special documentary on the history of Latin American ballplayers ("Baseball With a Latin Beat", produced by WNBC-TV, New York, October 1989). The claim was probably moot, however, not so much in light of Robinson's celebrated career, but rather in view of Hi Bithorn's totally obscure sojourn on the big league diamond of Chicago. Yet another Latin pitcher of only modest talents, Bithorn preceded de la Cruz by two full seasons and outlasted him by that many as well. He showed promise with a 9-14 (3.68 ERA) 1942 rookie campaign, was the staff ace (18-12, 2.60 ERA) for the fifth-place Cubbies during the war-cheapened season of 1943 (pacing the senior circuit in shutouts that year), then lost two seasons to wartime naval service (Puerto Ricans, unlike Cubans, were not draft exempt). While sustained on navy chow Bithorn unfortunately ballooned to 225 pounds, developed a sore arm, and kissed goodbye to his promising big league career. Perhaps the most noteworthy events marking the career of Hiram Bithorn were the fact that he teamed with Cuban backstop Sal Hernandez to provide the 1942 Cubs with baseball's first all-Latino battery, and the distressing fact that he was gunned down under mysterious circumstances by a police officer in Mexico City on New Year's Day of 1952. But not many fans or baseball historians ever noticed.

One baseball historian and scribe did lift his comfortable racial blinders long enough to take note, however, and that scribe was one of the game's most celebrated and respected—none other than venerable Fred Lieb. Pausing in his marvelous 1977 autobiography to comment on baseball's rich ethnic mix, Lieb recalls a personal puzzle he once faced regarding the case of the swarthy Puerto Rican pitcher with the wartime Cubs. Lieb's full account is eye-opening for its candor:

Late in the winter of 1946-7, when I was working

in St. Louis, I was invited to see a performance of Katherine Dunham's all-black dance troupe. I did not know the man who had arranged for me to sit in the wings throughout the performance. During the intermission he brought over one of the women dancers and introduced her to me. "She is a first cousin to Hi Bithorn, the pitcher," he explained to make conversation. "Yes," the girl volunteered immediately. "My mother and Hi's mother are sisters."

Hi Bithorn

Lieb then continues his narrative with a speculation that perhaps the conversation had been arranged "to tell me something" (given his advantageous position in the baseball press), reporting that "it had been rumored among baseball writers and in clubhouses when Bithorn came up in 1942 that he was part black" (Lieb 1977, 260). Lieb, for all his candor, was still a company man, however—which baseball writers of his generation were not!—and could only conclude that "I have been assured by a Puerto Rican baseball authority that Bithorn was *not* black, despite my curious experience."

If the greatest of the Cuban Black ballplayers who sprung forth in the decades between the two wars were fated to live out their glorious careers in the relative obscurity of island winter ball and hidden Negro League play, at least their image was not totally obliterated by the winds of fate. They would indeed emerge—eventually—among the game's great legends, thanks in large part to the work of literary champions like John Holway and Jules Tygiel. Of course, it is still arguable that Dihigo and Torriente and Luis Tiant, Sr., and others of immortal stature within their own native Cuba and Puerto Rico were robbed by long delays of reputations that might have rivaled perhaps Cobb's or Walter Johnson's. And their eventual enshrinement came far too late for their own personal savouring. But it was, indeed, some of their dark-skinned compatriots who—due perhaps to their lesser talents—snuck briefly through baseball's loose racial barriers who suffered what now seems an even crueler fate. Why is it that Robinson was deified and vilified while Hi Bithorn and Jack Calvo and Alex Carrasquel provoked more of mild amusement and stifled yawns than any threats of banishment? Is it merely that the latter were mysterious island swarthy princes while the former was an upstart and disrespectful "son of a slave" who didn't know his place? Was it that those Black Cubans who enjoyed brief cups of espresso in the big time were simply never good enough ballplayers to receive much notice? Was it that fans and owners alike—perhaps like characters in Hemphill's novel—were actually fooled by protestations of local management that these dark-skinned "foreigners" weren't really black men of the same bloodlines as Georgia Negroes? Likely it was some shifting combination of all the above.

No serious baseball historian would dare to contend that Jackie Robinson does not deserve every bit of his huge and still-growing legend as baseball superstar—as an athlete of incomparable grace, skill and magnetism; and as a bold racial pioneer of unmatched courage and integrity. It should not be forgotten that once Robinson left the playing field he carried on still another all-consuming crusade (one that most likely cost him his health and his life) against racial bigotry across the land, dedicating himself to the battle with an intensity shown by few Americans of any color or creed. During the course of his decade-long big league career Robinson enjoyed the perfect forum for his conquest of sport's inexcusable racist traditions—playing in the New York baseball capital, wearing the uniform of the colorful Dodgers, dancing his magic upon the basepaths at the very moment when television's magical eye first captured images of the World Series. With the notoriety and exposure he enjoyed, Robinson took upon his lonely shoulders the full burden of racial hatred and the full weight of the integration struggle; as a result he enjoyed in large measure the full (and perhaps somewhat unmerited) credit for dismantling baseball's most unforgivable tradition. While Robinson wore his rebellion on his sleeve, other quiet pioneers like Campanella, Doby and Newcombe undoubt-edly did as much for the cause simply by sustaining their cheerful and infectious enthusiasms for the sport.

Yet in an era when baseball's historians quibble at length over whether fine-tuned adjustments in rule interpretation or record keeping might justify taking away a batting title earned four decades ago, or adjusting the statistical measures of some long bygone player's relative impact on the game, it would seem appropriate as well that factual inaccuracies of more far-reaching consequences for baseball's sociological history would also need to be set straight. Should there not be a place in our narratives to recognize the historical significance of a handful of men of color who crossed baseball's odious color barrier even before Jackie Robinson?

References

Allen, Lee. *The Cincinnati Reds*. New York: G.P. Putnam's Sons, 1948.

Bealle, Morris A. *The Washington Senators: The Story of An Incredible Fandom*. Washington, D.C.: Columbia Publishing Company, 1947.

Bjarkman, Peter C. "First Hispanic Star? Dolf Luque, of Course" in: *Baseball Research Journal* 19 (1990), 28-32. Society for American Baseball Research.

Bjarkman, Peter C. "Washington Senators–Minnesota Twins: Expansion-Era Baseball Comes to the American League" (Chapter 13) in: *Encyclopedia of Major League Baseball Team Histories, American League (Volume 1)*. Westport, Connecticut: Meckler Books, 1991, 487-534.

Bjarkman, Peter C. "Cincinnati Reds–Cincinnati's Hometown Game, from the Red Stockings to the Big Red Machine" (Chapter 4) in: *Encyclopedia of Major League Baseball Team Histories, National League (Volume 2)*. Westport, Connecticut: Meckler Books, 1991, 181-238.

Hemphill, Paul. *Long Gone*. New York: Viking Press, 1979.

Holway, John B. *Blackball Stars: Negro League Pioneers*. Westport, Connecticut: Meckler Books, 1988.

Lieb, Fred. *Baseball As I Have Known It*. New York: Coward, McCann and Geoghegan Publishers, 1977.

Oleksak, Michael M. and Mary Adams Oleksak. *Beisbol: Latin Americans and the Grand Old Game*. Grand Rapids, Michigan: Masters Press, 1991.

Thorn, John and Jules Tygiel. "Jackie Robinson's Signing: The Real, Untold Story" in: *The National Pastime: A Review of Baseball History* 10 (1990): 7-12. Society for American Baseball Research.

Tygiel, Jules. *Baseball's Great Experiment: Jackie Robinson and His Legacy*. New York: Oxford University Press, 1983.

Wheeler, Lonnie and John Baskin. *The Cincinnati Game*. Wilmington, Ohio: Orange Frazier Press, 1988.

The IBA and the World Amateur Baseball Movement

Bob Rybarczyk

The United States might have made it a science, and many in Japan, Mexico and Cuba play it scientifically, but did you know that baseball is being played these days in Italy? And Israel? And India? It's true. In fact, baseball is played around the world by people of all ages. And one organization has been working diligently for many years to take baseball's worldwide popularity to greater heights— the International Baseball Association, or IBA.

In 1975, the IBA, then known as the International Association of Amateur Baseball (AINBA), was formed as the result of a merger of two international baseball organizations that encompassed 39 baseball-playing countries. Since that time, the IBA has had a tremendous impact on the growth of baseball around the world. It has increased the number of players and teams, developed baseball in public school systems, and helped nations organize baseball federations. The IBA has also helped improve the playing levels and umpiring of its member countries. So far, the IBA has met with great success, and even greater success is yet to come. At Barcelona in 1992, baseball will be an official Olympic medal sport for the first time.

The drive for official Olympic status officially began with AINBA's creation, since a sport must have one recognized governing body to be considered for medal status in the Olympic Games. In 1979, international baseball leaders met in Los Angeles for an AINBA Congress in order to develop a plan for baseball to take its place in world-level sport.

Spearheading the plan was current IBA President Dr. Robert E. Smith, who helped organize its first phase:

Bob Rybarczyk *serves as a publications intern with the International Baseball Association (IBA) in Indianapolis and is making his debut here as a published baseball historian.*

bringing baseball back to the Olympics as a demonstration sport in 1984. Baseball had been a demonstration sport six times prior to 1979, the most recent being in 1964 at the Tokyo Games. However, the American national game had not been able to secure a permanent position in the Olympic structure.

Smith and the IBA Executive Committee, along with help from such figures as Major League Baseball Commissioner Bowie Kuhn, Los Angeles Dodgers owner Peter O'Malley, University of Southern California baseball coach Rod Dedeaux, and Los Angeles Olympic Organizing Committee Chairman Peter Ueberroth, helped persuade International Olympic Committee President Juan Antonio Samaranch to make baseball a demonstration sport in 1984.

The '84 Olympic baseball competition turned out to be an unqualified success, as more than 350,000 fans attended the games at Dodger Stadium and saw Japan, the United States and Chinese Taipei win the gold, silver and bronze medals, respectively. The 1984 Olympic baseball tournament also proved to be a turning point for international baseball. Its success (along with an assist from President Ronald Reagan, who lobbied the Republic of Korea's president on baseball's behalf) helped bring baseball back as a demonstration sport at the 1988 Seoul Olympics, where the United States, Japan and Puerto Rico won the gold, silver and bronze medals.

The 1984 Olympic tournament's success also proved to be the single most important factor in the IOC's vote in 1986 to include baseball as a medal sport at the 1992 Barcelona Olympics. The goal of making baseball an official Olympic sport had finally been realized. Eight teams will meet in Barcelona to play for the first official baseball gold medal. Chinese Taipei, Cuba, the Dominican Republic, Italy, Japan, Puerto Rico, the United States and host Spain eventually qualified for the inaugural baseball competition, which is scheduled to take place from July 26 to August 5, 1992.

In 1985, AINBA officially changed its name to the International Baseball Association, and in 1986, the IBA established its headquarters in Indianapolis, Indiana, and hired Indiana native David Osinski as its executive director. From Indianapolis, the IBA works with its member federations in planning events such as the Olympic baseball competition, the Intercontinental Cup, the President's Cup, World Championships for three age levels and worldwide baseball development programs.

In 1992, the IBA will introduce the Merit Cup, competition which is open only to the national teams of developing IBA member nations. The first IBA Merit Cup will be held at Cocoa Expo Sports Center in Cocoa, Florida, September 8-20, 1992.

Another event staged by the IBA is the World All-Star Game, which was played for the first time in Fulton County Stadium in Atlanta in 1990. The 1991 game was held in Dodger Stadium in Los Angeles. The IBA World All-Star Game was born at the suggestion of Richard Cecil, president of Eagle Sports Group, Ltd., when in 1986, he and John Cooper met with IBA President Smith to devise a long-term plan for the growth of international amateur baseball. Cecil and Cooper advised the IBA that an all-star game, which would spotlight the best players from IBA member countries, would, in fact, promote the game in the countries in which it is played and would offer the possibility for worldwide television exposure.

The game was first proposed by Eagle and Associates to several groups. While reaction to the proposal was positive, financial support was not forthcoming. In 1989, Cecil and Smith approached Billy Payne, president of the Atlanta Organizing Committee for the 1996 Olympics, and offered Atlanta the opportunity to host the inaugural IBA World All-Star Game in August of 1990. Such an event provided the city a chance to host an important international competition one month before the final decision would be announced as to the location of the 1996 Olympic Games. The 1990 inaugural event attracted athletes from 25 countries, and the '91 game featured players from 28 nations. The games have served their purpose by heightening interest in several baseball countries through television exposure.

In addition to staging baseball events, the IBA also publishes *IBA World Baseball* magazine, the official voice of the international amateur baseball movement, and *IBA Report*, a bi-monthly newsletter. The IBA regulates as well the organization and structure of senior and youth world tournaments, addresses the communication needs of its 72 member countries, and works to develop and improve the technical level and the promotional aspects of baseball throughout the world.

Antonio Pacheco of Cuba at the Second IBA All-Star Game at Dodger Stadium

The greatest factor in baseball's current rate of growth, however, is the IOC's vote to make baseball an Olympic medal sport. That vote triggered a groundswell of interest in baseball that has reached most parts of the world and continues unabated into the 1990s. Gold medal dreams of Olympic glory certainly are a large part of the story, but they don't account for all of the new interest in the game. Along with Olympic status comes funding to pay for the practical side of those dreams: needed monies for balls, bats, gloves, fields and instruction.

The vote uncovered a latent interest in baseball in many parts of the world. Since the IOC decision in 1986, the IBA has added the Soviet Union, Romania, Bulgaria, Zimbabwe, Nigeria, Guam, the Marshall Islands, American Samoa, Israel, the Democratic People's Republic of Korea and New Zealand to its growing list of member countries. Other countries such as Norway, Estonia, Lithuania and Zambia have indicated they will join soon. South Africa has also been readmitted to the IBA now that its national baseball union represents the aspirations of all the 25,000 youth and adults (white and black alike) playing the sport within that nation.

Eastern Europe and Africa are opening up to baseball, as evidenced by the many requests for assistance the IBA receives annually from Bulgaria, Romania, Poland, Czechoslovakia and Hungary, and the formation in 1990 of the Africa Baseball and Softball Association (ABSA), headed by Malcolm Burne of Zimbabwe. With the formation of ABSA in Nigeria in 1990 and the creation of the Baseball Confederation of Oceania in Guam the previous year, international amateur baseball possesses a structure that corresponds to the five Olympic regions.

In the Americas, the Confederation of Pan American

Baseball, headed by Mexican Baseball President Alonso Perez, controls regional events in youth and adult categories ranging from the Pan American Games baseball competition to America-wide youth championships held every two years. North America and the Caribbean historically have been strong baseball regions, and efforts are underway to improve the level of play in many less baseball-crazed South and Central American nations such as Honduras, Costa Rica, El Salvador, Peru, Argentina, Brazil, Ecuador and Chile.

Several of the South American countries have made significant progress in recent years:

- In 1991, Peru competed in the annual Jose Antonio Heregla tournament in Cuba.

- Brazil won a silver medal in the 1990 IBA AA World Youth Championship for 13-15-year-olds in Mexico.

- El Salvador defeated perennial champion Nicaragua in the 1990 Central American Games to win the gold medal and a berth in the 1991 Pan American Games.

- Argentina hosted the inaugural IBA President's Cup, in which top teams from Japan, the Republic of Korea and Chinese Taipei competed for the first time in South America.

In Asia, the Asian Baseball Federation has provided high level regional competition for several of the strongest baseball countries in the world—Japan, Republic of Korea and Chinese Taipei—since 1954. The BFA also allows its neighbors from Oceania—Australia and Guam—to compete in its Olympic classification tournaments. Asian officials, directed by Jong Nak Kim of the Republic of Korea, have targeted Mongolia and Thailand as the newest expansion grounds for baseball in the Far East. Also, the Philippines, India, Sri Lanka and the People's Republic of China have responded to the Olympic challenge by accelerating baseball development.

The European baseball community, which now embraces over twenty-one baseball countries, provides an efficient promotion/relegation system for its national adult teams. New baseball nations must win the biennial "B" pool competition to be able to play at "A" level and compete for the right to represent Europe at the World Championships and the Olympic Games. Also, European youths now compete at several levels with the aim of allowing players to experience international competition and measure their progress against their peers.

In Africa, the heterogeneous nature of the continent's nations contrasts sharply with Europe as new baseball countries such as Tunisia, Nigeria, Zimbabwe and Zambia overcome distance, communication difficulties and resource limitations to make baseball an African sport. Nigeria, site of the ABSA headquarters, sets the standard as its two-year-old federation has managed to send a team to an IBA world championship and build the first international standard baseball facility on the continent.

In Oceania, New Zealand is energetically building a baseball program, and Australian baseball is reaching top-level status, as evidenced by the Aussies' second-round victory over Japan in the 1991 Asian Baseball Championships, an Olympic qualification event. In 1989, the Baseball Confederation of Oceania was formed, an important step in upgrading baseball development among the many widespread island nations of the region. Guam and Australia dominate the Baseball Confederation of Oceania as their national federations must disseminate coaching and umpiring techniques to the islands that dot the Pacific. American Samoa, the Marshall Islands and Micronesia are recipients of international expertise which, when channeled to their national programs, will enable the regions to form a competitive structure.

As the IBA heads into 1992, its member nations and executives look forward to an historic year for baseball. With the sport's first appearance as an official Olympic medal sport, worldwide popularity of international baseball is expected to accelerate rapidly. The IBA will help to turn this increased attention into renewed growth which will continue to make baseball one of the world's most popular player and spectator sports.

Baseball-playing Countries

Am. Samoa	Chile	Finland	Malaysia	Peru	Sri Lanka
Argentina	PR of China	France	Malta	Philippines	Suriname
Aruba	Chinese Taipei	Germany	Marshall Is.	Poland	Sweden
Australia	Colombia	Great Britain	Mexico	Puerto Rico	Switzerland
Austria	Costa Rica	Guam	Morocco	Rep. of Korea	Tunisia
Bahamas	Cuba	Guatemala	Netherlands	Romania	Uruguay
Belgium	Czechoslovakia	Honduras	Neth. Antilles	San Marino	United States
Bolivia	Denmark	India	New Zealand	Singapore	U.S. V. I.
Brazil	Dominican Rep.	Indonesia	Nigeria	Somalia	Venezuela
British V.I.	DPR of Korea	Israel	Nicaragua	Soviet Union	Yugoslavia
Bulgaria	Ecuador	Italy	Pakistan	El Salvador	Zimbabwe
Canada	Egypt	Japan	Panama	Spain	

Brits in the Baseball Hall of Fame

Jack Kavanagh

With traditional bulldog determination, the British have resisted all attempts to transplant the hybrid we call America's "National Pastime." They cling to the tradition of cricket. They are content to have given us the ancient game of rounders, the seedling from which our own native game has sprouted. Fans' passions are inflamed in the British Isles not by men in flannel but by bruisers in short pants. Rugby and soccer serve to rally spectator enthusiasm. However, by having brought their ancient game of rounders to export quality, and sent several of their native sons to nurture its growth, the impact of Brits on our national game has been immense. It has resulted in three sons of Britain being enshrined in the Baseball Hall of Fame in Cooperstown: Henry Chadwick, Harry Wright, and Tommy Connolly.

It is hardly necessary to remind a SABR readership of the irony that baseball's Hall of Fame itself is found in Cooperstown as the result of Albert Spalding's jingoistic insistence that baseball could only have been invented by an American. The rigged Mills Report—with less substance than a Geraldo Rivera investigative TV inquiry—created a comfortable myth. The baseball establishment happily conned itself into believing a youth named Abner Doubleday scribbled the entire rule book in the dirt of a pasture in a sleepy upstate New York town to while away a summer's afternoon in 1839. Even so, the evidence that the early English game of rounders was baseball's ancestor was so obvious that not even the creators of baseball's ultimate theme park in Cooperstown could justify the Yankee Doodle Doubleday myth. When

the Baseball Museum and Hall of Fame opened in 1939, timed to a hoaxed up "Centennial" tie-in, Henry Chadwick was on an inside plaque. Abner Doubleday, the local boy who grew up to be a Union General in the Civil War, was relegated to the small ballpark built in Cooperstown by the WPA to generate employment in the Depression years.

Henry Chadwick is the only baseball writer ever elected to the Hall of Fame. (The Writer's Wing and accompanying Broadcaster's niche are in the library next door, and members aren't in the Baseball Hall of Fame proper.) English born Chadwick, whose parents brought

Henry Chadwick

Jack Kavanagh *is vice president of SABR and author of numerous baseball history articles, plus juvenile sports biographies of Rogers Hornsby, Dizzy Dean, footballer Barry Sanders and others.*

---

him to Brooklyn as a young boy, began as a newspaper stringer turning in cricket match scores to *The New York Times* just before the Civil War years. He created public awareness of the fledgling sport and became its arbiter of rules. A boxscore evolved largely with his input to become baseball's most treasured source of research data. Although repeatedly threatened with extinction as a newsprint feature, Henry Chadwick's boxscore will survive because baseball as a recorded historic activity cannot endure without it.

Henry Chadwick was a prolific writer and innovator of baseball guides, histories, and statistical compilations, and he contributed widely in the general press into the early years of the twentieth century. He did more than any writer to shape baseball and expand its popularity. He had a broad scope of interests, covering other sports ranging from sailing to billiards and chess. He was a musician, wrote songs, played piano, was a drama critic and—briefly—a Civil War correspondent. Henry Chadwick was a prophet unhonored in his native land but revered by those who recognized him as a true father of American baseball.

Another Englishman who crossed the Atlantic as a youth accompanying his parents was Harry Wright. His father, Sam Wright, was a professional cricketeer, whose fame had spread from the British Isles to America. In the 1840s cricket was the preferred sport of the toffs at the fashionable St. George Cricket Club on Staten Island, New York. The club imported Sam Wright to run its program. America got his oldest son as a bonus. The Wrights' next two sons were born in America. They were George, who is also a member of the Baseball Hall of Fame, and Sam, Jr., who appeared only briefly in major league games.

The oldest son, Harry, and his young brothers scandalized their father by deserting the traditional British game of cricket for the emerging local game of baseball. Harry became a member of the New York Knickerbockers, a social and athletic club of young city gentlemen which had included Alexander Cartwright. Cartwright is usually credited with codifying the rules of the time and with laying out a diamond with the presciently perceived "perfect dimensions" of 90 feet equally separating four bases.

As baseball developed, Harry Wright emerged as a good player and even better organizer. When the City Fathers of Cincinnati decided a winning baseball team would create good publicity for their fast growing metropolis at the close of the Civil War, they called in Harry Wright. They gave him a free hand and an open purse to bring together the best team that money could buy. He was told to form the first openly, fully professional baseball team. It wasn't nepotism that induced Harry to sign his young brother George first and pay him the most. George, less single-minded about baseball than Harry, was the best player in the game. The result of Harry's recruiting was the undefeated 1869 Red Stockings. Their 56-game nationwide tour spread the popularity of the game. A full professional league was inevitable and Harry Wright went to Boston to form the team which dominated it. From 1872 to 1875 he led the Boston Red Stockings to four National Association pennants.

Filled with a prodigal's pride in the American game of baseball, Harry Wright joined with Albert G. Spalding in 1874 to lead an All Star squad to England. The British were bored with the spectacle which resulted. Only when Harry taught a few rudiments of cricket to his new chums from the USA and beat the English at their own game were the locals impressed. But then only at the athletic ability of their visitors. The urbanity of the cricket club was undisturbed by this first in a long series of attempts to spread the American game. The new gospel of roundball failed to convert the British to baseball.

The National Association gave way to a stronger professional organization when the National League supplanted it in 1876. Harry Wright then began an 18-year NL managerial career in Boston, Providence and Philadelphia. Wright was an early devotee of using playing statistics to anticipate how upcoming games would be played. He pored over newspaper accounts of every game, looking for the hot players, those whose play was off their usual standard and interpreting stats to every advantage he could gain. He kept his own boxscores, neatly transferred into leather bound notebooks in a precise copperplate style. Harry Wright studied statistics so avidly he lost his sight for a year in 1890.

Harry Wright was a pioneer in the development of America's National Pastime. He was a key factor in the transition from "a gentleman's game" to the unabashed professional era. As a strategist, he is credited with having players back up each other on fielding plays. Henry Chadwick is entitled to be called, "The Father of Baseball" but it was Harry Wright who reared the American version of rounders well into adolescence.

Baseball was a lusty, growing sport when the Connollys crossed the Atlantic Ocean from Manchester, England where the 13-year old Tommy had been born to Irish parents. A scrawny five-foot seven, the lightweight teenager conceded he lacked the size to play the new game he found when his family settled in Natick, Massachusetts in 1893. However, he took joy in the game's rules and became a sandlot umpire whose fearless impartiality caught the attention of Tim Hurst, a top National League arbiter. Hurst passed the word of his protege on to Tim Murnane, New England's most influential baseball personality. Known as "The Silver King," Murnane had founded and ruled the New England League for 30 years. He hired young Tommy Connolly as an umpire. Murnane had been one of the players Harry Wright and Albert G. Spalding had taken to England on the 1874 visit. He became a prominent Boston sports editor as well as a ruling hand directing the development of the National Pastime in New England.

Tom Connolly

For four seasons Connolly held single-handed sway over games between New England's smokey industrial cities. Then, in 1900, to appease some team owner's wishes, the league did not back Connolly in a dispute about a player's actions. Connolly put his ball and strike indicator in his pocket and went home to Natick. The league put out the story he was ill. He did not argue. He was sick of the way umpires were treated. They were bullied, sometimes assaulted and, without the league to back them with fines and suspensions of their attackers, were left vulnerable. Connolly, who had married and was raising a brood that would total seven children, looked for a more certain kind of work.

The founding of the American League saved Tommy Connolly for a continuing baseball career and eventual election to the Baseball Hall of Fame. Ban Johnson, the American League's founder, insisted its umpires must be respected. The National League had degenerated to a level of play in which games were often decided by which team could best intimidate the umpires.

It was Connie Mack, then a tall, thin young manager whose Philadelphia Athletics would become the American League's first dynasty, who recommended Connolly. He based his endorsement on his fellow New Englander's reputation. Actually, Mack had not seen young Tommy work a game but trusted those who praised his work. When the American League began its premier season in 1901 Tommy Connolly was one of its four umpires. Only one umpire would be assigned to games among the eight teams. When three of the season's opening games were rained out, Tommy gained the unique distinction of umpiring the first American League game ever played. The sun shone in Chicago where he was the single umpire. Later in his career Tommy Connolly would also umpire the first modern World Series game, in 1903.

Despite Ban Johnson's backing and his own bantam rooster response to the taunts of players and fans,

Tommy Connolly was beleaguered. Joe McGinnity, a spit-ball pitcher with Baltimore once spat in Connolly's face. Irate Red Sox fans chased Connolly into a row boat that he paddled to safety in Boston Harbor. This led to Connolly heading off arguments by quickly bouncing belligerent players and his reputation for quick-triggered response grew.

The turning point came in 1922. Babe Ruth had been suspended by Commissioner Kenesaw Mountain Landis for ignoring a ban on post season barnstorming by players who had appeared in the World Series. Ruth missed spring training and the first six weeks of the season. When he was slow to round into form, the New York fans rode him hard. The Babe did not take the insults gracefully. He tried to climb into the stands to reach a heckler only to have umpire Connolly thrust his 150 pounds in the way. Ruth allowed himself to be pushed away and led from the field.

Both men seem to have been affected by the incident. It marked a point in the careers of both. From that time on, Babe Ruth was never thrown out of a game, nor did Tommy Connolly ever banish a player. He explained his forbearance: "The fans are entitled to see the players. They didn't come out to see me dust off home plate."

Tommy Connolly continued to push this point of view through his long life in baseball. He retired as an active umpire in 1931 when he was 60. He then served as the supervisor of American League umpires until he was 83, working from an office in Chicago and constantly touring the American League ball parks. He kept his crews under a watchful eye to be sure they followed the examples he had set. He was not only the reigning authority on how an umpire should work a game, he was recognized as the preeminent authority on the rules of baseball. He even became chairman of baseball's Rules Committee.

Tommy Connolly finally announced his retirement in 1954. The year before, he and Bill Klem, his counterpart from the National League, had received the ultimate honor of election to the Baseball Hall of Fame, the first umpires to be inducted. It was an achievement for a man to contemplate during his final years. Unlike Henry Chadwick and Harry Wright who were elected posthumously, Tommy Connolly experienced the honor in his lifetime. He lived to be 90, alert, among a large family in the house he had built in Natick, Massachusetts. It was a life whose formative years had been spent in England but was enriched by his career in baseball.

The three Brits whose plaques hang in the gallery of the Baseball Hall of Fame made unique contributions to America's "National Pastime." Perhaps now Henry Chadwick, Harry Wright and Tommy Connolly contemplate from somewhere above with a satisfied air, as they watch the marvelous game they helped nurture from British roots transplanted in American soil—a game now poised to spread widely across the planet as the new International Pastime.

Untold Saga of Europe's Big Leaguers

David L. Porter

"The Giants win the pennant! The Giants win the pennant! The Giants win the Pennant!" yelled New York Giants broadcaster Russ Hodges. The Giants and Brooklyn Dodgers had finished the 1951 regular season in a first place tie and had split the first two games of the three-game National League playoff series. The Dodgers led the Giants, 4-2, with one out in the bottom half of the ninth inning in the decisive third game. Outfielder Bobby Thomson, a native of Glasgow, Scotland, hit a dramatic three-run homer, the "shot heard 'round the world," off Dodger pitcher Ralph Branca on October 3, 1951, giving New York the National League title. Sports fans still cite the Giants' unbelievable comeback as the most memorable event in major league baseball history. Thomson and many other European-born figures left a significant impact on the development of American baseball. What European-born figures played major roles in the unfolding of America's national pastime? What major contributions did they make?

English-born figures made the earliest impact on American baseball. Henry Chadwick, originally from Exeter, England, became the dean of American sportswriters and was called "the Father of Baseball." The Brooklyn, New York resident became a baseball fan after witnessing a game in 1856 between two skilled New York teams and quickly realized baseball's potential to become the national pastime. For a half century, Chadwick wrote extensively about baseball for over 20 newspapers and magazines. He served on the editorial staff of the Brook-

lyn *Eagle* as a baseball writer from 1856 to 1894 and wrote baseball articles for the New York *Clipper*, an amusement sports weekly, from 1857 to 1888. In 1860 Chadwick prepared the first baseball guide, *Beadle's Dime Base Ball Player*. His other activities included editing *Haney's Base Ball Book of References* from 1866 to 1870, *DeWitt's Base Ball Guide* from 1869 to 1880, and *Spalding's Base Ball Guide* from 1881 until his death in 1908. Chadwick authored *The Game of Base Ball* (1868), the first hardback book devoted exclusively to baseball, and other books and pamphlets on hitting, fielding, base running, baseball language, and other topics. He chaired the Rules Committee of both the National Association of Base Ball Players (1858 to 1870) and the National League, writing numerous rule changes. Box scores were perfected and a scoring system devised, allowing reporters to describe games in greater depth. National League rules were instituted against gambling, excessive drinking, and rowdy behavior by players and fans alike. The National Baseball Hall of Fame enshrined Chadwick in 1938.

Harry Wright, a native of Sheffield, England, fathered professional baseball and paved the way for the first professional league. He came to Staten Island, New York as an infant when his father, Samuel, joined the St. George Cricket Club. Although originally a cricket player, Harry joined the amateur New York Knickerbockers as an outfielder in 1857 and organized the Cincinnati Base Ball Club in 1866. Wright, who managed and played center field for the Red Stockings, quit playing cricket when Cincinnati paid him a commensurate salary and authorized him to recruit the first openly paid team. These professionals, wearing knickers designed by Wright, won the Midwestern championship in 1868. In 1869 Harry signed

David L. Porter *is Shangle Professor of History at William Penn College in Iowa and editor of the multi-volume* Biographical Dictionary of American Sports *published by Greenwood Press.*

his brother, George, a superb hitting and fielding short-stop. The legendary 1869 Red Stockings finished undefeated on a 66 game national tour from Boston to San Francisco, spreading the popularity of baseball. The Cincinnati club disbanded after the 1870 season, but triggered the simultaneous formation of the National Association. Wright piloted the Boston Red Stockings of the National Association to 225 wins and 60 losses from 1871 to 1875, capturing titles the final four campaigns. In 1874, he sponsored baseball's first tour of his native England. When the National League began in 1876, the Boston Red Caps retained Wright as manager and won titles in 1877 and 1878. Wright piloted the Providence Grays in 1882 and 1883 and the Philadelphia Phillies from 1884 to 1893. In 18 National League seasons, his team recorded 1,042 victories and lost 848 contests. Wright, an early-day Connie Mack, demonstrated integrity, fairness, and firmness as a pilot and was elected to the National Baseball Hall of Fame in 1953.

Alfred Reach, who was born in London, England, contributed to the development of baseball as a player, executive, and sporting goods magnate. He grew up in Brooklyn, New York and entered baseball in 1855 with the newly-formed Eckford team. In 1865, Reach became the first paid baseball player upon joining the Philadelphia Athletics at a $25-a-week salary. The left-hander played mainly second base for the Athletics from 1865 to 1875, batting .252 overall during the last five seasons in the National Association. In 1871, his stellar .348 batting average helped Philadelphia garner the first National Association crown. Under Reach as manager, Philadelphia compiled 33-23 and 53-20 win-loss marks in 1874 and 1875, respectively. In 1883, Reach organized and helped finance the new Philadelphia Phillies National League club. He served as Phillies team president from 1883 to 1902 and later partly owned the Philadelphia Athletics American League team. His A. J. Reach & Company, a large sporting goods firm founded in the 1870s, made him a multi-millionaire. Reach's company manufactured baseballs, using a machine he developed to wind them more tightly. In 1893 he began publishing *Reach's Official Base Ball Guide*, which encouraged fan interest in baseball records and statistics. Six years later, the Spalding Sporting Goods Company purchased Reach's business. Reach held an executive position at the Spalding firm until 1892 and worked as an ambassador for baseball until his death in 1928. He served in 1907 and 1908 on the National Commission, whose questionable findings on the American origins of baseball enabled the infant sport to secure its recognized position as the national pastime.

Tom Connolly, originally from Manchester in England, became dean of American League arbiters. Connolly migrated in 1885 at age 15 to Natick, Massachusetts, where he served as batboy for a local baseball team. The baseball rule book fascinated him, and he soon became the nation's leading authority on the subject. Connolly um-

Harry Wright

pired National League games from 1898 to 1900, but quit when president Nicholas Young failed to defend his rulings. The upstart American League hired Connolly in 1901 as umpire for its inaugural campaign. Connolly officiated the first American League game ever played (a Cleveland Blues-Chicago White Sox contest at Comiskey Park), the initial junior circuit contests at Shibe Park in Philadelphia and Fenway Park in Boston, and the first modern World Series game in 1903 between Boston's Pilgrims and Pittsburgh's Pirates. He also umpired seven other Fall Classics, ranking among the finest all-time major league umpires. Players respected the fairness and patience of Connolly, who once went a full decade without ejecting a ballplayer. In 1931, new American League president Will Harridge designated Connolly the first American League umpire-in-chief. Based in Chicago, Connolly evaluated and advised umpires, scouted the minor leagues for umpiring talent, and advised Harridge on playing rules until retiring in 1954. Thereafter, he served on the league's Rules Committee until his death in 1961. In 1953, he and National Leaguer Bill Klem were the first umpires named to the National Baseball Hall of Fame in Cooperstown.

Outfielders George Hall and Tom Brown, catcher Harry Smith, and infielder Dave Brain also all hailed from the British Isles. Hall, a journeyman who left a mixed impact on baseball history, hit .309 in the National Association from 1871 through 1875, and .345 in the National

League during the next two seasons. His best performance came with the Philadelphia A's in 1876, when he batted .366 and became the senior circuit's first home run king with five. In 1877, Hall figured prominently in baseball's biggest nineteenth-century scandal as a member of the Louisville Grays. Louisville had led the National League for most of the 1877 season, but then lost several crucial road games in suspicious ways. Gamblers had bribed four Louisville players, including Hall, to lose key games, prompting National League President William Hulbert to banish them permanently. Brown, a native of Liverpool, batted .265 with nearly 2,000 hits spanning 17 seasons from 1882 to 1898 in the American Association, National League, and Players League. With the Boston Reds in 1891, Brown batted a career-high .321 and led the American Association in runs scored (177), hits (189), triples (21), and stolen bases (106). The fleet-footed Brown covered much ground defensively and stole 657 career bases, including a National League leading 66 for the Louisville Colonels in 1893. Smith, from Yorkshire, England, a light-hitting reserve National League catcher from 1902 to 1910 and a practical joker, was the first European-born player to appear in a modern World Series as a member of the 1903 Pittsburgh Pirates. Brain came originally from Hereford, England, and batted .252 as a third baseman and shortstop with six major league clubs from 1901 to 1908. The inconsistent-hitting, erratic-fielding Brain demonstrated impressive power, slugging 15 triples for the 1903 St. Louis Cardinals and leading the National League with ten home runs in 1907 for the Boston Braves. His career featured 97 doubles, 52 triples, 27 home runs, and 303 RBIs.

Irishmen contributed just as much as Englishmen to the early development of American baseball. Pitcher Tony Mullane, an ambidextrous athlete from Cork, Ireland, headed an illustrious group of Irish-born major leaguers. Although mainly a right-handed hurler, he could pitch, field and throw with either hand. His best performance came in the American Association from 1882 to 1884 and 1886 to 1888. Mullane recorded five consecutive 30-victory seasons from 1882 to 1887, highlighted by a brilliant 35-15 mark with the St. Louis Browns in 1883. In 1884, the free-spirited pitcher, already under contract with the Browns, violated the reserve clause by signing contracts with both the St. Louis Maroons of the Union Association and the Toledo Blue Stockings of the American Association. The American Association suspended Mullane for the entire 1885 season when he refused to return to the St. Louis Browns. The remainder of his career was spent mainly with the Cincinnati Red Stockings of the American Association. His impressive 13-year major league career from 1881 to 1894 included 284 wins, 220 losses, a 3.05 ERA, and 1,803 strikeouts in over 4,500 innings pitched. Mullane's 30 shutouts included the first American Association no-hitter, a 2-0 masterpiece for Louisville against Cincinnati in

Tony Mullane

September 1882. He twice led the American Association in shutouts (1884, 1887) and once each in games started (1882), strikeouts (1882), and winning percentage (1883). A .243 lifetime batter, Mullane played every defensive position except catcher. He epitomized the nineteenth century baseball hero with his flair, independence, and all-around athletic ability. The popular hurler, nicknamed "The Count" for his colorful attire, sported a handle-bar mustache and married several times.

Pitcher Tommy Bond from Granard, Ireland, compiled a 193-115 win-loss record and 2.25 ERA in ten major league seasons between 1874 and 1884 and remains the only major leaguer since 1876 to win at least 40 games three consecutive seasons. Wildness plagued Bond as a rookie with the Brooklyn Atlantics of the American Association in 1874, but then Candy Cummings taught him how to throw a curve ball. Bond won 31 of 44 decisions for the Hartford Charter Oaks of the newly-formed National League in 1876, registering a career-best 1.56 ERA.

Before the 1877 season, the Boston Red Stockings signed him to replace ace pitcher Albert Spalding. Bond toiled over 500 innings each of the next three campaigns, helping Boston capture National League pennants in 1877 and 1878 and finish second in 1879. During that span, he led the National League three times in shutouts, twice each in wins, winning percentage, strikeouts, and ERA, and once each in appearances and complete games. In 1877, Bond became the first major league pitcher to pace a major league in victories (40), strikeouts (170), and ERA (2.11) in the same season. National League statistics also list him with the best winning percentage (.702) and most shutouts (6) that year. The 1878 campaign featured Bond repeating as league leader in victories (40), winning percentage (.678), shutouts (9), and strikeouts (182). In 1879, he recorded a career-high 43 triumphs, paced the National League in ERA (1.96), and hurled twelve of the league's 42 shutouts. A sore arm forced Bond's initial retirement following the 1881 season. After managing Worcester in 1882 and umpiring in the New England League in 1882 and 1883, Bond attempted a comeback with Boston of the Union Association and Indianapolis of the American Association in 1884. He worked from 1891 to 1926 in the Boston City Assessor's Office and helped coach baseball at Harvard University, tutoring pitchers John Clarkson and Timothy Keefe.

Theodore Sullivan, originally from Country Clare, Ireland, excelled as a baseball league organizer and promoter from the late 1870s into the twentieth century. Sullivan in 1878 formed the Dubuque, Iowa Rabbits baseball club and signed Charles Comiskey to his first professional contract. In 1879 he organized the Northwestern League, perhaps the first minor league, to furnish steady competition for his club. The Northwestern League folded that July because Dubuque, led by ace pitcher Charles Radbourne, decimated all opponents. First baseman Comiskey learned from Sullivan how to play off the bag and stretch for throws. In 1883 Sullivan managed the St. Louis Browns of the American Association to a 53-26 win-loss mark and coined the term "fanatics" to describe people who bothered him constantly with opinions and suggestions about baseball. He acquired players for the 1884 Union Association and managed the St. Louis Maroons and Kansas City entries. Sullivan's subsequent activities included helping to organize and promote the first Western League, numerous Eastern and Southern Leagues, and several revivals of the Texas League. Besides being an excellent recruiter of young talent, he also introduced Ladies Day to increase attendance at games and attempted to play night games. Sullivan worked many years for Comiskey's Chicago White Sox American League club and directed Comiskey's White Sox-New York Giants World Tour after the 1913 season.

Jack Doyle, a native of Killorgin, Ireland, was one of only 20 major league players to have performed in at least 100 games at four different positions. Nicknamed "Dirty Jack," he played mainly as a first baseman and occasionally as a catcher, outfielder, and second baseman with ten major league clubs from 1889 to 1905. The lifetime .299 batter hit over .300 six seasons, including five consecutively with the New York Giants, Baltimore Orioles, and Washington Senators of the National League from 1893 to 1897. His best performance came in 1894, when he batted .367 in 105 games for the New York Giants. Doyle knocked in 924 career runs and in 1892 became the first major league pinch hitter, singling for the Giants. He briefly managed the 1895 Giants and 1898 Senators, piloted Milwaukee of the American Association in 1907, umpired in the Eastern League in 1910, National League and New England League in 1911, American Association in 1915, Pacific Coast League in 1916, and Three-I League in 1919, and scouted for the Cleveland Indians in 1913 and Chicago Cubs from 1920 until his death in 1958.

Jimmy Archer of Dublin, Ireland and Jimmy Walsh of Kallila, Ireland were two of only three European-born players to appear in more than one World Series. Archer ranked among the best throwing major league catchers of the early 1900s. Hot tar had burned his right arm severely in an industrial accident. The muscles shortened and strengthened during the healing process, enabling him to throw out baserunners attempting to steal from a squat position. Archer batted .249 lifetime, spending most of his twelve major league seasons between 1904 and 1918 with the Chicago Cubs. In 1912, he led National League catchers in assists and achieved career-highs in batting average (.283), hits (109), doubles (20), home runs (5), and RBIs (58). Archer performed in the 1907 World Series for the Detroit Tigers and 1910 World Series for the Cubs. Walsh, a reserve infielder, batted .333 for the Philadelphia Athletics in the 1914 World Series and appeared briefly for the Boston Red Sox in the 1916 fall classic. The fleet-footed .232 lifetime hitter spent six seasons in the major leagues, mostly with Philadelphia, and twice scored from second base in the same game when Eddie Collins placed squeeze bunts beyond pitcher Walter Johnson of the Washington Senators.

Andrew Jackson Leonard, originally from County Cavan, Ireland, played outfield with several charter clubs. He participated on the legendary 1869 Cincinnati Red Stockings, the initial openly all-professional team, and for the 1871 Washington Olympics of the National Association, the first professional league. A July 1871 game featured Leonard scoring three runs in one inning against the Ft. Wayne Kekiongas. Leonard batted over .300 for the Boston Red Stockings each season from 1872 to 1875, helping them capture four consecutive National Association pennants. His .341 career-high batting average came in 1872. He also was a charter member of the National League, performing for the Boston Red Stockings from 1876 to 1878. Boston captured National League pennants in 1877 and 1878. Failing vision forced

Leonard's retirement in 1880 after brief stints with Rochester and the American Association Cincinnati Red Stockings. Other Irish-born major league players included journeyman shortstop-outfielder Jimmy Hallinan in the 1870s, second baseman Reddy Mack during the late 1880s, and light-hitting catcher Jack O'Neill from 1902 to 1906.

Wales produced noteworthy major leaguers Edward "Ted" Lewis and Jimmy Austin. Lewis, a right-handed pitcher born in Machynlleth, Wales, compiled an impressive 94-64 record and 3.53 ERA in six major league seasons from 1896 to 1901. The 1896 Princeton graduate joined the starting rotation with Kid Nichols and Fred Klobedanz for the Boston Beaneaters in 1897 and won 21 of 33 decisions, helping his club win the National League pennant. His best season came in 1898 with a 26-8 record, as his .765 winning percentage paced the National League. Although compiling winning records in 1889 and 1900, Lewis contemplated retirement. Nicknamed "Parson," he earned a master's degree from Williams College in 1899 and was soon an ordained minister. Lewis pitched for the new Boston Pilgrims American League entry in 1901, hurling the club's first shutout ever, at Cleveland in May, and authoring a two-hitter in his final appearance. He retired following that season at age 29 and taught English at Columbia University, Williams College, and the University of Massachusetts. Lewis served as president of the University of Massachusetts in the 1926-1927 academic year and the University of New Hampshire from 1927 until his death in 1936.

Austin, of Swansea, Wales, ranked among the best American League defensive third basemen from 1909 to 1922, mostly with the St. Louis Browns. He led American League third basemen five times in total chances per game, four times in double plays, twice each in putouts and assists, and once in fielding percentage. The .246 lifetime batter walked frequently and stole 244 career bases. Austin, who managed the Browns briefly in 1913, 1918, and 1923, coached for the Browns from 1923 to 1932 and for the Chicago White Sox from 1933 to 1940. His greatest fame came as the fielder in a well-known picture showing Ty Cobb of the Detroit Tigers sliding into third base with spikes high.

Two Glasgow, Scotland, natives, pitcher Jim McCormick and outfielder Bobby Thomson, made stellar major league performances. McCormick, a burly right-handed pitcher hurled for six major league clubs from 1878 to 1887. He was the mainstay of the Cleveland staff from 1879 to 1884 and managed the Blues in 1879 and 1880. McCormick's pinnacle occurred in 1880, when he led National League pitchers in appearances (74), complete games (72), wins (45), and innings pitched (658) and finished second in strikeouts (260) and shutouts (7). Ten of his 28 losses that season resulted when the Blues were held scoreless. In 1882, McCormick paced the National League in victories (36), appearances (68), in-

nings pitched (596), and, for the third consecutive campaign, complete games (65) with Cleveland. His estimated 1.84 ERA and .700 winning percentage topped the National League in 1883. McCormick and two Cleveland teammates defected for Cincinnati of the Union Association during the 1884 season. At Cincinnati, McCormick won 21 of 24 decisions and led the Union Association in both ERA (1.54) and shutouts (7). He helped the Chicago White Stockings capture National League pennants in 1885 with a 20-4 slate and in 1886 with a 31-11 mark, but was sold to the Pittsburgh Allegheny club for violating regulations against drinking. In 494 career games, McCormick completed 466 contests, amassed 265 victories, struck out 1,704 batters in 4,275.2 innings, hurled 33 shutouts, and registered a 2.43 ERA. Besides triumphing at least 40 times twice, he won 20 or more games each season from 1879 to 1886. McCormick's teams unfortunately scored no runs in 43 of his 214 career losses.

Bobby Thomson gained more notoriety than any other European-born major leaguer, hitting the most dramatic home run in baseball history. The youngest of six children of a Scottish professional soldier, he had emigrated with his family at age 2 to Staten Island, New York. The 6 foot 2 inch, 180 pounder with deceptively fast, loping strides was the New York Giants regular center fielder from 1947 to 1953. Thomson's bat produced over 100 RBI four seasons between 1949 and 1953 and 24 or more home runs in six of his seven full campaigns with the Giants. His greatest acclaim occurred in the 1951 National League playoffs, when he hit the dramatic ninth-inning, pennant-winning three run homer off Ralph Branca of the Brooklyn Dodgers. Often forgotten is that Thomson also belted a two-out, two-run roundtripper off Branca in the fourth inning of the first playoff game, enabling the Giants to triumph, 3-1. In 1952 his grand slam home run with two outs in the bottom of the ninth inning gave the Giants a 7-6 victory over the St. Louis Cardinals. New York traded Thomson in February 1954 to the Milwaukee Braves for pitcher Johnny Antonelli, who helped the Giants take the 1954 National League pennant. Thomson broke an ankle in spring training camp in 1954 and never regained his earlier effectiveness. In 1969 he was named to the Giants all-time outfield with superstars Mel Ott and Willie Mays. A lack of intensity prevented Thomson, an excellent low ball hitter, from achieving superstar status. His productive career resulted in a .270 batting average, 1,026 RBIs, 267 doubles, and 264 home runs in 1,779 games.

German-born figures also influenced the early development of American baseball. Christian von der Ahe, originally from Hille, Germany, gained notoriety as the most flamboyant nineteenth century baseball team owner. The St. Louis saloon keeper knew very little about baseball. In 1882 he helped found the American Association, which rivalled the established National League through 1891. Von der Ahe owned the St. Louis Browns and selected Charles Comiskey as manager in 1883. St. Louis easily captured four straight American Association titles from 1885 to 1888 and defeated the Chicago White Stockings in the 1886 World Series. Von der Ahe, who earned around $75,000 annually during the 1880s, loved lavish ceremony and treated his players and fans regally. His players often took open carriages to home games at Sportsman's Park. Von der Ahe ceremoniously transported game receipts each day to a bank in a wheelbarrow, flanked by armed guards, and introduced hot dogs to ballpark concession stands. He also spent sizeable sums taking St. Louis fans to road World Series games against Chicago in 1885 and 1886 and the Detroit Wolverines in 1887. The Browns traded several stars and lost others to the Players' League in 1890, languishing in the second division of the twelve-team National League from 1892 to 1898. The early day Bill Veeck installed merry-go-rounds, beer gardens, artificial lakes, and other attractions in Sportsman's Park and used numerous promotions and publicity gimmicks to attract spectators. Personal and business reversals forced the spendthrift von der Ahe to sell the Browns in 1898 to attorney G. A. Gruner, who represented Frank and Stanley Robison.

Right-handed pitcher Charlie Getzien was the best German-born major league player, compiling a 145-139 win-loss mark, three 20-game-victory seasons, and a 3.46 ERA in the National League from 1884 through 1892. He struggled with the Detroit Wolverines in 1884 and 1885, but sculpted a superb 30-11 slate in 1886. Detroit, which had purchased superstars Dan Brouthers, Hardy Richardson, Jack Rowe, and Jim White from Buffalo, led Chicago for most of the 1886 campaign before fading down the stretch. In 1887, Getzien's stellar 29-13 record helped Detroit capture its only National League pennant. Getzien pitched brilliantly with his curve ball during the last half of the 1887 campaign, and gave his club an undisputed lead with a 5-3 victory over Chicago on August 16. He led the National League with a .690 winning percentage and posted four of the Wolverines' ten victories in the 15-game touring World Series against the St. Louis Browns of the American Association. His performances included a 2-1 13-inning victory in dramatic game three and a 9-0 shutout in his next contest. Getzien enjoyed only one winning season thereafter, compiling a 23-17 record and a ten-game winning streak in July for the 1890 Beaneaters. Nicknamed "The Pretzel Twirler," he finished his major league career with the beleaguered St. Louis Browns. Other German-born major league players included journeyman third baseman Willie Kuehne in the

Bobby Thomson

1880s and first baseman Heinz Becker, who appeared briefly for the Chicago Cubs in the 1945 World Series.

Two Eastern European natives made significant impacts on major league baseball history. Elmer Valo, originally from Ribnik, Czechoslovakia, appeared in three decades in the major leagues, mostly with the Philadelphia Athletics. After joining the Athletics in 1939, he walked as a pinch hitter in the season's final game. His name, however, did not appear in the official scorebook because he had not yet signed a major league contract. Valo started in the outfield for Philadelphia in 1942 and hit .307 upon his return from military service in 1946. A left-handed line drive hitter, he batted .300 or better in five of his twenty major league seasons and attained a career-high .364 average as a part-time player in 1955. Valo belted two bases-loaded triples on May 1, 1949 against the Washington Senators at Philadelphia and hit a single, double, triple, and home run on August 2, 1950 against the White Sox at Chicago. Defensively, he chased fly balls with reckless abandon and frequently crashed into fences. Three of his teams shifted franchises. Valo accompanied the Philadelphia Athletics to Kansas City in 1955, the Brooklyn Dodgers to Los Angeles in 1958, and the Washington Senators to Minnesota in 1961. No other major leaguer performed on two separate major league teams with 20-game winless streaks. His 1943 Athletics lost 20 consecutive contests, while his 1961 Philadelphia Phillies suffered 23 straight defeats. Valo blossomed into an outstanding pinch hitter in the twilight of his career, walking a record 91 times. In 1960 for the New York Yankees and Washington Senators, he set major league records for most games (81), walks (18), and times reaching first base (33) by a pinch hitter in a single season. His .282 lifetime batting average included 90 pinch hits, among the major league best. Valo coached for the Cleveland Indians in 1963 and 1964 and later served as a hitting instructor and scout for the Philadelphia Phillies.

Moe Drabowsky, a right-handed pitcher born in Ozanna, Poland, logged seventeen major league seasons with seven teams from 1956 to 1972. In 1956, the Chicago Cubs paid a $50,000 bonus to sign the Trinity College (Connecticut) ace. Drabowsky wielded an impressive 2.47 ERA as a rookie with Chicago that year, but demonstrated considerable wildness. In 1957 he struck out a career-high 170 batters, second best among National League hurlers, while amassing a 13-15 record for a seventh-place club. The same season, Drabowsky led the National League in hit batsmen (10) and tied a major league mark by beaning four Cincinnati Reds batters in a June 2 contest. A sore arm, suffered in 1958, limited his effectiveness the next seven seasons. Drabowsky in 1958 surrendered Stan Musial's 3,000th career hit and in 1963 was the losing pitcher when Early Wynn recorded his 300th major league victory. In 1966 Drabowsky's situation dramatically improved with the Baltimore Orioles, as he

won all six decisions, saved seven games, and sported a 2.81 ERA. In game one of the 1966 World Series against the Los Angeles Dodgers, Moe relieved Dave McNally with one out and the bases loaded in the third inning and yielded only one hit the remaining 6.2 innings to win the contest. His eleven total strikeouts included six in succession, a fall classic record. Drabowsky won his first twelve decisions as an Oriole and authored impressive 1.60 and 1.91 ERAs in 1967 and 1968, respectively. In 1969, he led the American League with 11 relief victories for the expansion Kansas City Royals and saved 11 other contests. After returning to the Orioles in June, 1970, Drabowsky posted a 4-2 slate with three saves and made two clutch relief appearances against Cincinnati in the World Series. Altogether, he registered an 88-105 win-loss mark and 3.71 ERA with 55 saves. The noted prankster once was rolled to first base in a wheelchair after being hit by a pitch and loved to rearrange the hand-operated scoreboard at Boston's Fenway Park, often pairing American League teams against National League clubs. In 1987, he returned to his native land to help Poland establish its first Olympic baseball team.

Few major league players were born in other European countries. Otto Hess, a native of Berne, Switzerland, pitched ten seasons with the Cleveland Naps and Boston Braves between 1902 and 1915. The erratic left-hander won only 70 of 160 decisions with a 2.98 ERA and appeared on the Braves roster in the 1914 World Series. His landmark season came in 1906 with a 20-17 record for Cleveland. Other major league players born on the European continent included Norwegian Arndt Jorgens, a reserve catcher behind Bill Dickey for the formidable New York Yankees of the 1930s, Italian Mario Pieretti, a relief pitcher in the late 1940s, and Italian Reno Bertoia, a reserve infielder in the 1950s.

In conclusion, European-born figures contributed to the development of American baseball in various ways. Henry Chadwick, Harry Wright, Alfred Reach, Theodore Sullivan, and Christian von der Ahe played key formative roles in organizing, promoting, and popularizing professional baseball as the national pastime, while Tom Connolly ranked among the all-time greatest major league umpires. Tony Mullane, Tommy Bond, Jim McCormick, Charlie Getzien, and Ted Lewis improved the calibre of pitching in major league baseball's formative years. Jack Doyle, Andrew Leonard, Tom Brown, and Elmer Valo proved skilled batsmen, while George Hall, Dave Brain, and Bobby Thomson exhibited impressive power at the plate. Jimmy Archer, Jimmy Austin, and other European-born players excelled defensively. Above all, European-born players performed well in crucial situations and provided baseball fans with memorable moments. The legendary heroics of Bobby Thomson and the sparkling 1966 World Series performance of Moe Drabowsky remain indelibly etched in baseball annals.

Forty years of Western-Hemisphere competition

Baseball in the Pan American Games

Mark Springer

Buenos Aires, February 27-March 8, 1951
An enthusiastic but somewhat undermanned group, composed mainly of Wake Forest University underclassmen, represented the United States baseballers at the inaugural Pan American Games in Buenos Aires, Argentina. The onset of World War II had postponed the planned games for nine years, yet the dream of intra-hemisphere competitions had finally become a reality. This inaugural version of the Pan Am Games was almost wiped out as well, however, not by man's wars but by Mother Nature's winds. A violent windstorm caused so much overnight damage to facilities and equipment that, although Opening Ceremonies went off as planned, the Games themselves had to be postponed a full day for repairs—not a very auspicious beginning!

The U.S. baseball team gathered in Argentina in 1951 was not at all the "all-star" squad that we normally equate with our international competitions. America was at the time deeply involved in yet another resource-draining military venture—the so-called Korean Conflict. Selection of athletes was thus hampered by the large number of young men again entering military service, and the selections committee ruled that it was truly impossible to elect a representative team from the nation's various amateur baseball organizations. However, an invitation was extended to Wake Forest, with its strong collegiate baseball program, and the Demon Deacon squad accepted.

Under the guidance of their coach, Taylor Sanford, the young Deacons (of the dozen ballplayers on the squad,

Mark Springer *is manager of communications with the Athletics Congress of the United States and a freelance writer who briefly appeared on camera as a player for the 1919 Cincinnati Reds in the movie* "Eight Men Out".

seven were sophomores with no previous experience at the varsity level) acquitted themselves nicely. They finished in a second-place tie with Mexico—both teams at 5-2—behind powerhouse Cuba, which earned the gold medal prize with a 6-1 overall record in round-robin competition. This established a pattern for future Pan American baseball play: Cuba as champions; the Americans as respectable also-rans.

In the ten days of competition, the U.S. squad pounded out victories over Argentina (who may have been weeping for themselves following an opening day 29-3 drubbing), Brazil (by an equally lopsided 23-4 count), Colombia (7-5), Venezuela (8-5) and Mexico (9-3). The American team soon enough lost a heartbreaker to Nicaragua, however, by a tight 9-8 count, then fell as well to the powerful Cubans, 8-1.

Fatigue may have played a role in the Americans' showing. With only eight position players and four pitchers on the roster, the young Deacons battled teams which, for the most part, enjoyed a full contingent of 20 players—with the next smallest rival squad consisting of 17 players. And, speaking of "bad breaks", Coach Sanford related the following in his post-game report:

> The U.S. got a very tough break in the opening game with Argentina when catcher Alton Brooks fractured his right thumb and had to retire from further competition. This necessitated moving the third baseman, Jack Liptak, to catcher, a position he had never played before, shifting Kent Rogers from center field to third base, and sending one of the extra pitchers into the outfield. This was the way the lineup ran the remaining six games. The fact that the U.S. players were

able to practice outdoors only three days prior to competing in the first international game meant that the team was handicapped in its training as compared with all its rivals, which had been playing baseball uninterrupted for at least two months.

In USOC General Manager J. Lyman Bingham's overall report following the Games, the leading U.S. official addressed the following concerns: "The teams and officials did very little complaining, but one of the justifiable complaints involved mosquitos. They were very bothersome during the night but fortunately were not of the disease-carrying type."

It appears obvious that the American baseball team was doing its share of swatting both on and off the field. Two of Coach Sanford's sophomores, in particular, must have gathered that the "buzzword" was hitting. Frank Wehner of College Point, New York, smacked 14 hits in 30 at-bats for a robust .467 average. Three of his projectiles left the park in fair territory. Jack Liptak of Bridgeport, Connecticut, was only a fraction behind, slugging out 12 safeties in 26 plate appearances (a .462 BA); Liptak also led the team with 12 RBI. Senior leadership was provided by Wiley Warren of Roanoke Rapids, North Carolina, who stroked the ball at an even .400 clip. Sophomore pitchers Stanley Johnson (Greensboro, North Carolina) and Don Woodlief (Wake Forest, North Carolina) were both perfect at 2-0 on the hill.

Pan Am baseball played to SRO crowds in Buenos Aires as average turnouts of 4,000-5,000 arrived for the contests—with some 8,000 showing up for the crucial USA-Cuba tilt (the second-to-last game for the American squad). The tiny stadium seated only about 2,000—the rest of the partisans were forced to stand ringed around the foul lines.

Mexico City, March 12-26, 1955

The 1955 U.S. baseball team that competed in the Pan American Games in Mexico City was staffed with 18 players—with representation from the Armed Services, the U.S. Amateur Baseball Federation, the American Baseball Congress, and even the collegiate ranks once again.

Even though the roster numbers were greater for this edition of the Games, the "team" wasn't a team in the truest sense of the word, for they had only assembled together as a unit when they arrived in Mexico City a couple of days in advance of their opening contest. And to make matters worse, their bats didn't arrive until much later, forcing manager A.J. Lewandowski from the University of Nebraska to go out and buy some Mexican bats for the team to use for practice prior to the Games' start-up. One wonders if this forced team members to take a "Mexican Bat Stance" when approaching home plate!

The format again was a double round-robin tournament involving Mexico, the Dominican Republic,

Venezuela, Netherlands Antilles, and the U.S. Play was held in the 30,000-seat "Social Security Baseball Park" located in downtown Mexico City.

In the first round-robin, the improved U.S. squad scored victories over Mexico (5-1), the Dominican Republic (6-5) and the outmanned Netherlands Antilles (12-6), before falling to the favored Venezuela team by an embarrassing 8-2 count.

The American team, although hitting robustly, was continually hampered by poor fielding (they made four errors in the first inning against Venezuela, the miscues leading to four unearned runs). Several key members of the team were also apparently suffering from dysentery. And to make matters still worse, one of the USA's top pitchers, Carl Thomas from the University of Arizona, had yet to pitch an inning thanks to an ill-timed sore arm. Thomas did, however, pinch-hit in the game against Venezuela, smacking a ninth-inning home run for the only USA highlight of the contest.

The second round of play was not a good one for the USA team, which took a 5-1 lead into the eighth inning against Mexico in their first game and saw it evaporate, "aided" by three errors. In all, Mexico scored eleven times in that disastrous frame and—hold on to your popcorn—ten of those came with two outs! The Mexicans went on to seal a demoralizing 12-5 victory over the young Yanks, who had outhit the Mexicans 13-8 in the contest, but to no avail as the USA led in the error tally as well, 5-0.

The Dominican Republic also paid back a first round loss by besting the Americans 10-6, with the losers again committing three costly errors. The bleeding stopped against Netherlands Antilles. Finally healthy, the USA squad pounded out 28 hits in a 27-6 pasting of their lesser opponents. Pitcher Bill Cary of Rollins College went the distance, allowing only eight scratch base hits.

The eighth and final game of the Series was against Venezuela, which had started the USA three-game losing skid. It was a must game for the North Americans if they entertained any hopes for a second place finish and medal. Cue the "Rocky" music. For the first time Carl Thomas was able to pitch—and did he ever! Thomas took a no-hitter into the seventh inning before tiring. Then the sore-armed ace handed matters over to Paul Ebert who closed things out for a 13-2 USA win. Thomas was a talented hurler whose entire career would be plagued with misfortune—the tall righthander from Minneapolis would lose his only major league appearance for the Cleveland Indians in 1960.

It was a gutty performance and a well-deserved silver medal for the USA team, which at 5-3, finished a mere game off the pace of the surprise gold medal contingent from the Dominican Republic. The Dominicans had lost but once to the USA in the opening round and again to the Mexicans in round two; Venezuela defeated Mexico for the third place bronze medal in the exceptionally well-balanced tournament finale.

Overall, the United States baseball team had dominated in most offensive categories, yet it had shot itself in the spikes on numerous occasions with 27 errors in but eight games. Afterwards team manager Lewandowski and coach John Kobs reported on the fine quality of the competition, saying that the opposing squads compared favorably with top-level college teams. Lewandowski: "It is true they do not have the same long distance hitting power, nevertheless, they would make up this difference in good defense, fine speed, and better than average pitching. Most of the pitchers we faced were primarily curve-ballers. Very few had real fastballs, and their reliance was primarily on control and an assortment of different pitches. It was a common practice for their pitchers to throw as many as eight curve balls in a row and from different deliveries, such as overhand, sidearm, and even underhand." It was obvious that the U.S. team was being graded on a curve; it was a lesson they would have to learn to advance to the next plateau.

Chicago, August 27-September 7, 1959

For the first time in its fledgling history, the Pan American Games were being conducted in the United States—and in one of the hotbeds of American baseball—Chicago. But by the time the 1959 Pan Am Games were concluded, America's baseball fans were undoubtedly wondering just whose "national pastime" this was, anyway.

After two silver medal finishes at the first and second Pan American Games, the 1959 U.S. team, made up primarily of collegiate athletes, took a step in the wrong direction, placing a disappointing third in action at Comiskey Park. Nine teams were involved in this the third edition of the Games, prompting a two-group tournament, with the top two finishers from each group advancing to the medal round.

The U.S. team, managed by John Kobs, started strong. In the first group, the U.S., Venezuela and Mexico all finished with 3-1 marks (Costa Rica at 1-3 and Brazil at 0-4 finished play at fourth and fifth), prompting a playoff for the two advancing spots. Venezuela drew a bye and the U.S. beat Mexico, 7-5, to advance. Qualifying from the second group was Puerto Rico at 3-0, and Cuba at 2-1. Defending PAG champion, the Dominican Republic, was ousted at 1-2, and Nicaragua was 0-3.

In the Championships round, the U.S. lost its opener to Venezuela, 11-6, before reeling off three consecutive wins against Mexico (2-1), Brazil (9-2) and Costa Rica (28-0). In the final round of play, Venezuela took the measure of Cuba (6-2), the U.S. (3-2) and Puerto Rico (6-2) for the gold. The U.S. finished this round at 1-2 (also losing to Puerto Rico, 9-5, and beating Cuba 3-2) for third place. Venezuela, which lost only once throughout the tournament, finished the Championship round 3-0, followed by Puerto Rico at 2-1.

Incidentally, a young outfielder who was the Southwest Conference batting champion hit a measly .100 (1 for 10) for the United States. The kid's name was Lou Brock.

Sao Paulo, April 20-May 5, 1963

Let's skip past 1963 pretty quickly, because there's better times ahead. This was a competition that saw the U.S. begin its climb back toward respectability with a silver medal showing, finishing behind Cuba, which won its first Pan American gold since the inaugural games.

Again, the U.S. squad was a mix of military and collegiate athletes, managed by Captain Wendell Lawrence of the U.S. Air Force. The Americans compiled a 5-3 record, behind Cuba's 7-1 showing. Mexico jumped in for the bronze with a 4-4 mark.

It was not an auspicious start for the Stars and Stripes, losing 13-1 to Cuba in the first game. U.S. victories were scored against Mexico (5-3), Venezuela (a 5-4 thriller in ten innings), and Brazil (13-3) before the team fell again to Cuba by a 3-1 score. Back on the plus side, the U.S. slipped past Mexico 4-3 and Venezuela (4-1) before succumbing to Brazil, 4-3. Now, on to 1967!

Winnipeg, July 23-August 6, 1967

It was the last gold medal awarded at the 1967 Pan American Games amidst a harvest of golds for the United States, but it was also the first for victory-starved U.S. baseball interests. And, for devotees of our national pastime, it may have been the most important.

It was a breakthrough year for U.S. baseball in Pan American competition—a gold medal secured in dramatic fashion against arch-rival Cuba. To complete the storybook finish, it was a relative unknown, the University of Connecticut's George Greer, who propelled the U.S. to gold with some late heroics in the final game of the playoffs.

The Championship round came down to a three-game playoff between the U.S. and Cuba, the series and Game Three were both knotted at 1-1. To heighten the drama, the decisive ninth inning was delayed, and the game almost washed out, by a sudden rainshower just as the USA was coming to bat. Cuba's ace, Manuel Alarcon, was pitching masterfully. But a walk, sacrifice bunt, walk and a single loaded the bases for Greer. He ended the drama abruptly, lacing Alarcon's first pitch into right field to score teammate Ray Blosse and hand the U.S. its first gold medal triumph.

The victory was even sweeter when one considers that Cuba had already beaten the U.S. – in the double round-robin schedule before they once more faced each other in the Championship round. Those 4-3 and 9-1 setbacks were the only ones suffered by the U.S. in round-robin play. After an opening tournament loss to Cuba, coach Martin (Ohio State) Karow's team bettered Mexico,

Puerto Rico and Canada by scores of 4-1, 8-3, and 14-0, before falling again to Cuba. The U.S. then disassembled the other three countries again by scores of 6-3 over Mexico, 7-3 over Puerto Rico, and 14-2 over Canada to finish with a 6-2 won-loss record. The Cubans topped out at 7-1, having been beaten once by Canada, 10-9. Ironically, it was the host country's only victory in the baseball competition.

This set up a three-game playoff for the gold. The USA took the early advantage—and gained some needed confidence—with a 8-3 win in Game One. Cuba rebounded with a 8-3 victory in Game Two to set the stage for Greer's Game Three heroics.

The U.S. triumph may be credited, in part, to an "attitude adjustment" by this team—and their overall approach to the Games. The 18-man squad, composed of 16 college undergrads and two U.S. Army officers, assembled in late June at Minneapolis and trained together vigorously prior to their departure for Winnipeg. The 1967 gold medal was truly a team effort.

Steve Sogge from Gardena, California, a compact 5-10, 182-pound catcher from USC, led U.S. hitters with a sterling .386 batting average, and the hero, Greer, a solid 6-3, 188-pounder, followed him with a .355 average. Incidentally, another player on the roster, Mark Marquess, was a future Stanford and Olympic baseball coach.

Cali, July 30-August 13, 1971

Cuba returned to the fore with a gold medal in the baseball competition at the 1971 Pan American Games. Perhaps still smarting from their loss to the USA in Winnipeg, Cuba roared through the nine-country round-robin competition with an unblemished 8-0 mark.

The U.S. accepted its usual silver with a respectable 6-2 standard. The American team of college undergraduates, coached by Arizona State's Bobby Winkles, took a very serious approach to these Games and the defense of the country's gold medal—playing 30 exhibition games before leaving for Colombia.

The crucial game for the U.S., which had opened play with wins over Nicaragua and Canada, was the third against Cuba. First baseman Jerry Tabb, left fielder Jerry Mims and center fielder Fred Lynn all hit home runs before an overflow crowd of 11,000 (in a section of Colombia where baseball was almost unknown). The U.S. led 2-0 in this contest until the fifth when Cuba knotted the score; errors led to two more Cuban tallies in the seventh. A ninth-inning U.S. rally could only plate one and Cuba came away with a 4-3 win. The only other U.S. loss would come at the hands of the Dominican Republic; victories also were scored against Colombia, Puerto Rico, Venezuela and Mexico.

Host Colombia finished with a surprising 4-4 record for the bronze medal. In addition to the silver, the U.S. also brought home some individual honors. Arizona State shortstop Alan Bannister was selected MVP of the tour-

nament. Joining Bannister on the All-Pan-Am team were pitcher Jay Smith, catcher Larry Calufetti, infielder Jeff Port and outfielder Lynn. The U.S. led all teams in home runs, and Lynn, with four, was the individual HR leader. Lynn also was the tournament's third leading batter with a .467 average.

Mexico City, October 12-26, 1975

For the fourth time, it was Cuba winning the gold at the Pan American Games. Cuba's strong suit was pitching, winning four games by shutouts. The U.S., which again captured the silver, saw their chances hampered by a disruption in their pitching rotation.

The U.S.-Dominican Republic contest, second on the round-robin schedule, was postponed due to rain and coach Hal (Florida Southern University) Smeltzly was forced to rearrange his pitching rotation. The game was played the following day and the U.S., owing in part to some crucial fielding errors, was unable to hold a 3-1 lead in the eighth inning, eventually losing 4-3.

Another come-from-behind 4-3 victory by Cuba in the USA's next-to-last game erased any hope for the gold. The final game against host Mexico would settle the question of the silver. With only one loss to date, Mexico could have vaulted into second place with a victory over the U.S. It was not to be, with the American's combination of pitching and hitting coming together for an 11-0 victory. Mexico then dropped its final contest to Cuba, 3-0.

A strong USA pitching corps headed by Bob Owchinko (Eastern Michigan), Steve Powers (Arizona), Pete Redfern (Southern Cal) and Rich Wortham (Texas) compiled the lowest ERA. The staff also included Scott Sanderson and Mike Scott. Top hitting performances were also turned in by third baseman Ron Hassey (Arizona), shortstop Wayne Krenchicki (Miami) and outfielder Steve Kemp (Southern Cal).

San Juan, July 1-15, 1979

The good news: at the 1979 Pan American Games in San Juan, Puerto Rico, the United States accumulated more gold medals (126) and more total medals (263) than any country in the history of the Games. The bad news: none of that treasure trove of medals was gathered by the U.S. baseball team—which was shut out in the medal count for the first time in eight Pan American Games.

The U.S., coached by the University of Arizona's Jerry Kindall, stockpiled one of its best pitching staffs ever, led by UCLA's Tim Leary, who had recently been the New York Mets' first-round selection in the '79 draft. The USA opened strong, with three consecutive wins, highlighted by superb hitting and dominant pitching. In the first contest, a 12-2 drubbing of the Bahamas, lefty Brian Snyder of Clemson tossed a two-hitter and fanned nine. Leary shut out Mexico, 18-0, on three hits in the next game. Arizona's Terry Francona, son of former major leaguer Tito Francona (and a future major leaguer himself) collected four hits to pace a 14-hit U.S. effort. Another future major leaguer, southpaw Craig Lefferts of Arizona, pitched a complete game, four-hit shutout against Canada. Indiana State's Greg Baker blasted his second homer of the Games, a grand slam, to ignite the 10-0 whitewashing.

A great pitchers' duel highlighted the next game against the Dominican Republic. Leary and Dominican ace Johnny Tavarez traded goose eggs for 8 innings. But in the ninth, Leary walked one batter and Enrique Cruz homered to end the game.

The U.S. rebounded to beat Venezuela, 7-2, but the wheels fell off with back-to-back losses to Cuba, 7-1, and Puerto Rico, 4-2, as the team fell out of gold medal contention. The U.S. squad finished play in fourth place with a 5-3 mark. The Dominican Republic and Puerto Rico, with records of 7-1 and 6-2, placed second and third, respectively, behind Cuba. Second baseman Mike Gallego of UCLA, an 18-year-old freshman, paced U.S. batters with a .423 average—fifth best of the Games. Francona was right behind with a .419 average.

Caracas, August 14-29, 1983

It was a case of highs and lows for the U.S. baseball team at the ninth Pan American Games. The team, under the tutelage of Fresno State's Bob Bennett, and featuring future major leaguers Jeff Ballard, Tim Belcher, Mark McGwire and B.J. Surhoff, cruised to a perfect 5-0 record in its first round-robin competition.

Falling like dominoes were the Dominican Republic (8-0), Canada (10-5), Nicaragua (9-5), Puerto Rico (11-2) and Brazil (17-6). The talented U.S. squad was apparently on a collision course—again—with Cuba, also 5-0 after its first round of play. The top three teams from each division advanced to the next round.

Three more U.S. wins (4-3 over Panama, 10-2 over Venezuela, and 11-2 over the Dominican Republic), and the showdown for the gold seemed imminent. Those were the highs—here come the lows! The U.S. squad fell to Nicaragua in an exact reversal of their earlier contest, 9-5. The Nicaraguans controlled the game from the outset, scoring six runs in the third (three coming on a bases-loaded triple off Stanford reliever Ballard). The score was 9-0 in the ninth, when the U.S. mounted a strong comeback, scoring five runs and leaving the bases loaded before succumbing.

Still, the U.S. had a chance for the gold with a win over Cuba in their final game. It was a classic contest through seven innings, with the U.S. leading 1-0 until the sixth, when Cuba scored twice, the second tally coming in on a passed ball. In the seventh, Cuban catcher Juan Castro knocked one out of the yard for a 3-1 lead, and they added five more in the eighth to break it open and seal the 8-1 victory—Cuba's fourth straight Pan Am title.

Nicaragua and the U.S. finished the playoff portion with identical 3-2 records, but Nicaragua was awarded the silver by virtue of its playoff win over the U.S. Coach Bennett bemoaned the loss to Nicaragua, saying "it kind of spoiled the tournament for us. We knew Cuba was a very, very tough team and we'd have to play them just right to beat them. But against Nicaragua we just weren't intense and tuned into the ballgame."

One player who tuned in for the whole competition was Southern Cal first sacker Mark McGwire, who slammed two home runs in the 10-2 playoff win against Venezuela, and totalled seven round trippers for the Games. Tim Belcher (Mt. Vernon Nazarene), the number one pick in the draft that year, struck out 13 in that contest.

Indianapolis, August 7-23, 1987

The U.S. baseball team was "back home again" in Indianapolis for the 1987 version of the Pan Am Games. Apparently, home-cooking agreed with the squad as the USA came very close to breaking the Cubans' four Games gold-medal winning streak.

In fact, the "Amazing Americans" of 1987 fell one game—or maybe just one starting pitcher—shy of the gold. Coach Ron Fraser's hammer was a pitcher named Cris Carpenter, who helped the U.S. cruise to an undefeated mark in the round-robin standings—handing Cuba their only setback and also beating Puerto Rico, Canada, Nicaragua, Aruba, Venezuela and Antilles.

Carpenter, in his first five relief appearances (16 innings) leading up to the gold medal game, didn't allow a run. He had given up only six hits and three walks while striking out 16. But he needed some help in the pen, and that was no longer available. The lack of quality starting pitching had forced Fraser to pull Gregg Olson from the bullpen and use him as a starter. This left all the closing chores to Carpenter, the St. Louis Cardinals first-round selection that year.

Coming into the gold medal contest on August 22, Carpenter had worked eight innings in the previous three days, including two innings the night before when Fraser had had to call upon him to seal a hotly-contested 7-6 win over Canada in the semifinals.

Carpenter was again called in during the sixth inning in the gold medal contest against Cuba—with the U.S. on top, 9-8. He threw BB's for two innings, retiring the Cubans in order on only 19 pitches (15 of them strikes!). But the innings finally took their toll in the eighth when Carpenter allowed two runs, and again in the ninth when he surrendered three more, to give the Cubans a 13-9 come-from-behind win for the gold. The U.S. settled for silver.

Havana, August 2-18, 1991

Perhaps looking ahead to Barcelona, the 1991 USA baseball squad, under the tutelage of coach Ron Polk of Mississippi State, slipped in the medal race at last year's Pan American Games in Havana, but it did qualify for the all-important Olympic Games berth.

After a dominating performance in the round-robin portion of the schedule, winning seven with the only blemish being a 3-2 loss to eventual champ, Cuba, the U.S. fell to Puerto Rico in the medal round, 7-1, then rebounded with a 15-inning squeaker over the Dominican Republic, 2-1, to capture the bronze. Ironically, the Americans had beaten both teams with relative ease in the round robin portion of the schedule. In fact, the Dominican Republic was the USA's first victim, falling 6-1 behind the complete-game pitching of Jeff Ware (Old Dominion). The USA rolled to two more easy wins—over Mexico (12-4) and Aruba (12-0), and undoubtedly anticipated more of the same against winless Netherlands Antilles.

It wasn't that easy. The USA trailed the fired-up Antilles squad, 4-3, with one out in the bottom of the ninth. Down two strikes, Jason Giambi fouled off four pitches before coaxing a walk. Chris Roberts, the USA's top power threat, ended the contest in dramatic fashion, pounding Edmond Martina's first pitch out of the yard for a USA 5-4 conquest.

A victory in the next game against Puerto Rico would guarantee the USA a place in the medal round and more importantly, perhaps, a trip to Barcelona in 1992. Lefty Jeff Granger pitched 7-2/3 innings, allowing only two unearned runs; Roberts hit another round-tripper (his third overall) and Jeffrey Hammonds smacked his first, as the USA rolled to a 10-3 victory.

Next up was the game with the highest marquee value—the USA vs. Cuba, perhaps a preview of the gold medal game? The more than 60,000 fans who squeezed into Estadio Latinoamericano were not disappointed. First sacker Lourdes Gurriel was the Cuban hitting dynamo, driving in a pair of runs with a double and homer. But U.S. baseball fans will forever remember "THE PLAY"—by Cuban shortstop German Mesa. And he certainly made a "mesa" the U.S. plans for gold! Trailing 3-2 in the top of the eighth, the USA mounted a comeback, loading the bases with nobody down and the meat of the lineup due up. Cuba's Omar Ajete struck out Giambi for the first out. Catcher Charles Johnson then tagged a pitch that seemed destined for center field—and at least a tie game. But Mesa made a diving stop and started a 6-4-3 twin killing that quelled the uprising.

The U.S. finished round-robin play with wins over Nicaragua (5-4) and Canada (9-5 in 11 innings) to set up a medal round showdown with Puerto Rico, and perhaps a rematch with Cuba. Puerto Rico had other plans, though, cruising to a 7-1 win that propelled it into the gold medal contest. The U.S. settled for the bronze medal game against the Dominicans.

Coach Polk said, "We're a little disappointed that we didn't get a chance to play Cuba for the gold, but I'm proud of our club. It's been a long summer. We did what we had to do and qualified for the Olympics. This club has nothing to hang its head about." So it's on to Barcelona! Where, ironically, Cuba will make its Olympic baseball debut after boycotting Olympic competition in 1984 and 1988.

Baseball's Latin Market

Milton Jamail

While players from Latin America are having an increasingly important impact on baseball in the United States, obstacles established by host governments and leagues to their signing, and a quota on the number of foreigners allowed to participate in U.S. professional baseball, limit the impact of the Latin market.

The Latin market, though it sounds like the name of a Hispanic grocery store, refers to the baseball industry's involvement in recruiting players from the Caribbean Basin and Mexico. All twenty-eight organizations are involved in Latin America (the first player signed to a Florida Marlin's contract was a sixteen year-old pitcher from the Dominican Republic, Clemente Nuñez) and all recognize its importance as a producer of players. Over twenty-five percent of all players signed to professional contracts in 1990 were from Latin America. Participation in the Latin market is no longer a luxury—these days, to not be active in the market is to concede an advantage to your competitor.

Why go to the Latin market?

"You go where the talent is," says Fred Claire, Executive Vice President of the Los Angeles Dodgers, one of the leading clubs in the Latin market. "It's not a case of 'why do we go there when the talent is here.' We are here because the talent is here and we are there because the talent is there. And so its really just in pursuit of talent."

Pat Gillick, General Manager of the Toronto Blue Jays, another pacesetting club in Latin America, echoes

Milton Jamail *is professor of Government at the University of Texas in Austin and a regular contributor on Latin American baseball topics for such publications as* USA Today Baseball Weekly *and* Baseball America.

Claire's remarks. "We just expect the Latin program to be a contributor. We have many phases of our program. We have the free agent draft and the professional draft in which we obtain some talent. We hope that all three of those areas feed our minor league system. We are not looking for anything dramatic out of the Latin American countries, we are just looking for a contribution."

Serious involvement in the Latin market requires a long range commitment. An organization must build the physical infrastructure, hire talented scouts who share the organization's vision, and have the patience to develop the Latin player. While every team is involved in the Latin market, the level of interest varies from team to team and among the countries. While the Dodgers, Blue Jays, Oakland, Montreal, Texas, and St. Louis lead the field in the Dominican Republic, Milwaukee and Pittsburgh stand out in Mexico, and the Houston Astros have emerged as front runners in Venezuela.

Although an organization must be willing to spend money in the Latin market, a shower of dollars alone will not bring success. Scouts, the gatekeepers of the Latin American dream, are the key to success. Latin America is open territory and many scouts describe working there in nostalgic terms, "the way it was in the U.S. before the draft." A player is sought, courted, sometimes hidden from other scouts, and signed. Projection as to the future potential of a player is more difficult to ascertain, and a scout's instinct is crucial—often a player must be signed on the spot before another scout shows up.

Over the past decade—really in the past five or six years—the Latin market has taken on added importance. "In 1976 when I went into Latin America there were seven teams scouting," says Luis Rosa, Chicago

Cubs Supervisor of Latin American Scouting. "Then all of a sudden it really took off and you had a large group of scouts coming in and asking 'what's happening?'"

Rosa's intimate knowledge of Puerto Rico has enabled him to stay ahead of much of the competition, and remain one of the dominant figures in the Latin market. Although he lost some of his advantage when Puerto Rico became subject to the free agent draft in 1990, he can still point to eighteen of his signees who have made it to the major leagues, including Ivan Calderon, Roberto Alomar, Sandy Alomar, Jr., Benito Santiago, Ozzie Guillen, Juan Gonzales and Ivan Rodriguez.

"There are a lot of people out there now that five or ten years ago were not in the market. Now it seems like everybody is in the market. So consequently any advantage that we had has been reduced. But I think we are competitive with the rest of them," says Gillick.

There is a general consensus among front office people that the quality of the talent from Latin America has continued to improve. There is no question that the quantity of players has increased. In 1950 there were four Latin-born players in the major leagues. In early July 1991, there were over 90, and the Texas Rangers last season fielded a team of which six of the eight position players were born in Latin America.

From the Rio Grande, on the U.S.-Mexico boundary, to the Rio Orinoco in Southern Venezuela, baseball is a national passion. Baseball is not played in all of Latin America, only those countries that border on the Caribbean. Take a quick look at a hurricane tracking chart and you will see the player exporting nations—the Dominican Republic, Puerto Rico, Venezuela, Cuba, Panama, Nicaragua, Mexico, and the Caribbean coasts of Colombia and Costa Rica.

Most organizations concentrate their efforts in the Latin market in four areas: Puerto Rico, the Dominican Republic, Venezuela, and to a lesser extent, Mexico. Restrictions or simply the lack of a critical mass of quality players make the necessary investment in the other countries less inviting.

Why does Latin America produce so many good players? First of all the region has talented young men, who play year around and who grew up dreaming of playing baseball in the U.S. In the Dominican Republic, where most foreign born players are reared, there are few economic opportunities for young men. But the Dominicans and other Latins are motivated by more than just this economic necessity—they bring a love for the game. "If I were rich, I'd tell you I play only because I love the game, but since I'm poor I play for love and money," explains Ramon Cedeño, former prospect in the Astros and Twins organizations.

Why does "America's Game" need to import players from Latin America. Don't we produce enough players here in the U.S.A.? Is there better talent abroad? Cheaper costs? If you answered yes to all three questions, you are correct. Latin players are good, cheaper to develop and fill a desperate need.

Why aren't more U.S. youngsters playing baseball? "I just think there are too many options for kids today," says Gerald Hunsicker, Director of Baseball Operations for the New York Mets. "And soccer has become a great youth sport. It enables any kid of any size to be able go out and compete and play. Skills for baseball are very difficult. It takes tremendous hand-eye coordination, tremendous dexterity to play baseball. Twenty years ago kids were playing baseball on the sandlots every weekend and seven days a week when they were out of school in the summer time. You don't see that any more."

"Kids want to play football where everybody pays attention to them, and there are cheerleaders and all that. In baseball there is no instant gratification," says former Cleveland Indian pitcher and Hall of Famer Bob Feller.

Most analysts agree with Hunsicker and Feller. They see sports talent in the U.S. as spread too thin, with U.S. youngsters opting to play other sports instead of baseball. Others believe U.S. kids to be too pampered, unwilling to put in the hard work necessary for baseball, choosing instead to spend their afternoons playing video games.

And more U.S. baseball players are choosing to attend college rather than turn pro out of high school. U.S. clubs prefer to work with younger players so that they can incorporate them into the organization and the availability of younger Latin players provides an added incentive for involvement in the market.

The bottom line is that the U.S. simply does not produce enough quality players to fill out the rosters of the minor league systems of the twenty-six organizations. One quarter of the U.S. players signed are not selected in the draft—that is, they were passed over by every club. This shortage of players will become even more acute with the addition of the Miami and Denver franchises.

Whatever the reasons, it is clear that the U.S. baseball talent pool is shrinking and it is necessary to look elsewhere for players. The most important area for baseball outside of the U.S. is Latin America, so the move south is only logical.

"We need players from anywhere in the world who can play in the major leagues. You have to put the best players possible on the field. There are so many good Latin players in baseball and developing for various organizations that it is wise for us to get heavy into that market also," says Roland Hemond, General Manager of the Baltimore Orioles.

Joe McIlvaine, San Diego Padres General Manager, sees the importation of talent from abroad as strengthening the U.S. game, and in the end providing a better product to the fans. "It's not that the talent here isn't good enough, but the talent in the Latin countries makes major league baseball what it is supposed to be—the best baseball in the world, and the best baseball players in the world. If there weren't Latin players we couldn't say it's the best baseball in the world."

An additional motivation to recruit in Latin America is the savings in costs. While the average signing bonus in the U.S. is above $50,000, in the Dominican Republic it is less than $5,000. In 1988 Oakland Athletics General Manager Sandy Alderson explained that his program in the Dominican Republic is "economically efficient." The costs both for signing and developing players is considerably less than it is in the U.S., and Alderson feels that if "you get one player every two and one-half years from your Latin program, it pays for itself." Alderson is ahead of the game. His Dominican program has produced three players who have reached the big leagues—pitcher Johnny Guzman, Luis Polonia, now with the California Angles and Felix Jose of the St. Louis Cardinals—in less than seven and one-half years, and there are several Dominican prospects progressing in the organization.

The Latin market has been opened for some time. Although Latin-born players did compete in the U.S. beginning in the 1870s, fewer than fifty—mostly light-skinned players—were allowed in prior to 1947. Black Latins played in the Negro Leagues. With integration, the door opened on the Latin market, but it has been slow to open completely.

Early ventures into the market concentrated on one country—Cuba. When political conditions in Cuba cut off the supply of players in the early 1960's, the emphasis shifted to the Dominican Republic where it remains.

The early Cuban market was dominated by one team, the Washington Senators, and one scout, Joe Cambria. The Giants and scout Alex Pompez prevailed in the Dominican Republic. By 1963 the Giants featured Juan Marichal who won twenty-five games, and the Alou brothers—Felipe, Matty and Jesus. During the next two decades, the Alou brothers, all outfielders, played a combined total of over forty-seven years. (The Giants had earlier ventured into Puerto Rico and signed Ruben Gomez, Orlando Cepeda, and Jose Pagan).

This trend of one scout, one country continued throughout the seventies. Howie Haak locked up the Dominican for Pittsburgh, and with the aid of scout Herb Rayborn (now Director of Latin American scouting for the Yankees) ventured into Panama. In Haak's path followed Epy Guerrero and Pat Gillick, first with Houston, then with the Toronto Blue Jays, Ruben Amaro with the Philadelphia Phillies and later with the Cubs and Detroit, and Ralph Avila with Los Angeles Dodgers.

Amaro, Guerrero, and Avila all opened what was to become the prototype of the institutionalization of the Latin market—the academy. Others soon followed, but there were academies and there were *academies*, ranging from facilities with prospects sleeping on cots under the grandstands, to the Campo Las Palmas facility opened by the Dodgers, which Baltimore's Hemond refers to as the Taj Majal.

The Dominican Republic continues to be the main fo-cus of U.S. teams, and is the only country where all twenty-six clubs have a presence—twenty have academies or camps there. While some teams concede leadership in the market to the Dodgers, Blue Jays, Expos and the A's, all of whom have invested or will invest considerable sums on their state-of-the-art academies, Houston, Atlanta, Texas, St. Louis, San Francisco, Kansas City, Cleveland, Milwaukee, Pittsburgh, Cincinnati, both New York teams, and a few other clubs still challenge the big boys. Every club has at least one full time scout presently working the island.

Is the Dominican Republic becoming oversaturated with scouts as many organizations believe? "It certainly seems to be the case with the emphasis of most major league clubs there. At the same time there is still talent there," says the Dodgers' Claire, adding a question, "Does saturation take away all of the resources, or help to create more players as young men are given more opportunities to display their talents?" Some scouts and player development people feel that you just have to look harder—going back in the more remote rural areas of the country—and work harder—teaching the basic skills.

And now the U.S. organizations have another competitor in the Dominican market. Late last year the Hiroshima Toyo Carp opened a multi-million-dollar complex at San Pedro de Macoris. At first glance, it looks like the Kansas City Royals' camp at Baseball City, Florida, or the Astros complex in Kissimmee.

Some U.S. organizations are concerned that the Japanese might begin to inflate the low signing bonuses in their competition for players, something ex-big-leaguer and Toyo Carp complex coordinator, Cesar Geronimo, insists will not happen.

But the Japanese are going to do two things U.S. organizations do not do: prepare players to go to Japan and sell players on the world market.

"We can trade players with North American organizations. And we envision other situations where our players would not only go to Japan," says Geronimo. Where would they go? "Right now Taiwan or Korea are alternatives. And it appears that these will expand even more in the future. Baseball is no longer exclusively for Latin America, the United States and Japan. There appears to be a world-wide movement toward professional baseball. Perhaps, in the not too distant future, there will be leagues organized in other parts of the world and professional baseball will expand there as well."

As the Dominican market becomes increasingly crowded, the baseball industry continues to look elsewhere. Venezuela may be the new El Dorado in the search for baseball talent. A downturn in the Venezuelan economy has made careers in baseball more appealing. Venezuelan youngsters are also attractive to U.S. clubs, since they are big, strong, fast and a bit more sophisticated, and are perceived to be more coachable than Dominican players.

The Houston Astros are leading the way in Venezuela with an academy at Valencia, and a satellite facility at Caracas. But Los Angeles, Baltimore, Montreal, Minnesota, Chicago's White Sox and New York's Yankees all now have facilities there as well. So much talent is being produced in Venezuela that beginning this year a summer development league sanctioned by Major League Baseball and the National Association is being planned.

Cuba still does not allow its players to sign professional baseball contracts, but each time the Cuban National team plays, U.S. scouts flock to the games and all clubs would be interested in the Cuban market if it were suddenly to open.

Puerto Rican players are now subject to the draft—which greatly limits the number entering professional ball. But scouts continue to find the talent, and the new wave of Puerto Rican talent entering the major leagues is impressive, including Juan Gonzalez and Ivan Rodriguez of the Rangers, the Pirates' Orlando Merced, the Orioles' Leo Gomez and Twins' Pedro Muñoz.

Entry of Mexican players to U.S. ball is limited by the Mexican League. "We don't really go into the Mexican market at all because we want to put our dollars where they count. We think our dollars count more in the Dominican, Puerto Rico and Venezuela. We don't think the dollars are well spent in Mexico," says Gillick. But here too, changes which will facilitate entry of Mexican players are likely.

Only a few teams allocate full-time scouts to Nicaragua, Colombia, Panama, or to the Dutch islands of Curacao and Aruba. Players from these countries are usually spotted in international tournaments or on periodic visits made by scouts.

There is a consensus among all organizations that the Latin market is increasing in importance. More organizations are committing more resources and producing more and better players. But no matter how many players the market produces, the final measure of success of an organization's investment there is the number of players who make it to the major league level. Most teams believe that the impact cannot be fully measured until all restrictions on the importation of players are finally lifted.

Jesus Alou, part of the brother trio that opened the floodgates of Dominican talent.

Hispanic Baseball Statistical Record

Peter C. Bjarkman

The roster of Latin Americans who have donned big-league uniforms over the past century and a quarter has continued to expand by leaps and bounds in recent seasons, as the importation of Latin talent has reached floodtide proportions during the past decade. 587 players born in Latin countries have now become big leaguers through the end of the 1991 season. The Dominican Republic (148) has closed the gap on Canada (154) as the reigning leader in production of "foreign-born" talent, and the island nation (U.S. possession?) of Puerto Rico (144, counting only island-born Puerto Ricans and not Ameri-cans of Puerto Rican descent) stands ready to move into second place. While several rosters of Hispanic players have recently been published, all contain errors and omissions. Following is an accurate list which may serve as a research guide for baseball scholars wishing to pursue the history of Latin American impact on big league play. Players are here listed in order by year of debut (including playing position and debut team as well). A special debt of gratitude is owed here to SABR member Robert F. Schulz of Fort Frances, Ontario, Canada for his invaluable assistance in preparing this updated player list.

Table of Latin American Player Debuts by Decades

Country	1900s	1910s	1920s	1930s	1940s	1950s	1960s	1970s	1980s	1990s
Dominican	0	0	0	0	0	2	22	37	64	23
Puerto Rico	0	0	0	0	2	14	24	41	46	17
Cuba	*1	12	5	3	22	36	35	4	8	1
Venezuela	0	0	0	1	1	4	9	10	29	8
Mexico	0	0	0	3	2	7	7	18	13	8
Panama	0	0	0	0	0	5	13	6	1	1
Virgin Islands	0	0	0	0	0	1	4	2	1	0
Nicaragua	0	0	0	0	0	0	0	2	3	0
Colombia	1	0	0	0	0	0	0	1	1	0
Spain	0	1	0	0	0	0	0	0	2	0
Honduras	0	0	0	0	0	0	0	0	1	0
Curacao	0	0	0	0	0	0	0	0	0	1
Belize	0	0	0	0	0	0	0	0	0	1
Decade Totals	**2**	**13**	**5**	**7**	**27**	**69**	**114**	**121**	**169**	**60**

*Enrique Esteban Bellan of Cuba debuted in the National Association in 1871.

Dominican Republic (148 players)

Name	Debut	Position	Debut Team
Ossie (Osvaldo) Virgil	1956	Infielder	New York Giants
Felipe Alou	1958	Outfielder	San Francisco Giants
Matty Alou	1960	Outfielder	San Francisco Giants
Julian Javier	1960	Infielder	St. Louis Cardinals
Juan Marichal	1960	Pitcher	San Francisco Giants
Rudy (Rudolph) Hernandez	1960	Pitcher	Washington Senators
Diomedes Olivo	1960	Pitcher	Pittsburgh Pirates
Chi Chi (Federico) Olivo	1961	Pitcher	Milwaukee Braves
Manny (Manuel) Jimenez	1962	Outfielder	Kansas City Athletics
Manny (Manuel) Mota	1962	Outfielder	San Francisco Giants
Amado Samuel	1962	Infielder	Milwaukee Braves
Jesus Alou	1963	Outfielder	San Francisco Giants
Pedro Gonzalez	1963	Infielder	New York Yankees
Rico (Ricardo) Carty	1963	Outfielder	Milwaukee Braves
Elvio Jimenez	1964	Outfielder	New York Yankees
Rick (Ricardo) Joseph	1964	Third Base	Kansas City Athletics
Roberto Peña	1965	Infielder	Chicago Cubs
Jose Vidal	1966	Outfielder	Cleveland Indians
Winston Llenas	1968	Infielder	California Angels
Rafael Robles	1969	Shortstop	San Diego Padres
Freddie (Federico) Velazquez	1969	Catcher	Seattle Pilots
Pedro Borbon	1969	Pitcher	California Angels
Santiago Guzman	1969	Pitcher	St. Louis Cardinals
Cesar Geronimo	1969	Outfielder	Houston Astros
Cesar Cedeño	1970	Outfielder	Houston Astros
Teddy (Teodoro) Martinez	1970	Infielder	New York Mets
Tom (Tomas) Silverio	1970	Outfielder	California Angels
Frank (Franklin) Taveras	1971	Shortstop	Pittsburgh Pirates
Elias Sosa	1972	Pitcher	San Francisco Giants
Pepe (Jesus) Frias	1973	Infielder	Montreal Expos
Rafael Batista	1973	First Base	Houston Astros
Mario Guerrero	1973	Shortstop	Boston Red Sox
Bill (William) Castro	1974	Pitcher	Milwaukee Brewers
Ramon de los Santos	1974	Pitcher	Houston Astros
Nino (Arnulfo) Espinosa	1974	Pitcher	New York Mets
Juan Jimenez	1974	Pitcher	Pittsburgh Pirates
Miguel Dilone	1974	Outfielder	Pittsburgh Pirates
Jose Sosa	1975	Pitcher	Houston Astros
Jesus de la Rosa	1975	Pinch Hitter	Houston Astros
Alfredo Ignacio Javier	1976	Outfielder	Houston Astros
Sam (Samuel) Mejias	1976	Outfielder	St. Louis Cardinals
Alex (Alejandro) Taveras	1976	Infielder	Houston Astros
Santo Alcala	1976	Pitcher	Cincinnati Reds
Joaquin Andujar	1976	Pitcher	Houston Astros
Juan Bernhardt	1976	Infielder	New York Yankees
Alfredo Griffin	1976	Shortstop	Cleveland Indians
Mario Soto	1976	Pitcher	Cincinnati Reds
Rafael Landestoy	1977	Infielder	Los Angeles Dodgers
Luis Pujols	1977	Catcher	Houston Astros
Silvio Martinez	1977	Pitcher	Chicago White Sox
Angel Torrez	1977	Pitcher	Cincinnati Reds
Jose Baez	1977	Second Base	Seattle Mariners
Pedro Guerrero	1978	Infielder	Los Angeles Dodgers
Nelson Norman	1978	Shortstop	Texas Rangers
Domingo Ramos	1978	Infielder	New York Yankees
Luis Silverio	1978	Outfielder	Kansas City Royals
Victor Cruz	1978	Pitcher	Toronto Blue Jays
Art (Arturo) de Freites	1978	First Base	Cincinnati Reds
Damaso Garcia	1978	Second Base	New York Yankees
Pedro Hernandez	1979	Third Base	Toronto Blue Jays
Rafael Vasquez	1979	Pitcher	Seattle Mariners
Rafael Ramirez	1980	Shortstop	Atlanta Braves
Jose Moreno	1980	Outfielder	New York Mets
Tony (Antonio) Peña	1980	Catcher	Pittsburgh Pirates
Julio Valdez	1980	Second Base	Boston Red Sox
Pascual Perez	1980	Pitcher	Pittsburgh Pirates
Manny (Esteban) Castillo	1980	Third Base	Kansas City Royals
Jesus Figueroa	1980	Outfielder	Chicago Cubs
George (Jorge) Bell	1981	Outfielder	Toronto Blue Jays
Rufino Linares	1981	Outfielder	Atlanta Braves
Alejandro Peña	1981	Pitcher	Los Angeles Dodgers
Alejandro Sanchez	1982	Outfielder	Philadelphia Phillies
Rafael Belliard	1982	Shortstop	Pittsburgh Pirates
Cecilio Guante	1982	Pitcher	Pittsburgh Pirates
Carmen (Carmelo) Castillo	1982	Outfielder	Cleveland Indians
Juan Espino	1982	Catcher	New York Yankees
Julio Franco	1982	Second Base	Philadelphia Phillies
Gilberto Reyes	1983	Catcher	Los Angeles Dodgers
Juan Samuel	1983	Infielder	Philadelphia Phillies
Rafael Santana	1983	Shortstop	St. Louis Cardinals
Jose DeLeon	1983	Pitcher	Philadelphia Phillies
Julio Solano	1983	Pitcher	Houston Astros
Tony (Octavio) Fernandez	1983	Shortstop	Toronto Blue Jays
Stan (Stanley) Javier	1984	Outfielder	New York Yankees
Vic (Victor) Mata	1984	Outfielder	New York Yankees
Junior (Milciades) Noboa	1984	Infielder	Cleveland Indians
Jose Uribe (Gonzalez)	1984	Shortstop	St. Louis Cardinals
Jose Rijo	1984	Pitcher	New York Yankees
Jose Roman	1984	Pitcher	Cleveland Indians
Ramon Romero	1984	Pitcher	Cleveland Indians
Denny (Denio) Gonzalez	1984	Infielder	Pittsburgh Pirates
Manny (Manuel) Lee	1985	Infielder	Toronto Blue Jays
Jose Gonzalez	1985	Outfielder	Los Angeles Dodgers
Andres Perez Thomas	1985	Shortstop	Atlanta Braves
Mariano Duncan	1985	Infielder	Los Angeles Dodgers
Ruben Rodriguez	1986	Catcher	Pittsburgh Pirates
Wil (Wilfredo) Tejada	1986	Catcher	Montreal Expos
Balvino Galvez	1986	Pitcher	Los Angeles Dodgers
Manny (Manuel) Hernandez	1986	Pitcher	Houston Astros
Hipolito Peña	1986	Pitcher	Pittsburgh Pirates
Sergio Valdez	1986	Pitcher	Montreal Expos
Juan Castillo	1986	Infielder	Milwaukee Brewers
Luis Polonia	1987	Outfielder	Oakland Athletics
Nelson Liriano	1987	Second Base	Toronto Blue Jays
Jose Mesa	1987	Pitcher	Baltimore Orioles
Jose Nuñez	1987	Pitcher	Toronto Blue Jays
Melido Perez	1987	Pitcher	Kansas City Royals
Felix Fermin	1987	Shortstop	Pittsburgh Pirates
Leo Garcia	1987	Outfielder	Cincinnati Reds
Felix Jose	1988	Outfielder	Oakland Athletics

Name	Debut	Position	Debut Team
Gibson Alba	1988	Pitcher	St. Louis Cardinals
Jose Bautista	1988	Pitcher	Baltimore Orioles
Ravelo Manzanillo	1988	Pitcher	Chicago White Sox
Ramon Martinez	1988	Pitcher	Los Angeles Dodgers
Jose Segura	1988	Pitcher	Chicago White Sox
Sil (Silvestre) Campusano	1988	Outfielder	Toronto Blue Jays
Luis de los Santos	1988	First Base	Kansas City Royals
Juan Bell	1989	Infielder	Baltimore Orioles
Ramon Peña	1989	Pitcher	Detroit Tigers
Sammy (Samuel) Sosa	1989	Outfielder	Texas Rangers
Jose Vizcaino	1989	Shortstop	Los Angeles Dodgers
Jose (Joselito) Caño	1989	Pitcher	Houston Astros
German (Geronimo) Berroa	1989	Outfielder	Atlanta Braves
Francisco Cabrera	1989	Catcher	Toronto Blue Jays
Junior Felix	1989	Outfielder	Toronto Blue Jays
Adujar Cedeño	1990	Shortstop	Houston Astros
Moises Alou	1990	Outfielder	Pittsburgh Pirates
Luis Encarnacion	1990	Pitcher	Kansas City Royals
Ramon Manon	1990	Pitcher	Texas Rangers
Jose Offerman	1990	Shortstop	Los Angeles Dodgers
Geronimo Peña	1990	Second Base	St. Louis Cardinals
Mel (Melaquides) Rojas	1990	Pitcher	Montreal Expos
Vic (Victor) Rosario	1990	Shortstop	Atlanta Braves
Andres Santana	1990	Infielder	San Francisco Giants
Rafael Valdez	1990	Pitcher	San Diego Padres
Efrain Valdez	1990	Pitcher	Cleveland Indians
Hector Wagner	1990	Pitcher	Kansas City Royals
Esteban Beltre	1991	Shortstop	Chicago White Sox
Braulio Castillo	1991	Outfielder	Philadelphia Phillies
Francisco de la Rosa	1991	Pitcher	Baltimore Orioles
Tony (Antonio) Eusebio	1991	Catcher	Houston Astros
Juan Guzman	1991	Pitcher	Toronto Blue Jays
Johnny Guzman	1991	Pitcher	Oakland Athletics
Josias Manzanillo	1991	Pitcher	Boston Red Sox
Luis Mercedes	1991	Outfielder	Baltimore Orioles
Andy Mota	1991	Infielder	Houston Astros
Jose Mota	1991	Infielder	San Diego Padres
Yorkis Perez	1991	Pitcher	Chicago Cubs

Puerto Rico (144 players—native-born only)

Name	Debut	Position	Debut Team
Hiram Bithorn	1942	Pitcher	Chicago Cubs
Luis Rodriguez Olmo	1943	Outfielder	Brooklyn Dodgers
Luis Marquez	1951	Outfielder	Boston Braves
Ruben Gomez	1953	Pitcher	New York Giants
Carlos Bernier	1953	Outfielder	Pittsburgh Pirates
Victor Pellot (Vic Power)	1954	First Base	Philadelphia Athletics
Niño (Saturnino) Escalera	1954	Outfielder	Cincinnati Reds
Jose "Pantalones" Santiago	1954	Pitcher	Cleveland Indians
Luis Arroyo	1955	Pitcher	St. Louis Cardinals
Roberto Clemente	1955	Outfielder	Pittsburgh Pirates
Roberto Vargas	1955	Pitcher	Milwaukee Braves
Felix Mantilla	1956	Shortstop	Milwaukee Braves
Juan Pizarro	1957	Pitcher	Milwaukee Braves
Valmy Thomas	1957	Catcher	New York Giants
Orlando Cepeda	1958	First Base	San Francisco Giants
Jose Pagan	1959	Shortstop	San Francisco Giants
Julio Gotay	1960	Infielder	St. Louis Cardinals
Ed Olivares	1960	Outfielder	St. Louis Cardinals
Ramon Conde	1962	Third Base	Chicago White Sox
Felix Torres	1962	Third Base	Los Angeles Angels
Julio Navarro	1962	Pitcher	Los Angeles Angels
Jose Palillo Santiago	1963	Pitcher	Kansas City Athletics
Sandy (Santos) Alomar	1964	Second Base	Milwaukee Braves
Santiago Rosario	1965	First Base	Kansas City Athletics
Arturo Lopez	1965	Outfielder	New York Yankees
Hector Valle	1965	Catcher	Los Angeles Dodgers
Felix Milan	1966	Shortstop	Atlanta Braves
Willie (Guillermo) Montañez	1966	First Base	California Angels
Angel Luis Alcaraz	1967	Infielder	Los Angeles Dodgers
Ramon Hernandez	1967	Pitcher	Atlanta Braves
Luis Alvarado	1968	Infielder	Boston Red Sox
Ellie (Eliseo) Rodriguez	1968	Catcher	New York Yankees
Mickey (Miguel) Fuentes	1969	Pitcher	Seattle Pilots
Jose "Coco" Laboy	1969	Infielder	Montreal Expos
Francisco Libran	1969	Shortstop	San Diego Padres
Angel Mangual	1969	Outfielder	Pittsburgh Pirates
Jerry (Julio) Morales	1969	Outfielder	San Diego Padres
Jose Ortiz	1969	Outfielder	Chicago White Sox
Luis Peraza	1969	Pitcher	Philadelphia Phillies
Juan Rios	1969	Infielder	Kansas City Royals
Jose Cruz	1970	Outfielder	St. Louis Cardinals
Rogelio Moret	1970	Pitcher	Boston Red Sox
Luis Melendez	1970	Outfielder	St. Louis Cardinals
Samuel Parrilla	1970	Outfielder	Philadelphia Phillies
Milton Ramirez	1970	Infielder	St. Louis Cardinals
Jorge Roque	1970	Outfielder	St. Louis Cardinals
Juan Beniquez	1971	Outfielder	Boston Red Sox
Manny Muñiz	1971	Pitcher	Philadelphia Phillies
Jimmy (Angel) Rosario	1971	Outfielder	San Francisco Giants
Rusty (Rosendo) Torrez	1971	Outfielder	New York Yankees
Jose Fernando Gonzalez	1972	Infielder	Pittsburgh Pirates
Pepe (Jose) Mangual	1972	Infielder	Montreal Expos
David Rosello	1972	Infielder	Chicago Cubs
Jesus Orlando Alvarez	1973	Outfielder	Los Angeles Dodgers
Hector Cruz	1973	Outfielder	St. Louis Cardinals
Tommy (Cirilo) Cruz	1973	Outfielder	St. Louis Cardinals
Eduardo Rodriguez	1973	Pitcher	Milwaukee Brewers
Otto Velez	1973	Outfielder	New York Yankees
Carlos Velasquez	1973	Pitcher	Milwaukee Brewers
Benny (Benigno) Ayala	1974	Outfielder	New York Mets
Ivan de Jesus	1974	Shortstop	Los Angeles Dodgers
Sergio Ferrer	1974	Shortstop	Minnesota Twins
Ed (Eduardo) Figueroa	1974	Pitcher	California Angels
Jesus Hernaiz	1974	Pitcher	Philadelphia Phillies
Sixto Lezcano	1974	Outfielder	Milwaukee Brewers
Luis Joaquin Quintana	1974	Pitcher	California Angels
Jesus ("Bombo") Rivera	1975	Outfielder	Montreal Expos
Ramon Aviles	1977	Infielder	Boston Red Sox
Luis Delgado	1977	Outfielder	Seattle Mariners
Gil (Gilberto) Flores	1977	Outfielder	California Angels
Julio Gonzalez	1977	Infielder	Houston Astros

Name	Debut	Position	Debut Team
Pedro Garcia	1977	Second Base	Milwaukee Brewers
Willie (Guillermo) Hernandez	1977	Pitcher	Chicago Cubs
Ed (Edgar) Romero	1977	Infielder	Milwaukee Brewers
Luis Rosado	1977	First Base	New York Mets
Alberto Lois	1978	Outfielder	Pittsburgh Pirates
Chico (Manual) Ruiz	1978	Infielder	Atlanta Braves
Tony (Antonio) Bernazard	1979	Second Base	Montreal Expos
Rafael Santo Domingo	1979	Pinch Hitter	Cincinnati Reds
Dickie Thon	1979	Shortstop	California Angels
Jesus Vega	1979	First Base	Minnesota Twins
Luis Aguayo	1980	Infielder	Philadelphia Phillies
Onix Concepcion	1980	Infielder	Kansas City Royals
Orlando Isales	1980	Outfielder	Philadelphia Phillies
Carlos Lezcano	1980	Outfielder	Chicago Cubs
Mario Ramirez	1980	Shortstop	New York Mets
Ozzie Virgil	1980	Catcher	Philadelphia Phillies
Juan Agosto	1981	Pitcher	Chicago White Sox
Juan Bonilla	1981	Second Base	San Diego Padres
Luis DeLeon	1981	Pitcher	St. Louis Cardinals
Candy (Candido) Maldonado	1981	Outfielder	Los Angeles Dodgers
Bert (Adalberto) Peña	1981	Infielder	Houston Astros
Orlando Sanchez	1981	Catcher	St. Louis Cardinals
Orlando Mercado	1982	Catcher	Seattle Mariners
Junior (Adalberto) Ortiz	1982	Catcher	Pittsburgh Pirates
Edwin Rodriguez	1982	Infielder	New York Yankees
Hedi (Heriberto) Vargas	1982	First Base	Pittsburgh Pirates
Edwin Nuñez	1982	Pitcher	Seattle Mariners
James (Jaime) Cocanower	1983	Pitcher	Milwaukee Brewers
Carmelo Martinez	1983	Outfielder	Chicago Cubs
Jose Oquendo	1983	Infielder	St. Louis Cardinals
German Rivera	1983	Infielder	Los Angeles Dodgers
Ivan Calderon	1984	Outfielder	Seattle Mariners
Francisco Melendez	1984	First Base	Philadelphia Phillies
Danny (Danilo) Tartabull	1984	Outfielder	Seattle Mariners
Edwin Correa	1985	Pitcher	Chicago White Sox
Jose Guzman	1985	Pitcher	Texas Rangers
Carlos Ponce	1985	First Base	Milwaukee Brewers
Juan Nieves	1986	Pitcher	Milwaukee Brewers
Luis Aquino	1986	Pitcher	Toronto Blue Jays
Rafael Montalvo	1986	Pitcher	Houston Astros
Edgar Diaz	1986	Shortstop	Milwaukee Brewers
Luis Quiñones	1986	Infielder	Oakland Athletics
Rey Quiñones	1986	Shortstop	Boston Red Sox
Luis Rivera	1986	Infielder	Montreal Expos
Benito Santiago	1986	Catcher	San Diego Padres
Ruben Sierra	1986	Outfielder	Texas Rangers
Joey Cora	1987	Second Base	San Diego Padres
Mario Diaz	1987	Shortstop	Seattle Mariners
Jose Lind	1987	Shortstop	Pittsburgh Pirates
Candy (Ulises) Sierra	1988	Pitcher	San Diego Padres
Sandy Alomar Jr.	1988	Catcher	San Diego Padres
Luis Alicea	1988	Second Base	St. Louis Cardinals
Roberto Alomar	1988	Second Base	San Diego Padres
Juan Gonzalez	1989	Outfielder	Texas Rangers
Jaime Navarro	1989	Pitcher	Milwaukee Brewers
Francisco Javier Oliveras	1989	Pitcher	Minnesota Twins

Name	Debut	Position	Debut Team
Carlos Baerga	1990	Infielder	Cleveland Indians
Rafael Novoa	1990	Pitcher	San Francisco Giants
Leo Gomez	1990	Third Base	Baltimore Orioles
Jose Melendez	1990	Pitcher	Seattle Mariners
Orlando Merced	1990	First Base	Pittsburgh Pirates
Pedro Muñoz	1990	Catcher	Minnesota Twins
Omar Olivarez	1990	Pitcher	St. Louis Cardinals
Mike Perez	1990	Pitcher	St. Louis Cardinals
Julio Valera	1990	Pitcher	New York Mets
Hector Villanueva	1990	Catcher	Chicago Cubs
Ricky Bones	1991	Pitcher	San Diego Padres
Jose Hernandez	1991	Infielder	Texas Rangers
Roberto Hernandez	1991	Pitcher	Chicago White Sox
Ivan Rodriguez	1991	Catcher	Texas Rangers
Rico Rossy	1991	Infielder	Atlanta Braves
Rey Sanchez	1991	Infielder	Chicago Cubs
Bernie Williams	1991	Outfielder	New York Yankess

Cuba (127 players)

Name	Debut	Position	Debut Team
Enrique Esteban Bellan	1871	Infielder	Troy Haymakers (NA)
Armando Marsans	1911	Outfielder	Cincinnati Reds
Rafael Almeida	1911	Outfielder	Cincinnati Reds
Mike (Miguel) Gonzalez	1912	Catcher	Boston Braves
Merito (Baldomero) Acosta	1913	Outfielder	Washington Senators
Jack (Jacinto) Calvo	1913	Outfielder	Washington Senators
Angel Aragon	1914	Infielder	New York Yankees
Adolfo Luque	1914	Pitcher	Boston Braves
Emilio Palmero	1915	Pitcher	New York Giants
Joseito Rodriguez	1916	Infielder	New York Giants
Manolo (Manuel) Cueto	1917	Outfielder	Cincinnati Reds
Eusebio Gonzalez	1918	Shortstop	Boston Red Sox
Oscar Tuero	1918	Pitcher	St. Louis Cardinals
Jose Acosta	1920	Pitcher	Washington Senators
Ricardo Torres	1920	Catcher	Washington Senators
Pedro Dibut	1924	Pitcher	Cincinnati Reds
Pafto "Mike" (Ramon) Herrera	1925	Infielder	Boston Red Sox
Oscar Estrada	1929	Pitcher	St. Louis Browns
Roberto Estalella	1935	Outfielder	Washington Senators
Mike (Fermin) Guerra	1937	Catcher	Washington Senators
Rene Monteagudo	1938	Pitcher	Washington Senators
Gilberto Torres	1940	Infielder	Washington Senators
Jack (Angel) Aragon	1941	Pinch Runner	New York Giants
Roberto Ortiz	1941	Outfielder	Washington Senators
Sal (Salvador) Hernandez	1942	Catcher	Chicago Cubs
Mosquito (Antonio) Ordenana	1943	Shortstop	Pittsburgh Pirates
Nap (Napoleon) Reyes	1943	Infielder	New York Giants
Tommy (Tomas) de la Cruz	1944	Pitcher	Cincinnati Reds
Preston (Pedro) Gomez	1944	Infielder	Washington Senators
Baby (Oliverio) Ortiz	1944	Pitcher	Washington Senators
Luis Suarez	1944	Third Base	Washington Senators
Santiago (Carlos) Ullrich	1944	Pitcher	Washington Senators
Roy (Rogelio) Valdez	1944	Pinch Hitter	Washington Senators
Jorge Comellas	1945	Pitcher	Chicago Cubs
Sid (Isidoro) Leon	1945	Pitcher	Philadelphia Phillies
Armando Roche	1945	Pitcher	Washington Senators

Name	Debut	Position	Debut Team
Adrian Zabala	1945	Pitcher	New York Giants
Jose Zardon	1945	Outfielder	Washington Senators
Reggie (Regino) Otero	1945	First Base	Chicago Cubs
Angel Fleitas	1948	Shortstop	Washington Senators
Moin (Ramon) Garcia	1948	Pitcher	Washington Senators
Enrique (Julio) Gonzalez	1949	Pitcher	Washington Senators
Minnie (Orestes) Minoso	1949	Outfielder	Cleveland Indians
Witto (Luis) Aloma	1950	Pitcher	Chicago White Sox
Sandy (Sandalio) Consuegra	1950	Pitcher	Washington Senators
Connie (Conrado) Marrero	1950	Pitcher	Washington Senators
Limonar (Rogelio) Martinez	1950	Pitcher	Washington Senators
Julio Moreno	1950	Outfielder	Washington Senators
Carlos Pascual	1950	Pitcher	Washington Senators
Cisco (Francisco) Campos	1951	Outfielder	Washington Senators
Willie (Guillermo) Miranda	1951	Shortstop	Washington Senators
Ray (Rafael) Noble	1951	Catcher	New York Giants
Sandy (Edmundo) Amoros	1952	Outfielder	Brooklyn Dodgers
Mike (Miguel) Fornieles	1952	Pitcher	Washington Senators
Hector Rodriguez	1952	Third Base	Chicago White Sox
Raul Sanchez	1952	Pitcher	Washington Senators
Carlos Paula	1954	Outfielder	Washington Senators
Camilo Pascual	1954	Pitcher	Washington Senators
Vicente Amor	1955	Pitcher	Chicago Cubs
Julio Becquer	1955	First Base	Washington Senators
Juan Delis	1955	Third Base	Washington Senators
Lino Donoso	1955	Pitcher	Pittsburgh Pirates
Vince (Wenceslao) Gonzalez	1955	Pitcher	Washington Senators
Roman Mejias	1955	Outfielder	Pittsburgh Pirates
Pedro Ramos	1955	Pitcher	Washington Senators
Joe (Jose) Valdivielso	1955	Shortstop	Washington Senators
Chico (Humberto) Fernandez	1956	Shortstop	Brooklyn Dodgers
Evelio (Gregorio) Hernandez	1956	Pitcher	Washington Senators
Cholly (Lazaro) Naranjo	1956	Pitcher	Pittsburgh Pirates
Rene Valdez	1957	Pitcher	Brooklyn Dodgers
Ossie (Oswaldo) Alvarez	1958	Infielder	Washington Senators
Pancho (Juan) Herrera	1958	First Base	Philadelphia Phillies
Dan (Daniel) Morejon	1958	Outfielder	Cincinnati Reds
Orlando Peña	1958	Pitcher	Cincinnati Reds
Freddy (Fernando) Rodriguez	1958	Pitcher	Chicago Cubs
Tony (Antonio) Taylor	1958	Infielder	Chicago Cubs
Rudy (Rodolfo) Arias	1958	Pitcher	Chicago White Sox
Mike (Miguel) Cuellar	1959	Pitcher	Cincinnati Reds
Zoilo Versalles	1959	Shortstop	Washington Senators
Borrego (Rogelio) Alvarez	1960	First Base	Cincinnati Reds
Joe (Joaquin) Azcue	1960	Infielder	Cincinnati Reds
Ed (Eduardo) Bauta	1960	Pitcher	St. Louis Cardinals
Leo (Leonardo) Cardenas	1960	Infielder	Cincinnati Reds
Mike (Miguel) de la Hoz	1960	Infielder	Cleveland Indians
Tony (Antonio) Gonzalez	1960	Infielder	Cincinnati Reds
Hector Maestri	1960	Pitcher	Washington Senators
Leo (Leopoldo) Posada	1960	Outfielder	Kansas City Athletics
Berto (Dagoberto) Cueto	1961	Pitcher	Minnesota Twins
Manny (Manuel) Montejo	1961	Pitcher	Detroit Tigers
Hector (Rodolfo) Martinez	1962	Outfielder	Kansas City Athletics
Marty (Orlando) Martinez	1962	Infielder	Minnesota Twins
Orlando McFarlane	1962	Catcher	Pittsburgh Pirates

Name	Debut	Position	Debut Team
Tony (Pedro) Oliva	1962	Outfielder	Minnesota Twins
Cookie (Octavio) Rojas	1962	Infielder	Cincinnati Reds
Diego Segui	1962	Pitcher	Kansas City Athletics
Jose Tartabull	1962	Outfielder	Kansas City Athletics
Jose Cardenal	1963	Infielder	San Francisco Giants
Marcelino Lopez	1963	Pitcher	Philadelphia Phillies
Tony (Gabriel) Martinez	1963	Infielder	Cleveland Indians
Aurelio Monteagudo	1963	Pitcher	Kansas City Athletics
Bert (Dagoberto) Campaneris	1964	Shortstop	Kansas City Athletics
Tony (Atanasio) Perez	1964	Infielder	Cincinnati Reds
Luis Tiant	1964	Pitcher	Cleveland Indians
Paul (Paulino) Casanova	1965	Catcher	Washington Senators
Tito (Rigoberto) Fuentes	1965	Outfielder	San Francisco Giants
Jackie (Jacinto) Hernandez	1965	Shortstop	California Angels
Jose Ramon Lopez	1966	Pitcher	California Angels
Minnie (Minervino) Rojas	1966	Pitcher	California Angels
Sandy (Hilario) Valdespino	1966	Outfielder	Minnesota Twins
Hank (Enrique) Izquierdo	1967	Catcher	Minnesota Twins
George (Jorge) Lauzerique	1967	Pitcher	Kansas City Athletics
Jose Arcia	1968	Infielder	Chicago Cubs
Chico (Lorenzo) Fernandez	1968	Infielder	Baltimore Orioles
Jose Martinez	1969	Infielder	Pittsburgh Pirates
Minnie (Rigoberto) Mendoza	1970	Infielder	Minnesota Twins
Oscar Zamora	1974	Pitcher	Chicago Cubs
Orlando Gonzalez	1976	First Base	Cleveland Indians
Bobby (Roberto) Ramos	1978	Catcher	Montreal Expos
Leo (Leonard) Sutherland	1980	Outfielder	Chicago White Sox
Barbaro Garbey	1984	Outfielder	Detroit Tigers
Jose Canseco	1985	Outfielder	Oakland Athletics
Rafael Palmeiro	1986	First Base	Chicago Cubs
Orestes Destrade	1987	First Base	New York Yankees
Nelson Santovenia	1988	Catcher	Montreal Expos
Israel Sanchez	1988	Pitcher	Kansas City Royals
Tony (Emilio) Fossas	1988	Pitcher	Texas Rangers
Ozzie Canseco	1990	Outfielder	Oakland Athletics

Venezuela (62 players)

Name	Debut	Position	Debut Team
Alejandro Carrasquel	1939	Pitcher	Washington Senators
Chucho (Jesus) Ramos	1944	Outfielder	Cincinnati Reds
Alfonso "Chico" Carrasquel	1950	Shortstop	Chicago White Sox
Pompeyo Davalillo	1953	Shortstop	Washington Senators
Ramon Monzant	1954	Pitcher	New York Giants
Luis Aparicio	1956	Shortstop	Chicago White Sox
Elio Chacon	1960	Infielder	Cincinnati Reds
Victor Davalillo	1963	Outfielder	Cleveland Indians
Cesar Tovar	1965	Infielder	Minnesota Twins
Nestor (Isaias) Chavez	1967	Pitcher	San Francisco Giants
Roberto Muñoz	1967	Pitcher	Kansas City Athletics
Jose Herrera	1967	Outfielder	Houston Astros
Gustavo Gil	1967	Infielder	Cleveland Indians
Angel Remigio Hermoso	1967	Infielder	Atlanta Braves
Angel Bravo	1969	Outfielder	Chicago White Sox
Ossie (Osvaldo) Blanco	1970	First Base	Chicago White Sox
David Concepcion	1970	Shortstop	Cincinnati Reds
Enzo Hernandez	1971	Shortstop	San Diego Padres

Name	Debut	Position	Debut Team
Damaso Blanco	1972	Infielder	San Francisco Giants
Gonzalo Marquez	1972	First Base	Oakland Athletics
Manny Trillo	1973	Infielder	Oakland Athletics
Pablo Torrealba	1975	Pitcher	Atlanta Braves
Manny Sarmiento	1976	Pitcher	Cincinnati Reds
Tony (Antonio) Armas	1976	Outfielder	Pittsburgh Pirates
Bo (Baudilio) Diaz	1977	Catcher	Boston Red Sox
Luis Aponte	1980	Pitcher	Boston Red Sox
Luis Leal	1980	Pitcher	Toronto Blue Jays
Luis Salazar	1980	Third Base	San Diego Padres
Fred Manrique	1981	Infielder	Toronto Blue Jays
Luis Mercedes Sanchez	1981	Pitcher	California Angels
Leonardo Hernandez	1982	Third Base	Baltimore Orioles
Cesar Gutierrez	1983	Shortstop	San Francisco Giants
Angel (Argenis) Salazar	1983	Shortstop	Montreal Expos
Alvaro Espinoza	1984	Shortstop	Minnesota Twins
Toby (Tobias) Hernandez	1984	Catcher	Toronto Blue Jays
Andres Galarraga	1985	First Base	Montreal Expos
Ossie (Osvaldo) Guillen	1985	Shortstop	Chicago White Sox
Gus (Gustavo) Polidor	1985	Infielder	California Angels
Urbano Lugo	1985	Pitcher	California Angels
Alexis Infante	1987	Shortstop	Toronto Blue Jays
Al (Alfredo) Pedrique	1987	Infielder	New York Mets
Miguel Angel Garcia	1987	Pitcher	California Angels
Ubaldo Heredia	1987	Pitcher	Montreal Expos
Les (Lester) Straker	1987	Pitcher	Minnesota Twins
Carlos Quintana	1988	First Base	Boston Red Sox
Tony (Antonio) Castillo	1988	Pitcher	Toronto Blue Jays
German Gonzalez	1988	Pitcher	Minnesota Twins
Osvaldo Peraza	1988	Pitcher	Baltimore Orioles
Angel Escobar	1988	Infielder	San Francisco Giants
Carlos Martinez	1988	First Base	Chicago White Sox
Johnny Paredes	1988	Infielder	Montreal Expos
Omar Visquel	1989	Shortstop	Seattle Mariners
Wilson Alvarez	1989	Pitcher	Texas Rangers
Julio Machado	1989	Pitcher	New York Mets
Oscar Azocar	1990	Outfielder	New York Yankees
Rich Garces	1990	Pitcher	Minnesota Twins
Carlos Garcia	1990	Outfielder	Pittsburgh Pirates
Carlos Hernandez	1990	Catcher	Los Angeles Dodgers
Luis Sojo	1990	Infielder	Toronto Blue Jays
Jose Escobar	1991	Infielder	Cleveland Indians
Amalio Carreno	1991	Pitcher	Philadelphia Phillies
Ramon Garcia	1991	Pitcher	Chicago White Sox

Mexico (58 players)

Name	Debut	Position	Debut Team
Mel Almada	1933	Outfielder	Boston Red Sox
Chili (Jose) Gomez	1935	Infielder	Philadelphia Phillies
Felipe Montemayor	1938	Outfielder	Pittsburgh Pirates
Jesse Flores	1942	Pitcher	Chicago Cubs
Beto (Roberto) Avila	1949	Second Base	Cleveland Indians
Tito Herrera	1951	Pitcher	St. Louis Browns
Chico (Vincio) Garcia	1954	Second Base	Baltimore Orioles
Bob (Robert) Greenwood	1954	Pitcher	Philadelphia Phillies
Memo (Guillermo) Luna	1954	Pitcher	St. Louis Cardinals

Name	Debut	Position	Debut Team
Ruben Amaro	1958	Infielder	St. Louis Cardinals
Marcelino Solis	1958	Pitcher	Chicago Cubs
Benny (Benjamin) Valenzuela	1958	Third Base	St. Louis Cardinals
Jorge Rubio	1966	Pitcher	California Angels
Aurelio Rodriguez	1967	Third Base	California Angels
Horacio Piña	1968	Pitcher	Cleveland Indians
Vicente Romo	1968	Pitcher	Los Angeles Dodgers
Bobby (Carlos) Treviño	1968	Outfielder	California Angels
Hector Torres	1968	Infielder	Houston Astros
Jose Peña	1969	Pitcher	Cincinnati Reds
Miguel Puente	1970	Pitcher	San Francisco Giants
Francisco Estrada	1971	Catcher	New York Mets
Rudy (Rodolfo) Hernandez	1972	Shortstop	Chicago White Sox
Jorge Orta	1972	Second Base	Chicago White Sox
Sergio Robles	1972	Catcher	Baltimore Orioles
Celerino Sanchez	1972	Infielder	New York Yankees
Cy (Cecilio) Acosta	1972	Pitcher	Chicago White Sox
Max (Maximo) Leon	1973	Pitcher	Atlanta Braves
Luis Gomez	1974	Shortstop	Minnesota Twins
Francisco Barrios	1974	Pitcher	Chicago White Sox
Aurelio Lopez	1974	Pitcher	Kansas City Royals
Mario Mendoza	1974	Shortstop	Pittsburgh Pirates
Sid (Isidro) Monge	1975	Pitcher	California Angels
Carlos Lopez	1976	Outfielder	California Angels
Andres Mora	1976	Outfielder	Baltimore Orioles
Enrique Romo	1977	Pitcher	Seattle Mariners
Alex Treviño	1978	Catcher	New York Mets
German Barranca	1979	Infielder	Kansas City Royals
Fernando Valenzuela	1980	Pitcher	Los Angeles Dodgers
Angel Moreno	1981	Pitcher	California Angels
Ernesto Escarrega	1982	Pitcher	Chicago White Sox
Salome Barojas	1982	Pitcher	Chicago White Sox
Houston Jimenez	1983	Shortstop	Minnesota Twins
Alfonso Pulido	1983	Pitcher	Pittsburgh Pirates
Teddy (Teodoro) Higuera	1985	Pitcher	Milwaukee Brewers
Vicente Palacios	1987	Pitcher	Pittsburgh Pirates
Randy Velarde	1987	Infielder	New York Yankees
Jose Cecena	1988	Pitcher	Texas Rangers
German Jimenez	1988	Pitcher	Atlanta Braves
Tony Perezchica	1988	Second Base	San Francisco Giants
Rosario Rodriguez	1989	Pitcher	Cincinnati Reds
Narciso Elvira	1990	Pitcher	Milwaukee Brewers
Matias Carrillo	1991	Outfielder	Milwaukee Brewers
Vinny Castilla	1991	Infielder	Atlanta Braves
Hector Fajardo	1991	Pitcher	Pittsburgh Pirates
Everardo Magellanes	1991	Infielder	Cleveland Indians
Armando Reynoso	1991	Pitcher	Atlanta Braves
Carlos Rodriguez	1991	Shortstop	New York Yankees
Jose Tolentino	1991	Outfielder	Houston Astros

Panama (26 players)
(* denotes Panama Canal Zone)

Name	Debut	Position	Debut Team
Humberto Robinson	1955	Pitcher	Milwaukee Braves
Hector Lopez	1955	Infielder	Kansas City Athletics
Webbo (Vibert) Clarke	1955	Pitcher	Washington Senators

*Pat Scantlebury	1956	Pitcher	Cincinnati Reds
*Tom (Thomas) Hughes	1959	Pitcher	St. Louis Cardinals
Bobby (George) Prescott	1961	Outfielder	Kansas City Athletics
Dave Roberts	1962	First Base	Houston Colt 45s
Rupe (Ruperto) Toppin	1962	Pitcher	Kansas City Athletics
Ivan Murrell	1963	Outfielder	Houston Colt 45s
Gil Garrido	1964	Infielder	San Francisco Giants
Adolfo Phillips	1964	Outfielder	Philadelphia Phillies
Chico (Ruthford) Salmon	1964	Infielder	Cleveland Indians
Ossie (Osvaldo) Chavarria	1966	Infielder	Kansas City Athletics
*Rod Carew	1967	Infielder	Minnesota Twins
Manny (Manuel) Sanguillen	1967	Catcher	Pittsburgh Pirates
Al (Allan) Lewis	1967	Outfielder	Kansas City Athletics
Ramon Webster	1967	First Base	Kansas City Athletics
Bill (William) Heywood	1968	Pitcher	Washington Senators
Eduardo Acosta	1970	Pitcher	Pittsburgh Pirates
Ben (Benjamin) Oglivie	1971	Outfielder	Boston Red Sox
Rennie (Renaldo) Stennett	1971	Second Base	Pittsburgh Pirates
Omar Moreno	1975	Outfielder	Pittsburgh Pirates
*Mike (Edward) Eden	1976	Infielder	Atlanta Braves
Juan Berenguer	1978	Pitcher	New York Mets
Roberto Kelly	1987	Outfielder	New York Yankees
Carlos Maldonado	1990	Pitcher	Kansas City Royals

Virgin Islands (8 players)

Name	Debut	Position	Debut Team
Joe Christopher	1959	Outfielder	Pittsburgh Pirates
Alvin McBean	1961	Pitcher	Pittsburgh Pirates
Elmo Plaskett	1962	Catcher	Pittsburgh Pirates
Horace Clarke	1965	Infielder	New York Yankees
Ellie (Elrod) Hendricks	1968	Catcher	Baltimore Orioles
Jose Morales	1973	First Base	Oakland Athletics
Henry Cruz	1975	Outfielder	Los Angeles Dodgers
Jerome Browne	1986	Infielder	Texas Rangers

Nicaragua (5 players)

Name	Debut	Position	Debut Team
Dennis Martinez	1976	Pitcher	Baltimore Orioles
Tony (Silvio) Chevez	1977	Pitcher	Baltimore Orioles
Al (Albert) Williams	1980	Pitcher	Minnesota Twins
David Green	1981	Outfielder	St. Louis Cardinals
Porfirio Altamirano	1982	Pitcher	Philadelphia Phillies

Colombia (3 players)

Name	Debut	Position	Debut Team
Luis Castro	1902	Infielder	Philadelphia Athletics
Orlando Ramirez	1974	Shortstop	California Angels
Jackie Gutierrez	1983	Shortstop	Boston Red Sox

Spain (3 players)

Name	Debut	Position	Debut Team
Alfredo Cabrera	1913	Shortstop	St. Louis Cardinals
Bryan Oelkers	1983	Pitcher	Minnesota Twins
Alberto Pardo	1985	Catcher	Baltimore Orioles

Honduras (1 player)

Name	Debut	Position	Debut Team
Gerald Young	1987	Outfielder	Houston Astros

Curacao, Netherlands Antilles (1 player)

Name	Position	Debut	Debut Team
Hensley Meulens	1990	Outfielder	New York Yankees

Belize (1 player)

Name	Debut	Position	Debut Team
Chito Martinez	1991	Outfielder	Baltimore Orioles

Latin American Managers (Chronological Listing)

Mike Gonzalez (Cuba) St. Louis Cardinals (1938, 1940)

Preston Gomez (Cuba) San Diego, Houston, Chicago (1969-72, 1974-75, 1980)

Marty (Orlando) Martinez (Cuba) Seattle Mariners (1986)

Cookie Rojas (Cuba) California Angels (1988)

Felipe Alou (Dominican Republic) Montreal Expos (1992)

Latin American Coaches (Alphabetical Listing)

Sandy Alomar (Puerto Rico) San Diego Padres (1986-1990)

Felipe Alou (Dominican Republic) Montreal Expos (1979-1980, 1984, 1989)

Jesus Alou (Dominican Republic) Houston Astros (1974)

Ruben Amaro (Mexico) Phil. Phillies (1980-1981), Chi. Cubs (1983-1986)

Tony Auferio (Cuba) St. Louis Cardinals (1973)

Leonel Carrion (Venezuela) Montreal Expos (1988-1990)

Orlando Cepeda (Puerto Rico) Chicago White Sox (1980)

Orlando Gomez (Dominican Republic) Texas Rangers (1991)

Preston Gomez (Cuba) Los Angeles Dodgers (1965-1968)

Mike Gonzalez (Cuba) St.L. Cards (1934-1940)—**1st Latin American coach**

Epy Guerrero (Dominican Republic) Toronto Blue Jays (1981)

Elrod Hendricks (Virgin Islands) Baltimore Orioles (1979-1991)

Luis Issac (Puerto Rico) Cleveland Indians (1988-1990)

Rafael Landestoy (Dominican Republic) Montreal Expos (1989-1991)

Winston Llenas (Dominican Republic) Toronto Blue Jays (1988)

Adolfo Luque (Cuba) New York Giants (1936-1945)

Jose Martinez (Cuba) K.C. Royals (1980-1987), Chi. Cubs (1988-1990)

Marty Martinez (Cuba) Seattle Mariners (1984-1986)

Minnie Mendoza (Cuba) Baltimore Orioles (1988)

Minnie Minoso (Cuba) Chicago White Sox (1976-1981)

Jose Morales (Virgin Islands) S.F. Giants (1986-1988), Cleve. Indians (1990)

Manny Mota (Dominican Republic) Los Angeles Dodgers (1980-1991)

Tony Oliva (Cuba) Minnesota Twins (1976-1991)

Reggie Otero (Cuba) Cincinnati Reds (1959-1965)

Tony Pacheco (Cuba) Cleveland Indians (1974), Houston Astros (1976-1982)

Camilo Pascual (Cuba) Minnesota Twins (1978-1980)

Tony Perez (Cuba) Cincinnati Reds (1987-1991)

Ben Reyes (Mexico) Seattle Mariners (1981)

Cookie Rojas (Cuba) Chicago Cubs (1978-1981)

Tony Taylor (Cuba) Philadelphia Phillies (1977-1979, 1988-1989)

Hector Torrez (Mexico) Toronto Blue jays (1981)

Ozzie Virgil (Dominican Republic) Giants, Padres, Expos, Mariners (1972-1988)

All-Time Season Leaders Among Latin American Major Leaguers

Latin American MVPs

Zoilo Versalles	1965	AL (Minnesota Twins)
Roberto Clemente	1966	NL (Pittsburgh Pirates)
Orlando Cepeda	1967	NL (St. Louis Cardinals)
Rod Carew	1977	AL (Minnesota Twins)
Guillermo Hernandez	1984	AL (Detroit Tigers)
George Bell	1987	AL (Toronto Blue Jays)
Jose Canseco	1988	AL (Oakland Athletics)

Latin American Cy Young Winners

Mike Cuellar	1969	AL (Baltimore Orioles)
Fernando Valenzuela	1981	NL (Los Angeles Dodgers)
Guillermo Hernandez	1984	AL (Detroit Tigers)

Latin American Rookies of the Year

Luis Aparicio	1956	AL (Chicago White Sox)
Orlando Cepeda	1958	NL (San Francisco Giants)
Tony Oliva	1964	AL (Minnesota Twins)
Rod Carew	1967	AL (Minnesota Twins)
Alfredo Griffin	1979	AL (Toronto Blue Jays)
Fernando Valenzuela	1981	NL (Los Angeles Dodgers)
Ozzie Guillen	1985	AL (Chicago White Sox)
Jose Canseco	1986	AL (Oakland Athletics)
Benito Santiago	1987	NL (San Diego Padres)
Sandy Alomar Jr.	1990	AL (Cleveland Indians)

Latin American Relief Pitchers of the Year

Mike Fornieles	1960	AL (Boston Red Sox)
Luis Arroyo	1961	AL (New York Yankees)
Minnie Rojas	1967	AL (California Angels)

Latin American Batting Champions

Roberto Avila	1954	AL (Cleveland Indians)	.341
Roberto Clemente	1961	NL (Pittsburgh Pirates)	.351
Roberto Clemente	1964	NL (Pittsburgh Pirates)	.339
Tony Oliva	1964	AL (Minnesota Twins)	.323
Roberto Clemente	1965	NL (Pittsburgh Pirates)	.329
Tony Oliva	1965	AL (Minnesota Twins)	.321
Matty Alou	1966	NL (Pittsburgh Pirates)	.342
Roberto Clemente	1967	NL (Pittsburgh Pirates)	.357
Rod Carew	1969	AL (Minnesota Twins)	.332
Rico Carty	1970	NL (Atlanta Braves)	.366
Tony Oliva	1971	AL (Minnesota Twins)	.337
Rod Carew	1972	AL (Minnesota Twins)	.318
Rod Carew	1973	AL (Minnesota Twins)	.350
Rod Carew	1974	AL (Minnesota Twins)	.364
Rod Carew	1975	AL (Minnesota Twins)	.359
Rod Carew	1977	AL (Minnesota Twins)	.388
Rod Carew	1978	AL (Minnesota Twins)	.333
Julio Franco	1991	AL (Texas Rangers)	.341

Latin American Home Run Leaders

Orlando Cepeda	1961	NL (San Francisco Giants)	46
Ben Oglivie	1980	AL (Milwaukee Brewers)	41
Tony Armas	1981	AL (Oakland Athletics)	22
Tony Armas	1984	AL (Boston Red Sox)	43
Jose Canseco	1988	AL (Oakland Athletics)	42
Jose Canseco	1991	AL (Oakland Athletics)	44

Latin American RBI Leaders

Orlando Cepeda	1961	NL (San Francisco Giants)	142
Orlando Cepeda	1967	NL (St. Louis Cardinals)	111
Tony Armas	1984	AL (Boston Red Sox)	123
George Bell	1987	AL (Toronto Blue Jays)	134
Jose Canseco	1988	AL (Oakland Athletics)	124
Ruben Sierra	1989	AL (Texas Rangers)	119

Latin American Stolen Base Leaders

Minnie Minoso	1951	AL (Chicago White Sox)	31
Minnie Minoso	1952	AL (Chicago White Sox)	22
Minnie Minoso	1953	AL (Chicago White Sox)	25
Luis Aparicio	1956	AL (Chicago White Sox)	21
Luis Aparicio	1957	AL (Chicago White Sox)	28
Luis Aparicio	1958	AL (Chicago White Sox)	29
Luis Aparicio	1959	AL (Chicago White Sox)	56
Luis Aparicio	1960	AL (Chicago White Sox)	51
Luis Aparicio	1961	AL (Chicago White Sox)	53
Luis Aparicio	1962	AL (Chicago White Sox)	31
Luis Aparicio	1963	AL (Baltimore Orioles)	40
Luis Aparicio	1964	AL (Baltimore Orioles)	57
Bert Campaneris	1965	AL (Kansas City Athletics)	51
Bert Campaneris	1966	AL (Kansas City Athletics)	52
Bert Campaneris	1967	AL (Kansas City Athletics)	55
Bert Campaneris	1968	AL (Oakland Athletics)	62
Bert Campaneris	1970	AL (Oakland Athletics)	42
Bert Campaneris	1972	AL (Oakland Athletics)	52
Frank Taveras	1977	NL (Pittsburgh Pirates)	70
Omar Moreno	1978	NL (Pittsburgh Pirates)	71
Omar Moreno	1979	NL (Pittsburgh Pirates)	77

Latin American ERA Champions

Adolfo Luque	1923	NL (Cincinnati Reds)	1.93
Adolfo Luque	1925	NL (Cincinnati Reds)	2.63
Luis Tiant	1968	AL (Cleveland Indians)	1.60
Juan Marichal	1969	NL (San Francisco Giants)	2.10
Diego Segui	1970	AL (Oakland Athletics)	2.56
Luis Tiant	1972	AL (Boston Red Sox)	1.91
Alejandro Peña	1984	NL (Los Angeles Dodgers)	2.48
Teodoro Higuera	1988	AL (Milwaukee Brewers)	2.45

Latin American Pitching Leaders (CareerGames Won)

Juan Marichal	243-142	.631 Pct.
Luis Tiant	229-172	.571 Pct.
Adolfo Luque	193-179	.519 Pct.

Latin American Appearance Leaders (Games Played by Pitchers)

Juan Marichal	744 Games
Diego Segui	639 Games
Elias Sosa	601 Games

Latin American Complete Games Leaders (Pitchers)

Juan Marichal	244 Games
Adolfo Luque	206 Games
Luis Tiant	187 Games

Latin American Strikeout Leaders (PItchers)

Luis Tiant	2,416 Strikeouts
Juan Marichal	2,303 Strikeouts
Camilo Pascual	2,167 Strikeouts

Latin American Shutout Leaders (Pitchers)

Juan Marichal	52 Shutouts
Luis Tiant	49 Shutouts
Camilo Pascual	36 Shutouts

Latin American Career ERA Leaders (Pitchers)

Juan Marichal	2.89 (3,506 IP)
Adolfo Luque	3.24 (3,221 IP)
Luis Tiant	3.30 (3,485 IP)

Latin American Saves Leaders (Pitchers)

Guillermo Hernandez	132 Saves
Aurelio Lopez	93 Saves
Pedro Borbon	80 Saves

Latin American Batting Leaders

Rod Carew	.328 BA
Roberto Clemente	.317 BA
Matty Alou	.307 BA

Latin American Hitting Leaders (Total Base Hits)

Rod Carew	3,053 Hits
Roberto Clemente	3,000 Hits
Tony Perez	2,732 Hits

Latin American Doubles Leaders (Batters)

Tony Perez	505 Doubles
Rod Carew	445 Doubles
Dave Concepcion	389 Doubles

Latin American Triples Leaders (Batters)

Roberto Clemente	166 Triples
Rod Carew	112 Triples
Luis Aparicio	92 Triples

Latin American Total Base Leaders (Batters)

Tony Perez	4,532 Total Bases
Roberto Clemente	4,492 Total Bases
Rod Carew	4,198 Total Bases

Latin American At-Bats Leaders

Luis Aparicio	10,230 ABs
Tony Perez	9,864 ABs
Roberto Clemente	9,459 ABs

Latin American Games Leaders (Appearances)

Tony Perez	2,777 Games
Luis Aparicio	2,599 Games
Rod Carew	2,469 Games

Latin American Home Run Leaders

Orlando Cepeda	379 Home Runs
Tony Perez	379 Home Runs
Tony Armas	251 Home Runs

Latin American RBI Leaders

Tony Perez	1,652 RBI
Orlando Cepeda	1,365 RBI
Roberto Clemente	1,305 RBI

Latin American Runs Scored Leaders

Rod Carew	1,424 Runs
Roberto Clemente	1,416 Runs
Luis Aparicio	1,335 Runs

Latin American Bases-on-Balls Leaders (Batters)

Rod Carew	1,018 Walks
Luis Aparicio	736 Walks
Cesar Cedeño	664 Walks

Latin American Stolen Base Leaders

Bert Campaneris	649 Steals
Cesar Cedeño	550 Steals
Luis Aparicio	506 Steals

Latin American Pinch Hitting Leaders

Manny Mota	150 Hits
Jose Morales	123 Hits
Vic Davalillo	95 Hits

**International baseball at the highest level:
Casey Stengel meets King George V
London, 1924.**